Ancient Egyptian Literature

VOLUME II: THE NEW KINGDOM

Published under the auspices of
The Gustave E. von Grunebaum Center
for Near Eastern Studies
University of California, Los Angeles

Ancient Egyptian Literature
A Book of Readings

by
Miriam Lichtheim

VOLUME II: THE NEW KINGDOM

UNIVERSITY OF CALIFORNIA PRESS

Berkeley   Los Angeles   London

UNIVERSITY OF CALIFORNIA PRESS
BERKELEY AND LOS ANGELES, CALIFORNIA
UNIVERSITY OF CALIFORNIA PRESS, LTD.
LONDON, ENGLAND
ISBN: 0-520-03615-8
LIBRARY OF CONGRESS CATALOG CARD NUMBER: 75-189225
COPYRIGHT © 1976, BY
THE REGENTS OF THE UNIVERSITY OF CALIFORNIA
PRINTED IN THE UNITED STATES OF AMERICA

2 3 4 5 6 7 8 9

Preface

This second volume of new translations is designed along the lines of the preceding one. In keeping with the ancient view, it defines literature broadly so as to include monumental inscriptions carved on stone and literary texts written on papyrus. Where the first volume outlined the gradual creation of Egyptian literary genres in the course of many centuries, the present one shows the elaboration of the genres within a single cultural period and in a relatively short span of time.

The literary production of the New Kingdom was much larger than that of the earlier periods. Hence even a whole volume devoted to it can do no more than focus on the highlights. Moreover, in the New Kingdom both the monumental inscriptions and the papyrus texts usually ran to greater length than their Middle Kingdom counterparts. The selection made from the vast quantity of stone-carved inscriptions contains famous pieces along with some less-renowned ones. Together they illustrate the principal topics that were deemed appropriate to the always functional monumental context. Similarly, the works written on papyrus have been selected to show the variety of themes and forms, and to single out those compositions that were outstanding in their day and have retained a timeless interest. Tales marred by major lacunae have been excluded; hence the absence, among others, of "The Capture of Joppa."

M. L.

Santa Monica, California
June 17, 1974

Contents

Indexes

Brief Chronology of the New Kingdom

Dynasties 18-20, ca. 1550-1080 B.C.

Eighteenth Dynasty	ca. 1550-1305
Nebpehtire Ahmose	
Djeserkare Amenhotep I	
Aakheperkare Thutmose I	(1506-1494)
Aakheperenre Thutmose II	
Makare Hatshepsut	
Menkheperre Thutmose III	(1468-1438)
Aakheprure Amenhotep II	
Menkheprure Thutmose IV	
Nebmare Amenhotep III	
Neferkheprure Amenhotep IV Akhenaten	(1365-1349)
Nebkheprure Tutankhamun	
Kheperkheprure Ay	
Djeserkheprure Haremhab	
Nineteenth Dynasty	ca. 1305-1195
Menmare Seti I	
Usermare-sotpenre Ramses II	(1290-1224)
Banere-meramun Merneptah	
Twentieth Dynasty	ca. 1195-1080
Usermare-meramun Ramses III	
Usermare-sekheperenre Ramses V	
Neferkare-sotpenre Ramses IX	
Menmare-sotpenptah Ramses XI	(1110-1080)

Note: Only kings named in the texts or notes of this volume are listed here, and only a few regnal dates are given to serve as guideposts.

Abbreviations and Symbols

AEO	A. H. Gardiner. *Ancient Egyptian Onomastica.* 3 vols. Oxford, 1947.
AJSL	*American Journal of Semitic Languages and Literatures.*
ANET	*Ancient Near Eastern Texts Relating to the Old Testament,* ed. J. B. Pritchard. Princeton, 1950; 2d ed., 1955; 3d ed., 1969.
ASAE	*Annales du Service des Antiquités de l'Égypte.*
BAR	J. H. Breasted. *Ancient Records of Egypt.* 5 vols. Chicago, 1906-1907. Reprint New York, 1962.
Bibliothèque d'étude	Institut Français d'Archéologie Orientale du Caire. Bibliothèque d'étude.
BIFAO	*Bulletin de l'Institut Français d'Archéologie Orientale.*
Bonnet, *RÄRG*	H. Bonnet. *Reallexikon der ägyptischen Religionsgeschichte.* Berlin, 1952.
Brunner-Traut, *Märchen*	E. Brunner-Traut. *Altägyptische Märchen.* Dusseldorf and Cologne, 1963. 2d ed., 1965.
Caminos, *LEM*	R. A. Caminos. *Late-Egyptian Miscellanies.* Brown Egyptological Studies, 1. London, 1954.
CdE	*Chronique d'Égypte.*
CRAIBL	*Comptes rendus de l'Académie des Inscriptions et Belles-lettres.*
Davies, *Amarna*	N. de G. Davies. *The Rock Tombs of El Amarna.* 6 parts. Egypt Exploration Society, Archaeological Survey, 13-18. London, 1903-1908.
Edel, *Inschriften*	E. Edel. *Zu den Inschriften auf den Jahreszeitenreliefs der "Weltkammer" aus dem Sonnenheiligtum des Niuserre.* Nachrichten der Akademie der Wissenschaften in Göttingen. Phil.-hist. Kl., 1961 no. 8 and 1963 nos. 4-5. Göttingen, 1961-1964.
Erman, *Literature*	A. Erman. *The Literature of the Ancient Egyptians,* trans. into English by A. M. Blackman. London, 1927. Reprint New York, 1966 as *The Ancient Egyptians; A Sourcebook of Their Writings.*

Erman, *Denksteine*	A. Erman. *Denksteine aus der thebanischen Gräberstadt.* Sitzungsberichte der Berliner Akademie der Wissenschaften. Phil.-hist. Kl., 1911, No. 49, pp. 1086-1110 and pl. 16. Berlin, 1911.
Fecht, *Zeugnisse*	G. Fecht, *Literarische Zeugnisse zur "Persönlichen Frömmigkeit" in Ägypten.* Abhandlungen der Heidelberger Akademie der Wissenschaften. Phil.-hist. Kl., 1965 no. 1. Heidelberg, 1965.
Galling Festschrift	*Archäologie und Altes Testament: Festschrift für Kurt Galling zum 8. Januar 1970,* ed. A. Kuschke and E. Kutsch. Tübingen, 1970.
Galling, *Textbuch*	*Textbuch zur Geschichte Israels,* ed. K. Galling. 2d ed., Tübingen, 1968.
Gardiner, *Chester Beatty I*	A. H. Gardiner. *The Library of A. Chester Beatty . . . The Chester Beatty Papyri, No. I.* London, 1931.
Gardiner, *Egypt*	A. H. Gardiner. *Egypt of the Pharaohs.* Oxford, 1961.
Gardiner, *Grammar*	A. H. Gardiner. *Egyptian Grammar.* Oxford, 1927; 3d ed., 1957.
Gardiner, *Hieratic Papyri*	A. H. Gardiner. *Hieratic Papyri in the British Museum, Third Series: Chester Beatty Gift.* 2 vols. London, 1935.
Gardiner, *LEM*	A. H. Gardiner. *Late-Egyptian Miscellanies.* Bibliotheca Aegyptiaca, 7. Brussels, 1937.
Gardiner, *LES*	A. H. Gardiner. *Late-Egyptian Stories.* Bibliotheca Aegyptiaca, 1. Brussels, 1932.
Gilbert, *Poésie*	P. Gilbert. *La Poésie égyptienne.* 2d ed., Brussels, 1949.
Helck, *Übersetzung*	W. Helck. *Urkunden der 18. Dynastie: Übersetzungen zu den Heften 17-22.* Berlin, 1961.
Hieroglyphic Texts	British Museum. *Hieroglyphic Texts from Egyptian Stelae etc.* 2d ed., London, 1961——.
JARCE	*Journal of the American Research Center in Egypt.*
JEA	*Journal of Egyptian Archaeology.*
JNES	*Journal of Near Eastern Studies.*
Kitchen, *Inscriptions*	K. A. Kitchen. *Ramesside Inscriptions, Historical and Biographical.* Oxford, 1969——.
LD	R. Lepsius. *Denkmaeler aus Aegypten und Aethiopien.* 12 vols. Berlin, 1849-1856.
Lefèbvre, *Romans*	G. Lefèbvre. *Romans et contes égyptiens de l'époque pharaonique.* Paris, 1949.
MDIK	*Mitteilungen des deutschen archäologischen Instituts,* Abteilung Kairo.

Mélanges Maspero I	*Orient Ancien.* Institut Français d'Archéologie Orientale du Caire. Mémoires, 66. Cairo, 1934-1938.
Möller, *Lesestücke*	G. Möller. *Hieratische Lesestücke für den akademischen Gebrauch.* 3 fascicles. Berlin, 1927. Reprint, 1961.
Müller, *Liebespoesie*	W. M. Müller. *Die Liebespoesie der alten Ägypter.* Leipzig, 1899.
OLZ	*Orientalistische Literaturzeitung.*
Pierret, *Recueil*	P. Pierret, *Recueil d'inscriptions inédites du Musée Égyptien du Louvre.* 2 vols. Paris, 1874-1878.
PM	*Topographical Bibliography of Ancient Egyptian Hieroglyphic Texts, Reliefs, and Paintings,* by B. Porter and R. L. B. Moss. 7 vols. Oxford, 1927-1951. 2d ed., 1960——.
Posener, *Ostr. hiér.*	G. Posener. *Catalogue des ostraca hiératiques littéraires de Deir el Médineh.* 2 vols. Institut Français d'Archéologie Orientale du Caire. Documents de fouilles, 1 and 18. Cairo, 1935-1972.
PSBA	*Proceedings of the Society of Biblical Archaeology.*
RdE	*Revue d'Égyptologie.*
RT	*Recueil de travaux relatifs à la philologie et à l'archéologie égyptiennes et assyriennes.*
Sagesses	*Les Sagesses du proche-orient ancien.* Colloque de Strasbourg 17-19 mai 1962. Paris, 1963.
Sandman, *Akhenaten*	M. Sandman. *Texts from the Time of Akhenaten.* Bibliotheca Aegyptiaca, 8. Brussels, 1938.
Schott Festschrift	*Festschrift für Siegfried Schott zu seinem 70. Geburtstag,* ed. W. Schenkel. Wiesbaden, 1968.
Schott, *Liebeslieder*	S. Schott. *Altägyptische Liebeslieder, mit Märchen und Liebesgeschichten.* Zurich, 1950.
Simpson, *Literature*	*The Literature of Ancient Egypt: An Anthology of Stories, Instructions, and Poetry,* ed. W. K. Simpson, with translations by R. O. Faulkner, E. F. Wente, Jr., and W. K. Simpson. New Haven, 1972. 2d ed., 1973.
Untersuchungen	Untersuchungen zur Geschichte und Altertumskunde Ägyptens.
Urk. IV	*Urkunden des ägyptischen Altertums, Abteilung IV: Urkunden der 18. Dynastie,* ed. K. Sethe and W. Helck. Fascicles 1-22. Leipzig and Berlin, 1906-1958.
Urk. deutsch	*Urkunden der 18. Dynastie, I,* bearbeitet und übersetzt von K. Sethe. Leipzig, 1914.
Wb.	*Wörterbuch der ägyptischen Sprache,* ed. A. Erman and H. Grapow. 7 vols. Leipzig, 1926-1963.
Wilson Festschrift	*Studies in Honor of John A. Wilson.* Studies in Ancient Oriental Civilization, 35. Chicago, 1969.

ZA   *Zeitschrift für Assyriologie und vorderasiatische Archäologie.*

ZÄS   *Zeitschrift für ägyptische Sprache und Altertumskunde.*

ZDPV   *Zeitschrift des deutschen Palästina-Vereins.*

Half brackets ⌐ ⌐ are used instead of question marks to signify doubt.

Square brackets [] enclose restorations.

Angle brackets < > enclose words omitted by the scribe.

Parentheses ( ) enclose additions in the English translations.

A row of three dots . . . indicates the omission in the English translation of one or two words. A row of six dots . . . . . . indicates a longer omission.

A row of three dashes --- indicates a short lacuna in the text. A row of six dashes ------ indicates a lengthy lacuna.

Introduction

Continuity and Change

The military campaigns of King Ahmose drove the Hyksos from the soil of Egypt, reunited the nation under a strong dynasty, and set in motion an expansionist policy of foreign conquests.

With the Hyksos expelled and Lower Nubia reconquered, King Amenhotep I devoted himself to the building of the new capital city, Thebes, and to its westbank where a vast necropolis of splendidly decorated rock-tombs began to rise. His successor, Thutmose I, embarked on far-flung conquests. In the south he passed beyond the strongly fortified border of the second cataract and campaigned in Upper Nubia. In the east he traversed Palestine and Syria and set his stelae on the shore of the Euphrates, thus claiming all of Syria for Egypt. His son, Thutmose II, campaigned in Nubia and Palestine, but his early death put a temporary stop to military activity.

The widow of Thutmose II, Queen Hatshepsut, after first ruling as regent for her young nephew, the future Thutmose III, took the crown in her own name; and for two decades this energetic woman, who legitimized her rule by claiming the god Amun as her father, reigned peacefully and splendidly. The architecture and art of her time are unexcelled in their elegance and good taste.

At her death, Thutmose III, so long held back from the throne, took his revenge by defacing and overturning her monuments and by usurping the twenty-one years of her reign in the dating of his records. When he came to the throne, Egypt's Asiatic possessions were threatened by an alliance between the rising kingdom of Mitanni and the princes of Palestinian and Syrian city-states led by the prince of Kadesh. Thus, in the very first year of his rule, he mounted a rapid campaign in Palestine which resulted in the defeat of the hostile coalition and the capture of the fortified city of Megiddo. Thereafter, over the next twenty years, Thutmose III conducted sixteen Syrian campaigns in which he twice sacked the city of Kadesh and even crossed the Euphrates, thus reaching into the heartland of Mitanni. In the south he extended Egypt's border to the town of Napata on the fourth cataract. The conquests were secured by an effective administration. Foreign princes were brought to Egypt for their education. Asiatic rulers who proved loyal were allowed to retain their territories. Egyptian garrisons held the strategically important towns, and Egyptian clerks turned the wheels of government abroad. Building activities at Thebes and elsewhere reached an unprecedented scale. Nubian gold, and goods imported from the empire, combined with the sheer inexhaustible output of Egypt's workshops, created a golden age of wealth and luxury.

The splendid reign of the great empire builder was followed by the strong rule of his son, Amenhotep II, who effectively defended the empire his father had created. In the reign of his son, Thutmose IV, the long struggle against Mitanni was resolved by peace, alliance, and the entrance of a Mitannian princess into the harem of the pharaoh, the alliance being designed to stem the forward march of the Hittites.

Luxurious living in a setting of peace reached its climax in the reign of Amenhotep III. This king never set foot in his Asiatic empire. Instead he acquired Mitannian, Babylonian, and other Asiatic princesses for his harem and lavished gold on his allies. Furthermore, he strove to surpass his predecessors in the number, size, and splendor of his buildings.

The age of empire meant more than power, wealth, and refined luxury. It fostered a broadening of the intellectual horizon. The sense of superiority over foreigners, while not abandoned, was mitigated by curiosity and tolerance. The scribes who ran the administration prided themselves on their knowledge of foreign places and peoples; and foreigners who had settled in Egypt could rise to high office. The royal archive found in the ruins of El Amarna revealed that Kings Amenhotep III and IV corresponded in Akkadian with Asiatic rulers. Hence many Egyptian scribes had to be bilingual; and it was fashionable to show off one's knowledge of foreign languages. Thus, in due course, numerous Semitic loanwords entered the Egyptian vocabulary.

Religious thinking was especially affected by the new internationalism. The great gods of Egypt became gods for all mankind. And this universalism allied itself to the growing tendency of viewing all gods as manifestations of the sun-god.

Amenhotep IV thought the consequences of religious universalism through to their ultimate conclusion: the sun-god who ruled the universe and all mankind was not only supreme; he was the sole god. There were no other gods beside him. This revolutionary conclusion threw the nation into turmoil; and as soon as the king had died, the offensive doctrine was swept away. But though monotheism had been defeated the universalist tendency remained alive.

The second half of the New Kingdom, the age of the Ramesside kings, brought a renewed struggle for the control of Palestine and Syria, where Egypt's hegemony was threatened by Hittite expansion and the ambitions of local rulers. Seti I and Ramses II campaigned vigorously and preserved the empire; and eventually the Hittite enemy became an ally. In his sixty-six years of reign, Ramses II broke all records in the quantity and size of his monuments. The taste for the colossal, already manifest under Amenhotep III, reached its climax. In literature too the Ramesside age was enormously prolific.

In the reign of Merneptah, the Indo-European "sea peoples" swept into the Near East and, allied with the Libyans, made a vigorous attempt to invade the Nile valley. They were beaten back, reappeared several decades later, and were again prevented from entering Egypt, this time by Pharaoh Ramses III, the last great king of the New Kingdom. But though they failed to gain Egypt, their sweep through the Near East broke the strength of the Hittites and contributed to the rise of new powers. Thus, after the death of Ramses III, Egypt lost its foreign possessions and was, moreover, weakened by internal conflicts and maladministration.

In the second half of the Twentieth Dynasty an economic decline became manifest. Workmen who had not obtained their rations went on strike. Royal tombs were looted and their valuables sold for bread. A succession of kings appeared unable to rule effectively. In the end, Ramses XI, the last of the Ramesside line, had to share the rule of Upper Egypt with Herihor, the high priest of Amun, and in the Delta with the regent Smendes. When the Theban official Wenamun undertook his journey to Byblos to buy timber on behalf of his master Herihor, the prince of Byblos, no longer a vassal of Egypt, received him with scorn. The age of empire was over.

The texts included in this volume illustrate the principal themes of the age. *The Autobiography of Ahmose Son of Abana* continues the ancient genre autobiography and is also the most important surviving source for the war against the Hyksos. It depicts the well-lived life, the life of service and material rewards. The *Prayers of Paheri*, on the other hand, sum up the expectations for a blessed afterlife. The text known as the *Installation of the Vizier* sets out the obligations and honors of the highest official in the land.

The royal monumental inscriptions enlarge upon such early prototypes as the building inscription and the annalistic historical account. Annalistic historiography reaches its full flowering in the *Annals of Thutmose III*. The hymn of victory on the *Poetical Stela of Thutmose III* proclaims imperial dominion in a poem of beautiful craftsmanship. The *Sphinx Stela of Amenhotep II* manifests the king's pride in his physical prowess. The *Building Inscriptions of Amenhotep III* reflect that king's love of architectural magnificence. In his *Boundary Stelae* at El Amarna Amenhotep IV consecrates his new city to the worship of the sole god, while the *Dedication Inscriptions of Seti I* breathe traditional piety and the spirit of restoration. Thus the basic types of royal inscriptions appear enlarged and diversified, and the themes are characteristic of the imperial age.

The *Kadesh Battle Inscriptions of Ramses II* break new ground in literary form; for the long section of the inscriptions known as *The Poem* is a *narrative poem*, an epic, and the first of its kind in Egypt. Heretofore poetry had served to celebrate and to instruct; it had not aimed at narration. The *Poetical Stela of Merneptah* is a second example of this new form of poetry.

The *hymns to the gods* are another genre in which the New Kingdom built on foundations of the Middle Kingdom and went beyond them. The hymns are found in great quantity both in the monumental context and on papyrus, and they mirror the trends of New Kingdom religiosity, in particular the evolution from an immanent view of the gods to a transcendent one. Transcendence and universalism go hand in hand: the transcendent god is truly the god of all. And though remote, he is accessible to the pious individual. Thus the elaborate hymns that come from the cultic context stand side by side with the short hymns and prayers of humble individuals.

It seems that the death of Osiris at the hands of Seth was viewed as a mystery too awesome and sacred to be narrated in detail. It could only be alluded to; and the most elaborate allusions to the fate of Osiris occur in the *Great Hymn to Osiris*, recorded on the stela of the official Amenmose.

The largest number of hymns are addressed to the sun-god in his several manifestations. The two long *Hymns to the Sun-God* of the brothers Suti and Hor show the widened universalist conception of sun worship and also the inclusion of the sun disk, the Aten, among the manifestations of the sun-god. This was the point that the worship of the Aten as a distinct deity had reached in the time of Amenhotep III.

The *Great Hymn to the Aten* recorded in the tomb of the courtier Ay presents in pure form the doctrine of the sole god worked out by Amenhotep IV Akhenaten. The king had taught it to his followers, and it is only through their hymns and prayers, carved in their tombs at El Amarna, that his monotheistic teaching has reached us. The Great Hymn and the shorter hymns and prayers in the Amarna tombs show how completely the doctrine of the one god had been enforced at Amarna. In recording their hopes for a blessed afterlife, the courtiers could no longer turn to Osiris and related comforting beliefs. Only the king, the son of the Aten, remained as guarantor of their survival.

From the workmen's village of Deir el-Medina come the *Penitential Hymns*, which express the personal piety so characteristic of the New

Kingdom. The same piety informs the short hymns and prayers, written on papyrus, which were transmitted as models to be used in schools. Individualism, inwardness, and humility characterize this piety which had evolved from the more social and cultic religiosity of the earlier periods.

The same inwardness underlies the *Instruction of Amenemope*. Here too the old values have undergone subtle changes. Life is still governed by *Maat*, the divine order; and as ever success depends on living in accord with *Maat*. But success is no longer described in terms of material rewards. The ideal man now is modest in status, and he is humble toward gods and men.

Continuity and change also characterize the *Mortuary Literature* of the New Kingdom. The *Book of the Dead* is a reworking and expansion of the Middle Kingdom *Coffin Texts*. Instead of being inscribed on coffins, the spells are now written on papyrus scrolls, grouped into chapters, and accompanied by vignettes. In addition, the scribes of the New Kingdom composed new works that were designed as "guides to the beyond." These works are only marginally "literature" and, moreover, they do not lend themselves to presentation in excerpts. Hence only the Book of the Dead is included here in a small sampling. Its most famous part, chapter 125, the judgment of the dead, mixes ancient and honorable moral values with the sorcerer's magic. Morality and magic, seemingly incompatible, were often linked in Egyptian thought and are here closely joined.

In the New Kingdom the education and training of scribes was much expanded and systematized, and the genre known as *School Texts* has no counterpart in the earlier periods. Since a large variety of compositions were used as models for instruction, the term "school texts" embraces a miscellany of works, including documents taken from archives. Within this variety, certain compositions are school texts in the specific sense of coming from the milieu of the schools and reflecting the student-teacher relationship. When such texts were strung together to make a book, we have a regular "school book," of which *Papyrus Lansing* is an example. More commonly, a papyrus roll contains a variety of compositions that are independent of each other. In one such medley, *Papyrus Chester Beatty IV*, there appears a short text in which a scribe lists some famous authors of the past and draws the astonishingly skeptical conclusion that the only immortality a man can expect is the immortality of the written word.

Lyric poetry was well developed in the Middle Kingdom; but *Love Lyrics* seem to be a creation of the New Kingdom. At least, no love poems older than the New Kingdom have come to light. The love poems are misunderstood if they are thought to be naïve and artless. For they are rich in elaborate wordplays, metaphors, and rare words and thereby indicate that they are crafted with deliberation and literate skill. The actual situations of life from which the poems may have arisen are concealed from our view. We do not know enough about the position of women, especially of young unmarried girls, to know how to interpret the free relations of the lovers that are depicted in so many of the poems.

The genre *Tales* was of course well developed in the Middle Kingdom. The New Kingdom adds new motifs, greater length and complexity, and broader horizons. The *Report of Wenamun*, though included among the tales, stands apart, since it is probably based on an actual report. Even if it is a work of fiction, the incidents are all in the realm of the possible, and the historical background is real.

We have seen continuity with the earlier periods in terms of the principal literary categories: private autobiographies, royal historical inscriptions, hymns and prayers, instructions, mortuary spells, and tales. The New Kingdom broadened the genres and added new themes, attitudes, and motifs. It also created two new genres: school texts and love lyrics.

As before, my translations are based on the conviction that the Egyptian authors worked in three styles: prose, poetry, and an intermediate style which I have termed symmetrically structured speech, or, orational style. The New Kingdom adds a new variety: the narrative poem. Thus, Egyptian poetry as a whole might be subdivided into hymnic, lyric, didactic, and narrative. It goes without saying that all our literary categorization is tentative. For after a century and a half of study, the contemporary scholar's understanding of the language and literature of ancient Egypt remains imperfect, incomplete, and subject to diverging views.

"Le temps conserve de préférence ce qui est un peu sec." This remark by Jacques Chardonne, quoted in the preface of Iris Origo's anthology *The Vagabond Path*, seems eminently applicable to the literature of ancient Egypt. Having been physically preserved by the dry sands of the desert, these ancient works endure by virtue of their sober strength. Even at their most lyrical, as in the love poems, the writings are never cloying or sentimental. Up to the end of the New Kingdom, the literature mirrors a society whose members lived in harmony with themselves and with nature. The cares of life could be met with confidence, for the gods ruled the world firmly and justly. Life was both hard and good.

PART ONE

Monumental Inscriptions

I. Inscriptions from Private Tombs

The three tomb inscriptions in this section are major representatives of their kind. The *Autobiography of Ahmose son of Abana* continues the traditional genre of tomb autobiography. Its special interest is historical, for it furnishes the principal account of the expulsion of the Hyksos. It is a wholly martial autobiography that describes the actions and career of a soldier. As such it is a rarity among Egyptian autobiographies, for most of them came from members of the civilian bureaucracy.

Ahmose began his career as a soldier on board a ship, stepping into the position that his father had held. Having come to the attention of King Ahmose, he was transferred to the north, where he saw action in the decisive battles against the Hyksos, first at Avaris and subsequently at Sharuhen in Palestine. Then he participated in the Nubian campaigns of Kings Amenhotep I and Thutmose I, where he so distinguished himself that he was promoted to the rank of commander of a crew and given substantial landholdings in his home town Nekheb, modern El-Kab. Finally he took part in the Syrian campaign of Thutmose I in which the king reached the Euphrates. Thus risen from the ranks, he was able to bequeath wealth to his descendants and to found a family which reached the upper echelons of the civil service. His son Itruri and his grandson Paheri became tutors of the king's sons, and Paheri attained the post of mayor of Nekheb and Iunyt. The style of the autobiography is simple, straightforward, and unadorned.

The grandson *Paheri*, whose career probably began under Thutmose I, built for himself the handsomest of the known tombs of El-Kab. In addition to being mayor of two towns, he was "scribe of the grain accounts" for an area extending north as far as Dendera. The fine reliefs in his tomb show him overseeing the various agricultural activities that were in his charge. His tomb does not contain an autobiographical prose narration. Instead he had the rear wall of the main hall inscribed with elaborate prayers and a recital of his virtues, the whole composition designed to help attain a blessed afterlife envisaged in considerable detail. This vision contains many of the features that were incorporated in the spells of the Book of the Dead.

The highest official of the state was the vizier. His duties were so important and so numerous that he was installed by the king in person, in a public ceremony in which the king gave him a formal charge. The text of this charge was inscribed on a wall of the sumptuous tomb of the *Vizier Rekhmire*, who served King Thutmose III. The same text with variants appears in two other Theban tombs of viziers of the Eighteenth Dynasty. The king's speech is composed in the orational style.

11

THE AUTOBIOGRAPHY OF AHMOSE SON OF ABANA

In his Tomb at El-Kab

The inscription is carved in two parts: lines 1-31 on the right-hand wall of the hall of the rock-tomb (east wall), and lines 32-40 on the left side of the door wall (south wall). Also on the right-hand wall is the standing relief figure of Ahmose accompanied by the small figure of his grandson Paheri.

A list of Ahmose's landholdings and slaves, not translated here, is inscribed on the right side of the door wall.

Publication: LD III, 12, b-d.   V. Loret, L'inscription d'Ahmès fils d'Abana, Bibliothèque d'étude, 3 (Cairo, 1910).   Urk. IV, 1-11.

Translation: BAR, II, §§ 1-16, 38-39, 78-82.   Urk. deutsch, pp. 1-6. B. Gunn and A. H. Gardiner, JEA, 5 (1918), 48-54.   J. A. Wilson in ANET, pp. 233-234 (excerpts).

Historical study: C. Vandersleyen, Les Guerres d'Amosis, fondateur de la XVIIIe dynastie, Monographies Reine Élisabeth, 1 (Brussels, 1971), pp. 17-87.   For additional references see PM V, 182 and Vandersleyen, op. cit., pp. 17-21.

(1) The Crew Commander Ahmose son of Abana,[1] the justified; he says. I speak to you, all people. I let you know what favors came to me. I have been rewarded with gold seven times in the sight of the whole land, with male and female slaves as well. I have been endowed with very many fields. The name of the brave man is in that which he has done; it will not perish in the land forever.[2]

He speaks as follows. I grew up in the town of Nekheb,[3] my father being a soldier of the King of Upper and Lower Egypt, Seqenenre,[4] the justified. Baba (5) son of Reonet was his name. I became a soldier in his stead on the ship "The Wild Bull" in the time of the Lord of the Two Lands, Nebpehtire,[5] the justified. I was a youth who had not married; I slept in . . .[6]

Expulsion of the Hyksos

Now when I had established a household,[7] I was taken to the ship "Northern," because I was brave. I followed the sovereign on foot when he rode about on his chariot. When the town of Avaris was besieged, I fought bravely on foot in his majesty's presence.[8] There-upon I was appointed to the ship "Rising in Memphis." Then there was fighting on the water in "Pjedku" of Avaris. I made a seizure (10) and carried off a hand.[9] When it was reported to the royal herald the gold of valor was given to me.

Then they fought again in this place; I again made a seizure there and carried off a hand. Then I was given the gold of valor once again.

Then there was fighting in Egypt to the south of this town, and I carried off a man as a living captive. I went down into the water—for he was captured on the city side—and crossed the water carrying him.

When it was reported to the royal herald I was rewarded with gold once more. Then Avaris was despoiled, and I brought spoil from there: one man, three women; total, four persons.[10] His majesty gave them to me as slaves.

(15) Then Sharuhen was besieged for three years. His majesty despoiled it and I brought spoil from it: two women and a hand. Then the gold of valor was given me, and my captives were given to me as slaves.

Nubian campaign of King Ahmose

Now when his majesty had slain the nomads of Asia, he sailed south to Khent-hen-nefer,[11] to destroy the Nubian Bowmen. His majesty made a great slaughter among them, and I brought spoil from there: two living men and three hands. Then I was rewarded with gold once again, and two female slaves were given to me.[12] His majesty journeyed north, his heart rejoicing in valor and victory. He had conquered southerners, northerners.

Destruction of the rebels Aata and Tetian

Then Aata came to the South.[13] (20) His fate brought on his doom. The gods of Upper Egypt grasped him. He was found by his majesty at Tent-taa.[14] His majesty carried him off as a living captive, and all his people as booty. I brought two young warriors[15] as captives from the ship of Aata. Then I was given five persons and portions of land amounting to five arurae in my town. The same was done for the whole crew.

Then came that foe named Tetian.[16] He had gathered the malcontents to himself. His majesty slew him; his troop was wiped out. Then I was given three persons and five arurae of land in my town.

Nubian campaign of King Amenhotep I

Then I conveyed King Djeserkare,[17] the justified, when he sailed south to Kush, to enlarge (25) the borders of Egypt. His majesty smote that Nubian Bowman in the midst of his army. They were carried off in fetters, none missing, the fleeing destroyed as if they had never been. Now I was in the van of our troops and I fought really well. His majesty saw my valor. I carried off two hands and presented them to his majesty. Then his people and his cattle were pursued, and I carried off a living captive and presented him to his majesty.

I brought his majesty back to Egypt in two days from "Upper Well," and was rewarded with gold. I brought back two female slaves as booty, apart from those that I had presented to his majesty. Then they made me a "Warrior of the Ruler."

Nubian campaign of King Thutmose I

Then I conveyed King Aakheperkare,[18] the justified, when he sailed south to Khent-hen-nefer, (30) to crush rebellion throughout the lands, to repel the intruders from the desert region. I was brave in his presence in the bad water, in the towing of the ship over the cataract. Thereupon I was made crew commander.

Then his majesty [ᒣwas informed that the Nubianᒧ] ––––––. At this his majesty became enraged like a leopard. His majesty shot, and his first arrow pierced the chest of that foe. Then those [enemies turned to flee], helpless before his Uraeus. A slaughter was made among them; their dependents were carried off as living captives. (35) His majesty journeyed north, all foreign lands in his grasp, and that wretched Nubian Bowman head downward at the bow of his majesty's ship "Falcon." They landed at Ipet-sut.[19]

Syrian campaign of King Thutmose I

After this (his majesty) proceeded to Retjenu, to vent his wrath[20] throughout the lands. When his majesty reached Nahrin, his majesty found that foe marshalling troops. Then his majesty made a great slaughter of them. Countless were the living captives which his majesty brought back from his victories. Now I was in the van of our troops, and his majesty saw my valor. I brought a chariot, its horse, and him who was on it as a living captive. When they were presented to his majesty, I was rewarded with gold once again.

(40) I have grown old; I have reached old age. Favored as before, and loved [by my lord], I [rest] in the tomb that I myself made.

NOTES

1. The name of his mother, variously transcribed by scholars as Eben, Ibana, Abana, or Abina.
2. A proverb which occurs twice more in inscriptions of Thutmose III (*Urk. IV*, 684 and 780); see B. Gunn, *JEA*, 12 (1926), 283.
3. The metropolis of the third nome of Upper Egypt, modern El-Kab.
4. Throne name of King Tao II of the Seventeenth Dynasty.
5. Throne name of King Ahmose, the founder of the Eighteenth Dynasty.
6. The meaning of *smt šnw* is unknown. The rendering "hammock of net" of Gunn and Gardiner, *op. cit.*, p. 49, lacks probability.
7. I.e., had married.
8. Ahmose is a marine rather than a sailor. Whether actual naval engagements took place at that time is doubtful. The ships served primarily to transport troops.

9. The seizure is a slaying, after which a hand of the dead enemy was cut off and brought back as proof of the killing. For bringing back live prisoners other terms are used.

10. Literally, "heads."

11. A name for a portion of Nubia south of the second cataract. See Vandersleyen, *op. cit.*, pp. 64-68.

12. All captives were presented to the king and he distributed some of them to his soldiers. In this incident Ahmose presents two men and receives two women as reward.

13. This enemy seems to have been a Nubian. The name Aata, which could be a title rather than a personal name, is discussed by Gunn and Gardiner, *op. cit*, p. 50 n. 3, and Vandersleyen, *op. cit.*, pp. 75 ff., who makes it plausible that the attack by this "rebel" takes place during or after the king's return journey, and to the north of the second cataract, i.e. in Egypt proper. The region of Lower Nubia between the first and second cataracts was considered to be Egypt by the Egyptians ever since it had been conquered by the kings of the Twelfth Dynasty, even though it had been lost during the Hyksos period and had only recently been reconquered.

14. Or Tjent-aa; the locality has not been identified, see H. Goedicke, *Kush*, 13 (1965), 104-105, and Vandersleyen, *op. cit.*, p. 79.

15. On *mg3* "young warrior," see Vandersleyen, *op. cit.*, p. 80.

16. This rebel was an Egyptian.

17. Throne name of King Amenhotep I.

18. Throne name of King Thutmose I.

19. The northern part of Thebes, modern Karnak.

20. Literally, "to wash his heart."

THE PRAYERS OF PAHERI

In his Tomb at El-Kab

Paheri's career probably began under Thutmose I and may have lasted through the reign of Queen Hatshepsut. He became a scribe of the treasury and also mayor of the towns of Nekheb and Iunyt (El-Kab and Esna).

The back wall of the main hall of his tomb was given the shape of a round-topped stela with a niche in its center. The niche was filled by three seated statues, and the surface of the stela was inscribed in horizontal lines with a text that begins in the rounded top and continues on the right and left sides of the niche. This is a mortuary text consisting of four parts: (1) the traditional prayer for offerings in a much enlarged version; (2) an elaborate vision of life in the beyond; (3) a recital of Paheri's virtuous conduct as an official; (4) an appeal to the living to recite the prayer for offerings, again much more elaborate than such appeals had been in the past.

Publication: J. J. Tylor and F. Ll. Griffith, *The Tomb of Paheri at El Kab*; bound with E. Naville, *Ahnas el Medineh*, Egypt Exploration Fund, 11th memoir (London, 1894), the text: pp. 27-31 and pl. 9. J. J. Tylor, *Wall Drawings and Monuments of El Kab: the Tomb of Paheri* (London, 1895), the text: pl. 16.   *Urk. IV*, 111-123.

Translation: *Urk. deutsch*, pp. 55-61.   G. Fecht, *ZÄS*, 92 (1965), 15-23 (lines 5-21).   For additional references see also PM V, 177-181.

The prayer for offerings

(1) An offering given by the King (to) Amun,
Lord of Thrones-of-the-Two-Lands,[1]
King of eternity, lord of everlastingness,
Ruler, lord of the two great plumes,
Sole one, primordial, eldest,
Primeval, without [equal],
[Creator] of men and gods,
Living flame that came from Nun,
[Maker] of light for mankind;
(And) Nekhbet, the White one of Nekhen,[2]
Mistress of heaven, lady of the Two Lands;
(And) Osiris Khentamentiu,
Lord of Thinis, great in Abydos;
(And) Hathor, mistress of the desert,
Strong of heart among the gods;
(And) Ptah-Sokar, lord of Shetyt,[3]
Anubis, lord of Rostau,[4]
(And) the Enneads, great and small.
May they give a thousand of bread, beer, beef and fowl,
A thousand of food-offerings,
A thousand of drink-offerings,
All the plants that sprout from earth,
A thousand of all things good and pure,
That are offered to the eternal lord;
To receive the bread that came before (him),
The milk that came upon the altar,
To drink the water that flows from Yebu,[5]

On the monthly feast, the sixth-day feast,
The half-monthly feast, the great procession,
The rise of Sothis, the *wag*-feast,
The Thoth-feast, the first-birth feast,
The birth of Isis, the procession of Min,
The procession of the *sem*-priest,
The evening meal, the rise of the river—
The feasts of heaven on their fixed days,
In accord with daily custom.
You are clothed in the robe of finest linen,
The garments that clad the flesh of the god;
You are anointed with pure oil,
You drink water from the altar's rim;

You partake of its possessions,
As a noble in front of the blessed;
For the *ka* of the Mayor of Nekheb,
The Scribe Paheri, the justified,
(5) The loyal trusty of his lord.

The life in the beyond

You come in, you go out,
Your heart in joy at the praise of the lord of gods;
A good burial after revered old age,
After old age has come.
You take your place in the lord-of-life,[6]
You come to the earth in the tomb of the west.
To become indeed a living *ba*,
It shall thrive on bread, water, and air;
To assume the form of phoenix, swallow,
Of falcon or heron, as you wish.
You cross in the ferry without being hindered,
You fare on the water's flowing flood.
You come to life a second time,
Your *ba* shall not forsake your corpse.
Your *ba* is divine among the spirits,
The worthy *ba*'s converse with you.
You join them to receive what is given on earth,
You thrive on water, you breathe air,
You drink as your heart desires.
Your eyes are given you to see,
Your ears to hear what is spoken;
Your mouth speaks, your feet walk,
Your hands, your arms have motion.
Your flesh is firm, your muscles are smooth,
You delight in all your limbs;
You count your members: all there, sound,
There is no fault in what is yours.
Your heart is yours in very truth,
You have your own, your former heart.
You rise to heaven, you open *dat*,[7]
In any shape that you desire.
You are summoned daily to Wennofer's altar,
You receive the bread that comes before (him),
The offering to the lord of the sacred land;
For the *ka* of the Mayor of Nekheb, the Mayor of Iunyt,[8]
Who counts the grain from Iunet[9] to Nekheb,

The watchful leader, (10) free of fault,
The Scribe Paheri, the justified.

You eat bread beside the god,
At the great terrace of the Ennead's Lord;
You turn from there to where he is,
In the midst of the leading council.
You walk about among them,
You consort with the Horus-servants;
You go up, you go down, unhindered,
You are not turned back at the gate of *dat*.
The portals of lightland open for you,
The bolts slide back of themselves;
You reach the Hall of the Two Truths,[10]
The god who is in it welcomes you.
You settle down in the netherworld,
You stride about in the city (15) of Hapy.[11]
Your heart rejoices as you plow
In your plot in the Field of Reeds;
You are rewarded with what you have grown,
You gather a harvest rich in grain.
The rope is roped for you in the ferry,
You sail as your heart desires.
You go outdoors each morning,
You return each evening.
The torch is lit for you at night,
Until the sun shines on your breast.
One says to you, "Welcome, welcome,"
In this your house of the living.
You see Re in heaven's lightland,
You watch (20) Amun as he dawns.
You waken gladly every day,
All afflictions are expelled.
You traverse eternity in joy,
In the favor of the god who is in you.[12]
Your heart is with you without failing you,
Your provisions remain in their place;
For the *ka* of the Scribe Paheri, the justified.

Paheri recalls his blameless conduct

He says:
I am a noble who served his lord,
One skilled and free of negligence.
I walked on the road I had explored,

I knew the outcome of life.
I reckoned the limits in the books,
The boundaries of the king's concerns,
All things that pertained to the palace,
Like Hapy in his course to the (25) sea.[13]
My mouth was firm in serving the lord,
I was fearful of deficiency;
I did not neglect making payment in full,
I did not take a slice of the expense.
I was guided by my own heart
On the road of those praised by the king.
My pen of reed made me renowned,
It gave me right in the council;
It made my nature, I ⌈surpassed⌉ the nobles,

My good character raised me high,
I was summoned as one who is blameless.
(30) Were I to be placed on the scales,
I would come out complete, whole, sound.
I came and went with a steady heart,
I told no lie to anyone.
I knew the god who dwells in man,
Knowing him I knew this from that.
I did the tasks as they were ordered,
I did not confuse the report with the reporter,
I did not speak with low-class words,
I did not talk to worthless (35) people.
I was a model of kindliness,
One praised who came praised from the womb.
The Mayor of Nekheb, Paheri, the justified,
Son of the tutor of the prince, the scribe Itruri, the justified,
Born of the Lady Kam, the justified.

The appeal to the living

He says:
Listen, all who now have being,
I speak to you without deceit;
You who live, who have existence,
Nobles, people, upon earth;
Servants of god, priests, attendants,
Every scribe who holds the palette,
Who is skilled in words of god;[14]
Whosoever is good to his subjects,

Whosoever excels in his (40) task:
Re, everlasting, will commend you,
Also Nekhbet, the White one of Nekhen,
And whoever guides your task.[15]
You will bequeath to your children,
If you say, "An offering, given by the king,"
In the form in which it is written;
"An invocation-offering," as said by the fathers,
And as it comes from the mouth of god.
Whosoever will bend his arm,
He will be on the path of truth.
To act as befits, as conforms to the rules,
Is to bear witness before this stela.
Your thousand of bread, your thousand of beer,
Your hundredthousand of all good things,
Offered pure to the Osiris,
Mayor of Nekheb, Mayor of Iunyt,
Trusty of the treasurer on the southern journey (45),
The worthy Scribe of the accounts, the justified Paheri.

I say to you, I let you know:
It is a recital without expense,[16]
It does not make poor, it makes no trouble;
It means no quarrel with another,
It is no coercing one who is needy.
It is a pleasing speech that uplifts,
The heart does not tire to hear it.
The breath of the mouth, it is not eaten,
There is no strain, no fatigue in it.
It is good for you when you do it,
You will find in it [profit] and (50) praise.
While I was in the land of the living,
No sin against god was reproached me.
I have become an equipped [blessed spirit],
I have furnished my place in the graveyard.
I have what I need in all things,
I shall not fail to respond.
The dead is father to him who acts for him,
He forgets not him who libates for him,
It is good for you to listen!

NOTES

1. The temple of Amun at Karnak.

2. In addition to being the goddess of the town of Nekheb, Nekhbet was closely associated with the town of Nekhen (Hieraconpolis), which faced Nekheb across the river.

3. Name of a sanctuary of Ptah-Sokar.

4. Term for the necropolis, often specifically that of Giza.

5. Elephantine, where the waters of the Nile were thought to emerge from the ground.

6. A metaphor for the coffin.

7. A region of the sky often identified with the netherworld.

8. Modern Esna.

9. Modern Dendera.

10. The hall in which the judgment of the dead took place as described in chapter 125 of the Book of the Dead.

11. Hapy, the Nile god, dwelled in the netherworld.

12. On the notion of the god who dwells in man see Bonnet, *RÄRG*, pp. 225-228.

13. This seems to mean that Paheri observed the proper limits in his administrative activities, just as the Nile stays on course.

14. I.e., in writing. The god Thoth had invented the art of writing.

15. The specific gods who were the patrons of the various professions.

16. I.e., the recitation of the offering formula is a simple and easy task that requires no exertion.

THE INSTALLATION OF THE VIZIER REKHMIRE

In his Tomb at Thebes

The reliefs and texts in this splendid tomb give a many-faceted account of the activities of the vizier Rekhmire, who served under King Thutmose III. The principal texts are: (1) the autobiography; (2) the king's installation speech; (3) the description of the duties of the vizier. Only the second text, the royal installation speech, is translated here. The text is carved in vertical columns on the west wall of the transverse hall. The accompanying relief shows Thutmose III enthroned. The figure of Rekhmire, who stood before the king, has been destroyed.

Publication: P. E. Newberry, *The Life of Rekhmara* (London, 1900), pls. 9-10.   A. H. Gardiner, *RT*, 26 (1904), 1-19.   K. Sethe, *Die Einsetzung des Viziers unter der 18. Dynastie*, Untersuchungen, 5/2 (Leipzig, 1912).   *Urk. IV*, 1086-1093.   N. de G. Davies, *The Tomb of Rekhmi-Reʿ at Thebes*, The Metropolitan Museum of Art Egyptian Expedition, vol. 11 (New York, 1944), pp. 84-88 and pls. xiv-xv.   R. O. Faulkner, *JEA*, 41 (1955), 18-29 (the best text copy).

Translation: *BAR*, II, §§665-670.

Legend accompanying the scene

(1) The charge placed upon the vizier Rekhmire. The council is brought into the hall of Pharaoh. The vizier Rekhmire is ushered in, newly appointed.

The speech of Pharaoh

His majesty said to him:
Look to the office of vizier,
(5) Watch over all that is done in it,
Lo, it is the pillar for the whole land.
Lo, being vizier,
Lo, it is not sweet,
Lo, it is bitter as gall.[1]
Lo, he is the copper that shields the gold of his master's house,
Lo, he is not one who bends his face to magistrates and councillors,
Not one who makes of anyone his client.
Lo, what a man does in his master's house will be his happiness,
Lo, he shall not act [⌜in the house⌝] of another.

Lo, petitioners come from the South and the North,
The whole land is eager for [the counsel of the vizier];
See to it that all is done according to law,
That all is done exactly right,
In [giving a man] his vindication.
Lo, the magistrate who judges in public,
Wind and water report all that he does,
Lo, there is none who ignores his deeds.
If he makes [⌜a mistake in deciding⌝] his case,
And fails to reveal it through the mouth of the clerk,
It will be known (10) through the mouth of him whom he judged,
Through his telling it to the clerk by saying:
"This is not the decision of my case."[2]
If the petitioner is sent ---
------ or magistrate,
One will not ignore what he did.
Lo, the magistrate's safety is acting by the rule,
In acting on a petitioner's speech;
Then the judged [cannot say]:
"I was not given my right."
⌜A proverb in the Book of Memphis says:
"Gracious king, lawful vizier."⌝[3]

Avoid what was said of the vizier Akhtoy,
That he denied his own people for the sake of others,

For fear of being falsely called [partial].
If one of them appealed a judgment,
That he had planned to do to him,
He persisted in denying him,
But that is excess of justice.
(15) Do not judge unfairly,
God abhors partiality;
This is an instruction,
Plan to act accordingly.
Regard one you know like one you don't know,
One near you like one far from you.
The magistrate who acts like this,
He will succeed here in this place.

Do not pass over a petitioner,
Before you have considered his speech.
When a petitioner is about to petition you,
Don't dismiss what he says as already said.
Deny him after you let him hear
On what account you have denied him.
Lo, it is said:
"A petitioner wants his plea considered
Rather than have his case adjudged."[4]
Do not scold a man wrongfully,
Scold where scolding is due.
Cast your fear, that you be feared,
The feared magistrate is a magistrate.
A magistrate's worth is that he does right,
But if a man makes himself feared a million times,
People think something is wrong with him,
And they don't say of him, "He is a man."

This too is said:
A magistrate (20) who lies comes out as he deserves.
Lo, you succeed in doing this office by doing justice,
Lo, doing justice is what is wanted in the actions of the vizier,
Lo, the vizier is its true guardian since the time of god.
Lo, what one says of the vizier's chief scribe:
"Scribe of Justice" one says of him.
As to the hall in which you judge,
It has a room full of [written] decisions.
He who does justice before all people,
He is the vizier.
Lo, a man remains in his office,
If he acts as he is charged,

Innocent is the man who acts as he is told.
Do not act willfully
In a case where the law is known;
For as regards the headstrong man,[5]
The Lord prefers the timid to the headstrong man.
Act then in accord with the charge given you.
Lo, [⌐it is laid upon you⌐].

Furthermore, pay attention to the plowlands when they are being confirmed. If you are absent from the inspection, you shall send the chief inspectors and chief controllers to inspect. If anyone has made an inspection before you, you shall question him. May you act according to your charge.[6]

NOTES

1. On the use of iterated *mk*, "lo," see my article in *JNES*, 30 (1971), 69-72.

2. The five lines are difficult and the translations differ widely.

3. On this passage see my note in the *Wilson Festschrift*, pp. 63-65, and also H. Goedicke's new interpretation in *JARCE*, 9 (1971/72), 69-72.

4. The same observation occurs in the *Instruction of Ptahhotep*, lines 268-269.

5. *Dmi n*, "touching upon," means "as regards"; it is the same evolution of meaning as in Hebrew *be-noge'a*. The *shm-ib* is the man who is willful, arrogant, violent, and the like.

6. This final passage is written in prose and fits better with the text called "duties of the vizier" which is carved on the wall opposite the "installation" text.

II. Inscriptions from Royal Monuments

OBELISK INSCRIPTIONS OF QUEEN HATSHEPSUT
In the Temple of Karnak

Queen Hatshepsut erected four obelisks in the temple of Amun at Karnak, two of which have disappeared entirely. Of the remaining pair, the northern one still stands in its original position, while its companion has fallen. The obelisks are of pink Assuan granite.

A column of inscription was carved on each of the four sides of the shaft, and subsequently side columns with offering scenes were added. The bases on which the obelisks rested were also inscribed on all four sides. The shaft and base inscriptions of the standing obelisk (except for the later additions to the shaft) are translated below. The obelisk is 97.5 feet high and is now the tallest standing obelisk in Egypt. The base inscription is a single text of thirty-two lines which circles the base beginning on the south side.

In the inscriptions the Queen makes several emphatic points: Her devotion to her divine father Amun and to her earthly father Thutmose I. The obelisks are erected to the glory of Amun and to the memory of Thutmose I. Furthermore, she wants it correctly understood that each obelisk consists of a single monolith of granite, and that their gilding had required inordinate amounts of the finest gold. Lastly, there is the theme of her right to the throne, an ever present concern in her inscriptions: her father Amun had destined her to be king. Masculine and feminine designations of her person alternate in her pronouncements: she is the son and the daughter of Amun.

Publication: LD, III, 22-24.   Urk. IV, 356-369.
Translation: BAR, II, §§308-319.

Shaft Inscriptions

Westside. Horus: Mighty-of-*ka*'s; Two Ladies: Flourishing-in-years; Gold-Horus: Divine-of-diadems; King of Upper and Lower Egypt, Lord of the Two Lands: *Makare.* She made as her monument for her father Amun, Lord of Thrones-of-the-Two-Lands, the erecting for him of two great obelisks at the august portal, "Amun-great-in-majesty." Wrought with very fine electrum,[1] they illuminate the Two Lands like Aten.[2] Never was the like made since earth's beginning. Made for him by the Son of Re, *Hatshepsut Khenemet-Amun,* given life like Re forever.

Southside. Horus: Mighty-of-*ka*'s; King of Upper and Lower Egypt: *Makare*, shining image of Amun, whom he made appear as King upon the throne of Horus, in front of the holies of the palace; whom the Great Ennead nursed to be mistress of the circuit of Aten. They have endowed her with life, dominion, and joy in front of the living; the Son of Re: *Hatshepsut Khenemet-Amun*, beloved of Amen-Re, King of Gods, given life like Re forever.

Eastside. Horus: Mighty-of-*ka*'s; King of Upper and Lower Egypt: *Makare*, beloved of Amen-Re. Her majesty has recorded the name of her father on this enduring monument. Inasmuch as favor was shown to the King of Upper and Lower Egypt, Aakheperkare,[3] by the majesty of this god, accordingly these two great obelisks were erected by her majesty for the first time. For it was said by the Lord of Gods: "Your father, the King of Upper and Lower Egypt, Aakheperkare, gave instruction to erect obelisks, and your majesty shall multiply monuments, so as to live forever."

Northside. Horus: Mighty-of-*ka*'s; Two Ladies: Flourishing-in-years; Gold-Horus: Divine-of-diadems; King of Upper and Lower Egypt, Lord of the Two Lands: *Makare*. Her father Amun has established her great name upon the august *ished*-tree.[4] Her annals are millions of years, united with life, stability, and dominion. The Son of Re, *Hatshepsut Khenemet-Amun*, beloved of Amen-Re, King of Gods, is [⌐the builder of this beautiful monument¬] which she made for him on the first occurrence of the jubilee, so that she will have life forever.

Base Inscription

(1) The Living Horus: Mighty-of-*ka*'s; Two Ladies: Flourishing-in-years; Gold-Horus: Divine-of-diadems; King of Upper and Lower Egypt: *Makare*; Daughter of Re: *Hatshepsut Khenemet-Amun*, who lives forever. The daughter of Amen-Re, his beloved, his only one who came from him; shining image of the Lord-of-all; whose beauty was fashioned by the powers of On; who holds the Two Lands like her maker; whom he created so as to wear his diadems; who has forms like Khepri, who rises like Harakhti; pure egg, splendid seed, whom the Two Magicians nursed; whom Amun himself made appear upon the throne of Southern On;[5] whom he chose as guardian of Egypt, as protector of nobles and commoners. The Horus who championed her father, the eldest of Kamutef; (5) whom Re begot so as to have beneficent offspring on earth, for the well-being of mankind. His living image, the King of Upper and Lower Egypt, *Makare*, the fine gold of kings.

She made as her monument for her father Amun, Lord of Thrones-of-the-Two-Lands, presiding over Ipet-sut, the making for him of two great obelisks of hard granite of the South, their upper side[6] being of electrum, of the best of all foreign lands. Seen on both sides of the river, their rays flood the Two Lands when Aten dawns between them, as he rises in heaven's lightland.

Speech of the Queen

I have done this with a loving heart for my father Amun;
Initiated in his secret of the beginning,
Acquainted with his beneficent might,
I did not forget whatever he had ordained.
My majesty knows his divinity,
I acted under his command;
It was he who led me,
I did not plan a work without his doing.
(10) It was he who gave directions,
I did not sleep because of his temple,
I did not stray from what he commanded.
My heart was Sia[7] before my father,
I entered into the plans of his heart.
I did not turn my back to the city of the All-Lord,
Rather did I turn my face to it.
I know that Ipet-sut is the lightland on earth,
The august hill of the beginning,
The Sacred Eye of the All-Lord,
His favored place that bears his beauty,
That gathers in his followers.

It is the King himself who says:
I declare before the folk who shall be in the future,
Who shall observe the monument I made for my father,
Who shall speak in discussion,
Who shall look to posterity—
It was when I sat in the palace,
And thought of my maker,
(15) That my heart led me to make for him
Two obelisks of electrum,
Whose summits would reach the heavens,
In the august hall of columns,
Between the two great portals of the King,
The Strong Bull, King Aakheperkare, the Horus triumphant.[8]
Now my heart turns to and fro,
In thinking what will the people say,
They who shall see my monument in after years,
And shall speak of what I have done.

Beware of saying, "I know not, I know not:
Why has this been done?
To fashion a mountain of gold throughout,
Like something that just happened."
I swear, as I am loved of Re,
As Amun, my father, favors me,
As my nostrils are refreshed with life and dominion,
As I wear the white crown,
As I appear with the red crown,
As the Two Lords have joined (20) their portions for me,
As I rule this land like the son of Isis,
As I am mighty like the son of Nut,
As Re rests in the evening bark,
As he prevails in the morning bark,
As he joins his two mothers in the god's ship,
As sky endures, as his creation lasts,
As I shall be eternal like an undying star,
As I shall rest in life like Atum—
So as regards these two great obelisks,
Wrought with electrum by my majesty for my father Amun,
In order that my name may endure in this temple,
For eternity and everlastingness,
They are each of one block of hard granite,
Without seam, without joining together!

My majesty began work on them in year 15, second month of winter, day 1, ending in year 16, fourth month of summer, last day, totaling seven months of quarry work. (25) I did it for him out of affection, as a king for a god. It was my wish to make them for him gilded with electrum. "Their foil[9] lies on their body," is what I expect people to say. My mouth is effective in its speech; I do not go back on my word. Hear ye! I gave for them of the finest electrum. I measured it by the gallon like sacks of grain. My majesty summoned a quantity beyond what the Two Lands had yet seen. The ignorant and the wise know it.

Not shall he who hears it say,
"It is a boast," what I have said;
Rather say, "How like her it is,
She is devoted to her father!"
Lo, the god knows me well,
Amun, Lord of Thrones-of-the-Two-Lands;
He made me rule (30) Black Land and Red Land as reward,
No one rebels against me in all lands.

All foreign lands are my subjects,
He placed my border at the limits of heaven,
What Aten encircles labors for me.
He gave it to him who came from him,
Knowing I would rule it for him.
I am his daughter in very truth,
Who serves him, who knows what he ordains.
My reward from my father is life-stability-rule,
On the Horus throne of all the living, eternally like Re.

NOTES

1. *D·m*, "electrum," or, "fine gold," designated the gold with a high silver content which was especially prized.

2. Early in the Eighteenth Dynasty, the sun disk, *itn*, achieved the status of a deity.

3. King Thutmose I, the father of Hatshepsut.

4. A tree revered as the tree of life, on whose leaves the names and years of kings were recorded by the gods. The scene of recording is often depicted in Ramesside temples. The tree is depicted as a leafy fruit-tree. Just what kind of tree the Egyptians thought of is not known.

5. Thebes was often called "Heliopolis of the South"; see H. Kees, *Orientalia*, 18 (1949), 434-436.

6. *Gs.sn ḥry*, "their upper side," seems to mean "their surface." In any case it does not mean "their summits." That is to say, not merely the summits of the obelisks were gilded, but rather the entire shafts.

7. The personification of the concept of understanding.

8. Thutmose I had built the two pylons now numbered IV and V, and a hypostyle hall between them. Hatshepsut removed its wooden ceiling, thus turning the hall into a colonnaded court, and erected her two obelisks in it.

9. Literally, "their side." The meaning seems to be that the gold foil forms a solid sheath.

FROM THE ANNALS OF THUTMOSE III

The First Campaign: The Battle of Megiddo

Beginning in the first year of his reign, and over a period of twenty years, Thutmose III conducted a series of at least sixteen campaigns in Asia by which he established Egypt's Asiatic empire. The year-by-year record of the campaigns was carved on the walls of two halls located behind Pylon No. VI in the temple of Karnak. The first campaign is narrated at length; the others are told more briefly. The "Annals," as these records are called, are written in a direct and factual manner. They are thus both a primary historical source and an example of Egyptian royal records at their most realistic and least rhetorical.

The account of the first campaign is carved in vertical columns on the north wall of the second, or eastern, hall. Many of the lines have lost portions at the top or bottom.

Publication: *Urk. IV*, 645-667.
Translation: B*AR*, II, §§391-443.   H. H. Nelson, *The Battle of Megiddo* (Chicago, 1913).   R. O. Faulkner, *JEA*, 28 (1942), 2-15. J. A. Wilson in *ANET*, pp. 234-238.   E. Edel in Galling, *Textbuch*, pp. 14-20.
Study: H. Grapow, *Studien zu den Annalen Thutmosis des Dritten.* Abhandlungen der deutschen Akademie der Wissenschaften, Berlin. Phil.-hist. Kl., 1947/2 (Berlin, 1949).

(1) Horus: Strong-Bull-arisen-in-Thebes; [Two Ladies: Enduring-in-kingship-like-Re-in-heaven; Gold-Horus: Mighty-in-strength, Majestic-in-appearance]; the King of Upper and Lower Egypt, Lord of the Two Lands: *Menkheperre*; the Son of Re, [of his body: *Thutmose*, given life forever].

His majesty commanded to record [the victories his father Amun had given him] by an inscription in the temple which his majesty had made for [his father Amun, so as to record] (5) each campaign, together with the booty which [his majesty] had brought [from it, and the tribute of every foreign land] that his father Re had given him.

Year 22,[1] fourth month of winter, day 25, [his majesty passed the fortress of] Sile on the first campaign of victory [to smite those who attacked] the borders of Egypt, in valor [strength, might, and right]. For a [long] period of years ------ (10) plunder, with every man [serving] ---. For it had happened in the time of other (kings) that the garrison there[2] was (only) in Sharuhen, while from Yerdj to the ends of the earth there was rebellion against his majesty.

Year 23, first month of summer, day 4, the day of the feast of the King's Coronation, (arriving) at the town of "Conquest-of-the-Ruler" [the Syrian name of which is] Gaza. [Year 23] (15), first month of summer, day 5, departure from this place in valor, [strength], might, and right, to overthrow that wretched enemy,[3] to extend the borders of Egypt, his father, mighty and victorious Amun, having commanded that he conquer.

Year 23, first month of summer, day 16, (arrival) at the town of Yehem. [His majesty] ordered a consultation with his valiant army, saying: "That wretched foe (20) of Kadesh has come and entered into Megiddo and is [there] at this moment. He has gathered to him the princes of [all] the foreign lands [that had been loyal] to Egypt, as well as those from as far as Nahrin, consisting of ---, Khor and Kedy, their horses, their armies, [their people]. And he says—it is reported— 'I shall wait [and fight his majesty here] (25) in Megiddo.' (Now) tell me [what you think]."

They said to his majesty: "How will it be to go [on] this road which becomes narrow, when it is [reported] that the enemies are waiting there [beyond and they] are numerous? Will not horse go behind [horse] (30) and [soldiers] and people too? Shall our vanguard be fighting while the [rearguard] waits here in Aruna,[4] unable to fight? There are two (other) roads here. One of the roads is [to our east] and [comes out] at Taanach. The other is on the (35) north side of Djefti, so that we come out to the north of Megiddo. May our valiant lord proceed on whichever of [these] seems best to him. Do not make us go on that difficult road!"

Then messages —————, which they had said before. The speech of the majesty of the palace: "I swear, (40) as Re loves me, as my father Amun favors me, as my nostrils are refreshed with life and dominion, my majesty shall proceed on this Aruna road! Let him of you who wishes go on those roads you spoke of. Let him of you who wishes come in my majesty's following. Or they will say, those (45) foes whom Re abhors: 'Has his majesty gone on another road because he is afraid of us?' So they will say."

They said to his majesty: "May your father Amun, Lord of Thrones-of-the-Two-Lands, who presides over Ipet-sut, do [as you wish]! We are followers of [your majesty] wherever your majesty goes! A servant follows his lord."

[His majesty ordered to] (50) tell the whole army: ["Your valiant lord will guide your steps on] this road which becomes narrow." [For his majesty had taken] an oath, saying: "I shall not let [my valiant army] go before me from [this place!" Thus his majesty resolved] that he himself should go before his army. [Every man] was informed (55) of his order of march, horse following horse, with his majesty at the head of his army.

Year 23, first month of summer, day 19, awakening in [life] in the royal tent at the town of Aruna. Northward journey by my[5] majesty with my father Amen-Re, Lord of Thrones-of-the-Two-Lands, [that he might open the ways] before me, Harakhti fortifying [the heart of my valiant army], (60) my father Amun strengthening [my majesty's] arm, and ——— protecting my majesty.

Coming out (of the pass) by his majesty [at the head of his army], grouped in many battalions, [without meeting] a single [enemy]. [Their] southern wing was at Taanach, and [their] northern wing on the [north][6] side [of the Qina valley. Then] (65) his majesty called to them: "—————, they are fallen! The wretched enemy ————— Amun —————. Give (70) [praise to him, extol the might] of his majesty, for his strength is greater than —————. [He has protected the rearguard of] his majesty's army in Aruna." Now while the rearguard of his majesty's valiant army was still at Aruna, the vanguard had come out into the Qina valley, and they filled the opening of the valley.

Then they said to his majesty: (75) "Lo, his majesty has come out with his valiant troops and they fill the valley. May our valiant lord listen to us this time. May our lord watch for us the rearguard of his army with its people. When the rearguard has come out to us in the open, then we shall fight against those foreigners; then we shall not be concerned about the rearguard of (80) our army!" His majesty halted in the open. He sat [down] there to watch the rear guard of his valiant army. Now when the last of the lead-troops had come out from this road, the shadow turned.[7]

His majesty arrived at the south of Megiddo, on the shore of the Qina brook, when the seventh hour was in (its) course of day. A camp was laid out for his majesty, and the whole army was told: "Prepare yourselves! Make your weapons ready! For one will engage in combat with that wretched foe in the morning; for one ------." Resting in the royal camp. Giving provisions to the officers, rations to the attendants. Posting the watch of the army; saying to them: "Steadfast, steadfast! Vigilant, vigilant!" Awakening in life in the royal tent. One came to tell his majesty: "The region is safe, and so are the troops of the south and the north."

The battle

Year 23, first month of summer, day 21, the exact day of the feast of the new moon. Appearance of the King at dawn. An order was given to the whole army to pass ---. (85) His majesty set out on a chariot of fine gold, decked in his shining armor like strong-armed Horus, lord of action, like Mont of Thebes, his father Amun strengthening his arm. The southern wing of his majesty's army was at a hill south of the Qina [brook], and the northern wing to the northwest of Megiddo, while his majesty was in their center, Amun protecting his person ⟨in⟩ the melee, and the strength of [Seth pervading] his limbs.

Then his majesty overwhelmed them at the head of his army. When they saw his majesty overwhelming them, they fled headlong [to] Megiddo with faces of fear, abandoning their horses, their chariots of gold and silver, so as to be hoisted up into the town by pulling at their garments. For the people had shut the town behind them, and they now [lowered] garments to hoist them up into the town. Now if his majesty's troops had not set their hearts to plundering the possessions of the enemies, they would have [captured] Megiddo at this moment, when the wretched foe of Kadesh and the wretched foe of this town were being pulled up hurriedly so as to admit them into their town. For the fear of his majesty had entered [their bodies], and their arms sank as his diadem overwhelmed them.

Then their horses were captured, and their chariots of gold and silver became an easy [prey]. Their ranks were lying stretched out on their backs like fish in the bight of a net, while his majesty's valiant army counted their possessions. Captured was the tent of that wretched [foe], which was worked [with silver]. ——————. Then the entire army jubilated and gave praise to Amun [for the victory] he had given to his son on [that day. They lauded] his majesty and extolled his victory. Then they presented the plunder they had taken: hands, living prisoners, horses, chariots of gold and silver and of [⌐painted work⌐].

Siege and surrender of Megiddo

(90) ——————. [Then his majesty] commanded his army, saying: "Grasp well, grasp well, [my] valiant [army]! Lo, [all the foreign lands] are placed [in this town by the will of] Re on this day. Inasmuch as every prince of every [northern] land is shut up within it, the capture of Megiddo is the capture of a thousand towns! Grasp firmly, firmly!" ——————. [Orders were given to] the troop-commanders to [provide for their soldiers and to let] every [man know] his place. They measured the town, surrounded (it) with a ditch, and walled (it) up with fresh timber from all their fruit trees. His majesty himself was on the fort east of the town, guarding [it day and night]. —————— [surrounded] by a thick wall —————— its thickness. It was given the name "Menkheperre-Encircler-of-Asiatics." Guards were placed at the camp of his majesty and were told: "Steadfast, steadfast! Vigilant, vigilant!" His majesty ——————. [No one] of them [was permitted to come] out beyond this wall, except for a coming out to ⌐knock⌐ at the gate of their fortress.[8]

Now all that his majesty did to this town and to the wretched foe and his wretched army was recorded on its day by the name of the sortie and by the name of the troop-commander. ——————. They are recorded on a roll of leather in the temple of Amun to this day.[9]

Now the princes of this foreign land came on their bellies to kiss the ground to the might of his majesty, and to beg breath for their nostrils, because of the greatness of his strength and the extent of the power of [Amun over (95) all foreign lands]. ——————, all the princes captured by his majesty's might bearing their tribute of silver, gold, lapis lazuli, and turquoise, and carrying grain, wine, and large and small cattle for his majesty's army; one group among them bore tribute on the journey south. Then his majesty appointed the rulers anew for [every town] ——————.

[List of the booty which his majesty's army brought from the town of] Megiddo. Living prisoners: 340. Hands: 83. Horses: 2,041. Foals: 191. Stallions: 6. Colts: ———. One chariot of that foe worked in gold, with a ⌐pole⌐ of gold. One fine chariot of the prince of [Megiddo], worked in gold. [Chariots of the allied princes: 30]. Chariots of his wretched army: 892. Total: 924. One fine bronze coat of mail belonging to that enemy. One fine bronze coat of mail belonging to the prince of Megiddo. [⌐ Leather ⌐] coats of mail belonging to his wretched army: 200. Bows: 502. Poles of *mry*-wood worked with silver from the tent of that enemy: 7. And the army of [his majesty] had captured [cattle belonging to this town] ――――: 387. Cows: 1,929. Goats: 2,000. Sheep: 20,500.

List of what was carried off afterward by the King from the household goods of the enemy of Yanoam, Inuges, and Herenkeru, together with the property of the towns that had been loyal to him which were captured by [the might of his majesty] ――――.
[*Maryan*-warriors][10] belonging to them: 38. Children of that enemy and of the princes with him: 84. *Maryan*-warriors belonging to them: 5. Male and female slaves and their children: 1,796. Pardoned persons who had come out from that enemy because of hunger: 103. Total: 2,503. In addition, bowls of costly stone and gold, and various vessels (100) ――――. One large jar of Syrian workmanship. Jars, bowls, plates, various drinking vessels, large kettles, knives: [x+]17, making 1,784 *deben*.[11] Gold in ⌐ disks ⌐ skillfully crafted, and many silver ⌐ disks ⌐, making 966 *deben* and 1 *kite*. A silver statue ――――. ―――― with a head of gold. Walking sticks with human heads:[12] 3. Carrying chairs of that enemy of ivory, ebony, and *ssndm*-wood worked with gold: 6. Footstools belonging to them: 6. Large tables of ivory and *ssndm*-wood: 6. One bed of *ssndm*-wood worked with gold and all costly stones in the manner of a *krkr*, belonging to that enemy, worked with gold throughout. A statue of ebony of that enemy worked with gold with a head of lapis lazuli. ――――, bronze vessels and much clothing of that enemy.

The fields were made into plots and assigned to royal inspectors in order to reap their harvest. List of the harvest which his majesty brought from the fields of Megiddo. Sacks of wheat: 207,300[+x], apart from what was cut as forage by his majesty's army. ――――.

NOTES

1. In reckoning his regnal years, Thutmose III incorporated the twenty-one years of Hatshepsut's rule. Thus "year 22" is in fact "year 1" of his reign.
2. In Palestine.
3. The prince of Kadesh.
4. The army is actually at Yehem. Aruna was the next stop, reached after a three day march, and it was there that the narrow mountain pass began.
5. The change into a first person narrative suggests that parts of the original document, in the form of a campaign diary, were written in the first person and the whole was subsequently transposed, with some inconsistency, into the more formal third person narration. The original diary is mentioned in line 94.

6. Sethe's restoration of "south" in line 64 (*Urk. IV*, 653) is impossible. If the enemy's northern wing had been on the south side of the Qina valley, the Egyptian army, coming up from the south, could not have entered the valley unobserved. Either "north" must be restored, or the restoration "of the Qina valley" should be questioned.

7. At noon.

8. In order to surrender.

9. This is the mention of the campaign diary; see n. 5.

10. The *Maryan* are thought to have been chariot warriors of Indo-Aryan descent.

11. The *deben* weighed 91 grams; it was divided into 10 *kite*.

12. I.e., with handles carved in the shape of human heads.

THE POETICAL STELA OF THUTMOSE III

From the Karnak Temple

Cairo Museum 34010

The finely carved stela was found in the Karnak temple, in the court to the north of the western "hall of annals." It is of black granite, 180 cm high. In the lunette the king is shown in two symmetrical scenes, presenting offerings to Amen-Re. The text below, written in twenty-five horizontal lines, is a speech by Amen-Re which consists of three parts. In the first twelve lines the god welcomes the king and recounts the victories he has given him. This part is written in the orational style. Thereafter, the god's speech takes the form of a triumphal poem composed of ten quatrains. Each quatrain consists of two distichs introduced by anaphoras, the first anaphora being, "I came to let you tread," and the second, "I let them see." Owing to the anaphoric pattern, the length of each metrical line is precisely established and made visible. Moreover, the scribe has used the graphic device of stichic writing: each distich occupies one half of the line, and the anaphoric words are spaced symmetrically below one another.

The hymn of triumph is followed by a conclusion in three lines (lines 23-25) in which the god's speech reverts to the orational style. Thus the triumphal poem is framed by a prologue and an epilogue.

The poem was evidently much admired, for three later kings, Amenhotep III, Seti I, and Ramses III, adapted it to their use. The version of Amenhotep III is translated below on pages 46-47.

Publication: P. Lacau, *Stèles du nouvel empire*, Vol. I, Catalogue général ... du Musée du Caire (Cairo, 1909), pp. 17-21 and pl. vii.   *Urk. IV*, 610-619.

Translation: B*AR*, II, §§655-662.   Erman, *Literature*, pp. 254-258. J. A. Wilson in *ANET*, pp. 373-375.   R. O. Faulkner in Simpson, *Literature*, pp. 285-288 (the poem only).

Prologue

(1) Speech of Amen-Re, Lord of Thrones-of-the-Two-Lands:
You come to me in joy at seeing my beauty,
My son, my champion, Menkheperre, everliving!

I shine for love of you, my heart exults
At your good coming to my temple.
My hands have endowed your body with safety and life,
How pleasant to my breast is your grace!
I placed you in my temple and did signs for you,
I gave you valor and victory over all lands.[1]
I set your might, your fear in every country,
The dread of you as far as heaven's four supports.
I magnified your awe in every body,
I made your person's fame traverse the Nine Bows.
The princes of all lands are gathered in your grasp,
(5) I stretched my own hands out and bound them for you.
I fettered Nubia's Bowmen by tenthousand thousands,
The northerners a hundred thousand captives.
I made your enemies succumb beneath your soles,
So that you crushed the rebels and the traitors.
For I bestowed on you the earth, its length and breadth,
Westerners and easterners are under your command.

You trod all foreign lands with joyful heart,
None could approach your majesty's vicinity,
But you, with me your guide, attained them.
You crossed the water of Nahrin's Euphrates,
In might and victory ordained by me,
Hearing your battle cry they hid in holes.
I robbed their nostrils of the breath of life,
And made the dread of you pervade their hearts.
My serpent on your brow consumed them,
She made quick booty of the evildoers.
(10) The lowlanders[2] she swallowed by her flame,
Asiatic heads she severed, none escaped,
The foes were tottering before her might.
I let your valor course through every land,
The gleaming diadem protected you,
In all that heaven circles none defy you.
They came bearing their tribute on their backs,
Bowed down before your majesty as I decreed.
The foes who came toward you I made weak,
Their hearts aflame, their bodies trembled.

The poem

I came to let you tread on Djahi's chiefs,[3]
    I spread them under your feet throughout their lands;

I let them see your majesty as lord of light,
    so that you shone before them in my likeness.

I came to let you tread on those of Asia,
    to smite the Asians' heads in Retjenu;
I let them see your majesty clad in your panoply,
    when you displayed your weapons on your chariot.

(15) I came to let you tread on eastern lands,
    to crush the dwellers in the realm of god's land;[4]
I let them see your majesty as shooting star,
    that scatters fire as it sheds its flame.

I came to let you tread on western lands,
    Keftiu, Isy[5] are in awe [of you];
I let them see your majesty as youthful bull,
    firm-hearted, sharp of horns, invincible.

I came to let you tread on lowlanders,[6]
    Mitanni's regions cringe in fear of you;
I let them see your majesty as crocodile,
    master of terror in the water, unapproached.

I came to let you tread on islanders,
    the sea-borne people hear your battle cry;[7]
I let them see your majesty as the avenger,
    standing in triumph on his victim's back.[8]

I came to let you tread on Tjehenu,
    the Utjentiu isles[9] are in your power;
I let them see your majesty as fearsome lion,
    as you made corpses of them in their valleys.

(20) I came to let you tread on earth's limits,
    what Ocean circles is enfolded in your fist;
I let them see your majesty as falcon-winged,
    who grasps what he espies as he desires.

I came to let you tread on border people,[10]
    to bind as captives those upon the sand;
I let them see your majesty as southern jackal,[11]
    the racer, runner, roving the Two Lands.

I came to let you tread on Nubians;
    as far as Shat[12] you hold them in your grasp;
I let them see your majesty as your Two Brothers,[13]
    whose hands I joined for you in victory.

Epilogue

I placed your sisters[14] behind you as guard,
My majesty's arms are raised to crush evil,
I give you protection, my son, my beloved,
Horus, Strong-Bull-arisen-in-Thebes,
Whom I begot in my divine body, Thutmose, everliving,
Who does for me all that my *ka* desires.
You have built my temple as a work of eternity,
Made longer and wider than it had been,
With its great gateway "Menkheperre-feasts-Amen-Re,"
Your monuments surpass those of all former kings.
I commanded you to make them,
I am satisfied with them;
I have placed you on the Horus-throne of millions of years,
That you may lead the living forever.

NOTES

1. Here and elsewhere in this text I have rendered the *sḏm·f* forms as past tenses. The stela was erected in celebration of the king's numerous and unprecedented victories. If the god's account of these accomplishments is rendered in the present tense, the enumeration ceases to refer to actual deeds and becomes mere rhetorical hyperbole.

2. The term *imyw nbwt.sn* which I render as "lowlanders," recurs in line 17 next to the mention of Mitanni and in clear distinction from the *imyw iww*, "islanders," of line 18. In J. Vercoutter's study of the term (*BIFAO*, 46 (1947), 125 ff., and *BIFAO*, 48 (1949), 107 ff.) the *nbwt* appear as remote marshy regions to the north and east. In some cases, however, the meaning "islands" is called for, as was maintained by Gardiner in *AEO*, I, 206*-208*.

3. It has been thought that the term Djahi designated Palestine as far as the Lebanon, while Retjenu meant Palestine and Syria together; see Gardiner, *AEO*, I, 142*-149*. But C. Vandersleyen, *Les guerres d'Amosis* (Brussels, 1971), pp. 90-100, has now shown that the name had a wider meaning: it included Palestine, Syria, and northern Mesopotamia.

4. "God's land" was a vague designation of regions south and east of Egypt and included the land of Punt.

5. Keftiu is generally held to be Crete. As to Isy, some scholars identify it with Cyprus, in preference to the identification of Irs=Alasiya with Cyprus. Note that the text here speaks of lands to the west of Egypt, which fits Crete but not Cyprus.

6. See note 2.

7. The word *hmhmt* already occurred in lines 4 and 8. In line 4 it has the meaning "fame," "renown"; examples for this meaning were assembled by J. Spiegel in *WZKM*, 54 (1957), 191 ff.

8. Horus victorious over Seth.

9. An unidentified region; "isles" in Egyptian texts are not always true islands.

10. Faulkner, *op. cit.*, p. 287, rendered *imyw ḥȝt tȝ* as "those who are in the Southland." It is true that *ḥȝt tȝ*, "front of the land," sometimes means "Southland," but this meaning does not suit here, since a term denoting "foreigners" is required. In the next sentence these foreigners are identified as "those upon the sand," i.e., desert nomads. Hence I suggest that "those who are before the land" means "people on the border."

11. Literally, "jackal of Upper Egypt." The warlike god Wepwaut, represented as a jackal or wolf, is meant.

12. Unidentified region of Nubia.

13. Horus and Seth, whose union represented the united kingship of Egypt.

14. Isis and Nephthys, the guardians of Osiris.

THE GREAT SPHINX STELA OF AMENHOTEP II AT GIZA

Originally carved to represent King Khafra, the great sphinx of Giza came to be worshiped as a manifestation of the sun-god Harmakhis (Horus-in-the-horizon). In memory of having frequently visited the spot, King Amenhotep II erected a monument on the sphinx's northeast side, where it was discovered in 1936. It is a round-topped limestone stela measuring 425 × 253 × 53 cm. The upper third, badly damaged so that the scenes have been almost entirely effaced, showed the king offering to the sphinx in two symmetrical scenes. Below is the well-preserved inscription in twenty-seven lines. The text consists of an introductory encomium of the king, written in the orational style, and a prose narration which relates the young king's feats as an oarsman, archer, and horseman. While allowance must be made for hyperbole, the claims of royal prowess have a basis in fact, for several other monuments of this king extol his feats as sportsman, and his mummy is that of an exceptionally tall and strongly built man.

The encomium consists of ornate phrases that have become stereotypes. In the New Kingdom such introductions became ever more elaborate. Yet the kings were not smothered by the ceremonial that surrounded their persons, and the narratives of their deeds, as distinct from the formal laudations, bear the stamp of their individual personalities.

Publication: S. Hassan, *ASAE*, 37 (1937), 129-134 and pls. I-II. A. Varille, *BIFAO*, 41 (1942), 31-38 and pl. I.   *Urk. IV*, 1276-1283.

Translation: Helck, *Übersetzung*, pp. 24-28.   J. A. Wilson in *ANET*, pp. 244-245 (without the encomium).   For additional references see Varille, *op. cit.*, p. 31.

Titulary and encomium

(1) The living Horus: Strong Bull, Great in vigor; Two Ladies: Rich in splendor, Arisen in Thebes; Gold-Horus: Who conquers all lands by his might; the King of Upper and Lower Egypt: *Aakheprure*; the Son of Re: *Amenhotep, Divine Ruler of On.* The son of Amun who raised him for himself; the offspring of Harakhti. Shining seed of the god's body; whose being Neith fashioned. Whom the most ancient god engendered, so that he would take the rule which he has taken.

Himself he[1] crowned him king upon the throne of the living,
Gave him the Black Land as his retinue,
The Red Land as his serfs;
Bestowed on him a heritage forever,
A kingship for all time.
He gave to him the throne of Geb,
The mighty rulership of Atum,
The Two Lords' portions,
The Two Ladies' shares,
Their years of life and of dominion.
He placed his daughter[2] upon his breast,
He fastened the uraeus upon his head,
He crushed the Bowmen under his feet.
The northerners bow to his might,
All countries are under his fear.

He[3] bound the heads of the Nine Bows,
He holds the Two Lands in his hand;
The people are in dread of him,
All the gods have love for him.
[Amun] himself made him rule what his eye encircles,
What the disk of Re (5) illuminates;
He has taken all of Egypt,
South and North are in his care.
The Red Land brings him its dues,
All countries have his protection;
His borders reach the rim of heaven,
The lands are in his hand in a single knot.

Risen as king upon the great throne,
He has joined the Great Magicians;[4]
The double-crown clings to his head,
Re's *atef*-crown to his brow.
His face is adorned with southcrown and northcrown,
He wears the headband and the helmet;
The tall-plumed *ibes*-crown is on his head,
The headcloth embraces his shoulders.
Gathered are the crowns of Atum,
Handed over to his image,
As ordained by the maker of gods,
[Amun], the most ancient, who crowned him.

He commanded him to conquer all lands without fail,
The Son of Re, Amenhotep, Divine Ruler of On,
Re's heir, [Amun's son], shining seed,

Divine flesh's holy egg, of noble mien.
Come from the womb he wore the crown,
Conquered the earth while yet in the egg;
Egypt is his, no one rebels,
In all that Amun's eye lights up.
The strength of Mont is in his limbs,
In power he equals the son of Nut;
He has joined the reed to the papyrus,
People north and south are under his feet.

His portion is that on which Re shines,
To him belongs what Ocean encircles;
There is no hindrance to his envoy,
Throughout all countries of the Fenkhu.[5]
(10) To the pillars of Horus[6] he has no peer,
⌈He is not hemmed in by other people;⌉
The southerners come to him bowed down,
The northerners on their bellies.
He has gathered them all into his fist,
His mace has crashed upon their heads,
As [Amen]-Re-Atum, Lord of Gods, has decreed,
He seized the lands in triumph once and for all.

The narration

Now then his majesty appeared as king,[7] as a beautiful youth who was well developed and had completed eighteen years upon his thighs in strength. He was one who knew all the works of Mont; he had no equal on the field of battle. He was one who knew horses; there was not his like in this numerous army. Not one among them could draw his bow; he could not be approached in running.

Strong of arms, untiring when he took the oar, he rowed at the stern of his falcon-boat as the stroke-oar[8] for two hundred men. Pausing after they had rowed half a mile, they were weak, limp in body, and breathless, while his majesty was strong under his oar of twenty cubits in length. He stopped and landed his falcon-boat only after he had done three miles of rowing without interrupting (15) his stroke. Faces shone as they saw him do this.

He drew three hundred strong bows, comparing the workmanship of the men who had crafted them, so as to tell the unskilled from the skilled. He also came to do the following which is brought to your attention. Entering his northern garden, he found erected for him four targets of Asiatic copper, of one palm in thickness, with a distance of twenty cubits between one post and the next. Then his majesty appeared on the chariot like Mont in his might. He drew his bow while holding four arrows together in his fist. Thus he rode northward shooting at them, like Mont in his panoply, each arrow coming out at the back of its target while he attacked the next post. It was a deed never yet done, never yet heard reported: shooting an arrow at a target of copper, so that it came out of it and dropped to the ground—(done) only by the King rich in glory, whom Amun made strong, the King of Upper and Lower Egypt, Aakheprure, a fighter like Mont.

Now when he was still a youth, he loved his horses and rejoiced in them. He was stout-hearted in working them, learning their natures, skilled in training them, understanding their ways. When it was heard (20) in the palace by his father, the Horus, Strong-Bull Arisen-in-Thebes, his majesty's heart was glad to hear it. Rejoicing at what was said of his eldest son he said in his heart: "He will make a ruler of the whole land whom no one can attack. He is eager to excel and rejoices in strength while as yet a charming youth without wisdom. Though not yet at the age to do the work of Mont, he ignores the thirst of the body and loves strength. It is the god who inspires him to act, so as to become the protector of Egypt, the ruler of the land."

His majesty said to those at his side: "Let him be given the very best horses from my majesty's stable in Memphis and tell him: 'Look after them, master them, trot them, and manage them if they resist you.'" Then the king's son was told to look after some horses of the king's stable. He did what he was told, and Reshef and Astarte[9] rejoiced over him as he did all that his heart desired.

He raised horses that were unequaled. They did not tire when he held the reins; they did not drip sweat in the gallop. He would yoke (them) with the harness at Memphis and would stop at the resting place of (25) Harmakhis. He would spend time there leading them around and observing the excellence of the resting-place of Kings Khufu and Khafra, the justified. His heart desired to make their names live. But he kept it to himself until there would occur what his father Re had ordained for him.[10]

After this his majesty was made to appear as king; the uraeus took its place on his brow; the image of Re was established on its post. The land, as before, was in peace under its lord, Aakheprure, who ruled the Two Lands, while all foreign countries were bound under his soles. Then his majesty remembered the place where he had enjoyed himself, in the vicinity of the pyramids and of Harmakhis. One[11] ordered to make a resting-place there and to place a stela of limestone in it, its face engraved with the great name of Aakheprure, beloved of Harmakhis, given life forever.

NOTES

1. Amen-Re.
2. Maat.
3. The king.
4. The crowns of Upper and Lower Egypt.
5. A Syrian people.
6. I.e., under the sky.
7. As coregent; see D. B. Redford, *JEA*, 51 (1965), 107-122.
8. The same word as in Papyrus Westcar 5,15.
9. The warlike Syrian gods who had entered the Egyptian pantheon.
10. I.e., when he would be king.
11. Circumlocution for the king.

STELA OF AMENHOTEP III

From his Mortuary Temple in Western Thebes

Cairo Museum 34025 (Recto)

Of black granite and over ten feet tall, the stela was set up in the mortuary temple of Amenhotep III which stood behind the so-called Colossi of Memnon. The text and scenes were defaced in the reign of Amenhotep IV but restored by orders of Seti I. Subsequently Merneptah had the stela removed to his mortuary temple and its *verso* inscribed with a poetic account of his victory over the Libyans. In the latter temple it was discovered in 1896.

The recto shows Amenhotep III libating to Amun in two symmetrical scenes. Below is the inscription in thirty-one lines. King Amenhotep III was a builder on the most lavish scale, and this record of some of his building activities typifies the style of this *roi soleil* and marks the splendor and luxury of the imperial age at its highest point. The account of his building activities is concluded by a poetic speech of Amun which borrows from the Poetical Stela of Thutmose III.

Publication: W. M. F. Petrie, *Six Temples at Thebes* (London, 1897), pp. 23-26 and pls. xi-xii.   W. Spiegelberg, *RT*, 20 (1898), 37-54 and pl. I.   P. Lacau, *Stèles du nouvel empire*, Vol. I, Catalogue général . . . du Musée du Caire (Cairo, 1909), pp. 47-52 and pls. xv-xvi.   *Urk. IV*, 1646-1657.

Translation: B*AR*, II, §§878-892.   J. A. Wilson in *ANET*, pp. 375-376 (excerpts).   Helck, *Übersetzung*, pp. 194-199.

(1) The living Horus: Strong Bull, Arisen in truth; Two Ladies: Giver of laws, Pacifier of the Two Lands; Gold-Horus: Great of strength, Smiter of Asiatics; the King of Upper and Lower Egypt: *Nebmare*; the Son of Re: *Amenhotep, Lord of Thebes*, beloved of Amen-Re, Lord of Thrones-of-the-Two-Lands, who presides over Ipet-sut, given

life; who rejoices as he rules the Two Lands like Re forever. The good god, lord of joy, very vigilant for his maker Amun, King of Gods; who enlarged his house and contented his beauty by doing his *ka*'s desire.

It pleased his majesty's heart to make very great monuments, the likes of which had not existed since the beginning of the Two Lands.

The Mortuary Temple

He made as his monument for his father Amun, Lord of Thrones-of-the-Two-Lands, the building for him of an august temple on the west side of Thebes,[1] a monument of eternity and everlastingness, of fine sandstone worked with gold throughout. Its pavements were made pure with silver, all its doors with fine gold. It is very wide and great and decorated enduringly. It is adorned with this very great monument,[2] and enriched with statues of the lord,[3] of granite from Yebu, of gritstone, and all kinds of costly (5) stones, worked in enduring workmanship. Their height rises to heaven. Their rays fall on the faces like Aten when he shines at dawn. It is equipped with a station of the lord,[4] worked with gold and many costly stones. Flagstaffs are set up before it, worked with fine gold. It resembles the horizon of heaven when Re rises in it.

Its pond is filled by great Hapy; it has fish and fowl and is adorned with plants. Its workhouse is filled with male and female slaves and with children of the princes of every foreign country that his majesty despoiled. Its storerooms [contain] goods that cannot be counted. It is surrounded by Syrian settlements, inhabited by the children of the princes. Its cattle are like the sands of the shore; they total millions. It holds the prow-rope[5] of the Southland and the stern-rope of the Northland.

Lo, his majesty is keen like Ptah, discerning like South-of-his-Wall,[6] in seeking out worthy deeds for his father Amen-Re, Lord of Gods. He made for him a very great pylon opposite Amun.[7] Its good name, which his majesty gave, is: "Who receives Amun and exalts his beauty." It is a resting-place for the Lord of Gods at his valley-feast, during the journey of Amun to the West, to see the gods of the West. In return may he give (10) to his majesty life and dominion.

The Luxor Temple

The King of Upper and Lower Egypt, Lord of the Two Lands: *Nebmare*, Heir of Re; the Son of Re, Lord of diadems: *Amenhotep, Lord of Thebes*, is content with the work for his father Amun, Lord of Thrones-of-the-Two-Lands, in Southern Ipet: of fine sandstone, wide, very great, and exceedingly beautiful. Its walls are of fine gold, its pavements of silver. All its gates are worked with the pride of lands.[8] Its pylons reach to the sky, its flagpoles to the stars. When the people see it they give praise to his majesty. King *Nebmare* gladdens the heart of his father Amun, Lord of Thrones-of-the-Two-Lands, who gave him all foreign countries; the Son of Re, *Amenhotep, Lord of Thebes*, beneficent [˹since˺] the day of birth.

The Viewing Place

Another monument that his majesty made for his father Amun was making for him a viewing-place[9] as a divine offering, opposite Southern Ipet, a place of relaxation for my father at his beautiful feast. I[10] erected a great temple in its midst, resembling Re when he rises on the horizon. It is planted with all kinds of flowers. Nun[11] is happy in its pond at every season. It has more wine than water, like overflowing Hapy.[12] An abode[13] of the Lord of eternity, rich in goods; a place for receiving the produce of all foreign countries, as many gifts are brought before my father from the tribute of all lands.

He has handed over to me the princes of the southern lands. (15) Southerners and northerners surpass one another (with) their silver, their gold, their cattle, all kinds of costly stones of their countries in millions, hundred thousands, ten thousands, and thousands. I act for my begetter with affection, inasmuch as he has appointed me as the Sun of the Nine Bows; the King of Upper and Lower Egypt, *Nebmare*, Image of Re; the Son of Re, *Amenhotep, Ruler of Thebes*.

The Bark of Amun

I made another monument for my father Amen-Re, Lord of Thrones-of-the-Two-Lands, who set me on his throne, in making for him a great bark upon the river, "Amen-Re-firm-of-brow,"[14] of new pine wood, cut by my majesty in the countries of god's land,[15] and dragged from the mountains of Retjenu by the chiefs of all foreign lands. It is very wide and great; the like has never been made. Its interior is made pure with silver; it is worked with gold throughout. A great shrine of fine gold fills the entire surface. Its projecting ends double (its) length and bear great *atef*-crowns. Their uraeus-serpents, coiled about their sides, provide their protection. Before it stand flagpoles worked with fine gold, and two tall obelisks between them. It is beautiful on all sides. The souls of Buto hail it, the souls of Nekhen praise it;[16] the two divine songstresses (20) do homage to its beauty. Its projecting ends make the water glitter, as when Aten rises in the sky, when it makes its goodly crossing at the feast of Ipet, at its crossing to the West of millions of years. The King of Upper and Lower Egypt, *Nebmare*; the Son of Re, *Amenhotep, Ruler of Thebes*, who is alert in seeking what is beneficent.

The Third Pylon at Karnak

The king made another monument for Amun in making for him a very great gate in front of Amen-Re, Lord of Thrones-of-the-Two-Lands, worked with gold throughout, (with) the god's shade in the likeness of a ram,[17] inlaid with real lapis lazuli and worked with gold and costly stones. The like had never been made. Its pavement was made pure with silver, the portal in its front firmly set; (there are) stelae of lapis lazuli, one on each side. Its twin towers reach to the sky, like the four supports of heaven. Its flagpoles shine skyward, being worked in fine gold. His majesty brought the gold for it from the land of Kry on his first victorious campaign of slaying vile Kush; the King of Upper and Lower Egypt, *Nebmare*, beloved son of Amen-Re; the Son of Re, *Amenhotep, Ruler of Thebes*.

Another temple of Amun

I made other monuments for Amun, whose like did not exist. I built for you your House-of-millions-of-years on the ground of Amen-Re, Lord of Thrones-of-the-Two-Lands, called "Risen-in-truth," a splendor of fine gold, a resting-place for my father in all his feasts.[18] It is built of fine sandstone, worked (25) with gold throughout. Its pavements are adorned with silver, all its portals with gold. It is equipped with two tall obelisks, one on each side, so that my father rises between them while I am in his retinue. I have assigned to him thousands of oxen, so as to present their choice cuts.

Amun's blessing to the King

Speech of Amun, King of Gods:[19]
My son, of my body, my beloved Nebmare,
My living image, my body's creation,
Born me by Mut, Ashru's Lady in Thebes,
Mistress of the Nine Bows,
Who nursed you to be sole lord of peoples!
My heart is very joyful when I see your beauty,
I did a wonder for your majesty,
You repeat your youth,
For I made you the Sun of the Two Shores.

Turning my face to the south I did a wonder for you,
I made the chiefs of wretched Kush surround you,
Carrying all their tribute on their backs.

Turning my face to the north I did a wonder for you,
I made the countries of the ends of Asia come to you,
Carrying all their tribute on their backs.

They offer you their persons and their children,
Beseeching you to grant them breath of life.

Turning my face to the west I did a wonder for you,
I let you capture Tjehenu, they can't escape!
Built is this fort and named after (30) my majesty,
Enclosed by a great wall that reaches heaven,
And settled with the princes' sons of Nubia's Bowmen.

Turning my face to sunrise I did a wonder for you,
I made the lands of Punt come here to you,
With all the fragrant flowers of their lands,
To beg your peace and breathe the air you give.

The King of Upper and Lower Egypt, Ruler of the Nine Bows, Lord of the Two Lands, *Nebmare*; the beloved Son of Re, *Amenhotep, Lord of Thebes*, who contents the heart of the gods with his monuments; may he be given life, stability, dominion, health, and joy, like Re forever.

NOTES

1. Although the temple was intended for the worship of the king after his death, the god Amun was associated with it and received worship in it.
2. The stela.
3. Statues of the king.
4. The place in which the king stood or sat during ceremonies.
5. Read *ḥ3tt* instead of *pḥtt*. The country is likened to a ship that is guided by the temple.
6. Epithet of Ptah.
7. This seems to be a building on the west bank, facing the east bank temple of Amun at Karnak. Whether it was a pylon (*bḫn*), and not rather a mansion (*bḫnt*), it formed part of the king's mortuary temple and served as a resting-place for Amun, when the statue of the god journeyed from his temple on the east bank to visit the shrines of the west.
8. Metaphor for gold.
9. On *m3rw*, "viewing-place," see A. Badawy, *JEA*, 42 (1956), 58-64. It was a sanctuary characterized by gardens and ponds.
10. Note the change into the first person, as so often in royal inscriptions, when the first and the final versions of the text were not completely harmonized.
11. The pond has ground water (Nun), as distinct from Nile water.
12. A rather confused simile; the abundance of wine is likened to the abundance of Nile water.
13. For *msn* read *msḫn*, as suggested by A. Massart, *Orientalia*, 27 (1958), 454.
14. The name of the bark.
15. In this instance "god's land" designates the Lebanon.
16. The falcon-headed gods of the northern town of Buto and the jackal-headed gods of the southern town of Hieraconpolis are the retinue of the great gods.

17. A relief of a ram, the animal sacred to Amun, was carved on the door of the pylon.

18. In *ANET*, p. 375, n. 9, Wilson referred to A. Varille's view that this building was yet another temple in the Karnak complex. In *Urk. IV*, 1654, Helck assumed that the temple of Soleb was meant.

19. This composition borrows from the Poetical Stela of Thutmose III; see page 35.

THE LATER BOUNDARY STELAE OF AMENHOTEP IV AKHENATEN

At El-Amarna

Early in his reign, Akhenaten chose a broad plain in the Hermopolitan nome as the site for a new royal city, where the worship of the Aten would flourish unimpeded. Building proceeded rapidly, and the town was formally dedicated to the Aten in a ceremony recorded on three boundary stelae. These stelae were carved into the limestone cliffs of the east bank, at the northern and southern ends of the town. They have suffered much damage, so that the greater part of their long text is now destroyed. The date is no longer legible but is now surmised to have been "Year 6." Subsequently eleven more stelae were cut into the cliffs, eight on the east side of the river and three on the west side. These bear the date of "Year 6." Together the fourteen stelae marked the boundaries of the city in all directions.

The earlier group of three stelae (called X, M, and K in the publications) had one and the same long text in which the king told how he planned the city and how he dedicated it to his heavenly father the Aten. The later eleven stelae also bear one basic text with some additions and variations. The purpose of the later stelae was to define the boundaries of the city with greater precision, and to reaffirm the king's determination to maintain the city as the property of the god and as the royal residence dedicated to the worship of the god. Furthermore, the king vows that he will not "pass beyond" the boundaries as marked by the stelae. This probably does not mean that he would never leave the residence, but rather that he would not alter its boundaries. The reason for this insistence is, however, not clear.

Five of the later stelae (called S, Q, U, A, and R) are preserved well enough to allow the restitution of the complete text. The translation follows the version of Stela S, which marked the southeastern boundary. It measures 100 × 60 inches and has four vertical columns and twenty-six horizontal lines of inscription. Above the inscription, the king, queen, and two small daughters are shown worshiping the Aten. The same scene occurs on the other stelae.

Publication: Davies, *Amarna*, V, 19-34 and pls. 25-28 and 37-43. Sandman, *Akhenaten*, pp. 119-131.   *Urk. IV*, 1981-1990.

Translation: *BAR*, II, §§959-969.   Helck, *Übersetzung*, pp. 344-347. On the "royal name" of the Aten, written in cartouches, see especially: B. Gunn, *JEA*, 9 (1923), 168-176.   G. Fecht, *ZÄS*, 85 (1960), 91-118.   R. Anthes, *ZÄS*, 90 (1963), 1-6.

(I) Year 6, fourth month of winter, day 13. The Good God, who is content with *Maat*, the Lord of heaven, the Lord of earth, the great living Aten who illuminates the Two Lands, the living, my father: *Re-Harakhti-who-rejoices-in-lightland In-his-name-Shu-who-is-Aten*, who gives life forever.[1] The great living Aten who is in jubilee, who dwells in the House-of-Aten in Akhet-Aten.

(1) The living Horus: Strong Bull beloved of Aten; Two Ladies: Great of kingship in Akhet-Aten; Gold-Horus: Who exalts the name of Aten; the King of Upper and Lower Egypt who lives by *Maat*, the Lord of the Two Lands: *Neferkheprure, Sole-one-of-Re*; the Son of Re who lives by *Maat*, the Lord of crowns: *Akhenaten*, great in his lifetime, given life forever.

> The Good God, Sole one of Re,
> Whose goodness Aten fashioned,
> Useful, truthful, to his maker,
> Who contents him with that which pleases his *ka*.
> Who serves him who begot him,
> Who guides the land for him who enthroned him,
> Who provisions his house of eternity
> With millions, hundredthousands of things.
> Who exalts Aten, magnifies his name,
> Who causes the land to belong to his maker:

The King of Upper and Lower Egypt who lives by *Maat*, the Lord of the Two Lands: *Neferkheprure, Sole-one-of-Re*; the Son of Re who lives by *Maat*, the Lord of crowns: *Akhenaten*, great in his lifetime, given life forever.

The Princess, great in the palace; the fair-faced, adorned with the two plumes; the mistress of joy, endowed with favor, at the sound of whose voice one rejoices; the Great Wife of the King whom he loves, the Mistress of the Two Lands: *Nefer-nefru-aten Nefertiti*, living forever.

(5) On that day one[2] was in Akhet-Aten, in the carpeted tent made for his majesty in Akhet-Aten, the name of which is "Aten is content." The king appeared mounted on the great chariot of fine gold, like Aten when he dawns in lightland and fills the Two Lands with his love.

Setting out on the good road to Akhet-Aten, on the first anniversary of visiting it,[3] which his majesty had done so as to found it as a monument to the Aten, according to the command of his father, *Re-Harakhti-who-rejoices-in-lightland In-his-name-Shu-who-is-Aten*, who gives life forever, to make for him a monument in its midst.

Making a great offering of bread and beer, large and small cattle, fowl, wine, fruit, incense, and all kinds of good herbs, on the day of founding[4] Akhet-Aten for the living Aten, who accepts praise and love for the sake of the life-stability-health of the King of Upper and Lower Egypt who lives by *Maat*, the Lord of the Two Lands,

Neferkheprure, Sole one of Re; the Son of Re who lives by *Maat*, the Lord of crowns, *Akhenaten*, great in his lifetime, given life forever.

Having proceeded southward, his majesty halted upon his great chariot before his father, *Re-Harakhti-who-rejoices-in-lightland In-his-name-Shu-who-is-Aten*, who gives life forever, at the southeastern mountain of Akhet-Aten, the rays of (10) Aten being upon him with life and health for the renewal of his body every day.

Oath spoken by the King of Upper and Lower Egypt who lives by *Maat*, the Lord of the Two Lands, *Neferkheprure, Sole one of Re*; the Son of Re who lives by *Maat*, the Lord of crowns, *Akhenaten*, great in his lifetime, given life forever:

As my father lives, *Re-Harakhti-who-rejoices-in-lightland In-his-name-Shu-who-is-Aten*, who gives life forever, and as my heart rejoices in the great royal wife and her children, and old age be granted to the great royal wife, *Nefer-nefru-aten Nefertiti*, living forever, in these millions of years, she being in the care of Pharaoh, and old age be granted to the princess Meretaten and to the princess Meketaten, her children, they being in the care of the Queen their mother, this is my oath of truth which my heart speaks and which I shall not say falsely ever:

The southern stela which is on the eastern mountain of Akhet-Aten, that is the stela of Akhet-Aten, which I shall let stand in its place. I shall not pass beyond it southward (15) ever. The south-western stela has been made to face it on the southern mountain of Akhet-Aten directly opposite.

The middle stela which is on the eastern mountain, that is the stela of Akhet-Aten, which I shall let stand in its place on the sunrise mountain of Akhet-Aten. I shall not pass beyond it eastward ever. The middle stela which is on the western mountain of Akhet-Aten has been made to face it directly opposite.

The northeastern stela of Akhet-Aten I shall let stand in its place. It is the northern stela of Akhet-Aten. I shall not pass beyond it northward ever. The northern stela which is on the western mountain of Akhet-Aten has been made to face it directly opposite.

As to Akhet-Aten, from the southern stela to the northern stela, measured from stela to stela on the eastern mountain of Akhet-Aten, it measures 6 *iter*,[5] 1¾ rods, and 4 cubits.

Likewise, from the southwest stela of Akhet-Aten to the northwest stela on the western mountain of Akhet-Aten, it measures 6 *iter*, 1¾ rods, and 4 cubits.

Now (20) within these four stelae, from the eastern mountain to the western mountain, is Akhet-Aten itself. It belongs to my father, *Re-Harakhti-who-rejoices-in-lightland In-his-name-Shu-who-is-Aten*, who gives life forever, with mountains, deserts, meadows, new lands, highlands, fresh lands, fields, water, settlements, shorelands, people, cattle, trees, and all other things that the Aten my father shall let be forever.

I shall not violate this oath which I have made to the Aten my father in all eternity. Rather it shall endure on the stela of stone of the southeastern boundary, also on the northeastern boundary of Akhet-Aten. It shall also endure on the stela of stone of the southwestern boundary, also on the northwestern boundary of Akhet-Aten. It shall not be erased. It shall not be washed out. It shall not be hacked out. It shall not be covered with gypsum. It shall not be made to disappear. If it disappears, if it vanishes, if (25) the stela on which it is falls down, I shall renew it again, afresh in this place in which it is.

Supplement

Renewal of this oath in year 8, first month of winter, day 8. One was in Akhet-Aten; Pharaoh appeared mounted on a great chariot of fine gold to inspect the stelae of the Aten which are on the [side] of the mountain on the southeastern boundary of Akhet-Aten.

NOTES

1. The interpretation of the name of the Aten is problematical, and the reader should consult the literature cited. I tend to think, as did R. Anthes, that the 'nḫ sign at the beginning of the first cartouche is a symbol only and not meant to be read as a grammatical element. In essentials I have adopted B. Gunn's interpretation of the name. As to the phrase dỉ 'nḫ, I take it to have the active sense here, since the passive meaning, "given life," is incongruous when applied to the god.

2. The king.

3. The tenses that describe the king's acts are ambiguous. I take them to mean that on the date recorded at the beginning the king, having spent the night on the outskirts of the previously founded new residence, rode into the town in the morning, performed a sacrifice to the Aten, and then traversed the town until he reached the southeastern mountain. Halting at the mountain he took an oath in which he affirmed the boundaries. If this was the order of events, the phrase *m sp tpy n gmtw.s ir.n ḥm.f r snt.s* cannot mean "on the first time of finding it which his majesty had done so as to found it," but must mean, "on the first *anniversary*, etc."

4. Here too the phrase *m hrw n snt* must mean "on the anniversary of founding," rather than "on the day of founding." Or the whole passage has to be taken as a reference to the original founding ceremony. If so, the grammar is extremely awkward.

5. The length of the *iter* is not known; it is thought to have been about one mile or considerably more, or to have varied in the course of time. Here a length of about one mile agrees with the actual distance between the northern and southern stelae.

DEDICATION INSCRIPTIONS OF SETI I

In the Rock Temple of Wadi Mia

This small rock temple of sandstone is situated in the eastern desert, thirty-seven miles to the east of the village of Redesiya, which lies on the east bank of the Nile some five miles south of Edfu. The temple has been variously called "Temple of Redesiyeh," "Temple of the Wadi Abbad," "Temple of the Wadi Mia," or "Al-Kanais." The sanctuary was erected by King Seti I to mark the site where, on his orders, a well had been dug to provide water for the expeditions that came to this part of the eastern desert to quarry gold and building stones. Along with the well and the temple, a permanent settlement had also been planned.

The reliefs of the vestibule show the king smiting Nubians and Asiatics. The inscriptions consist of three interrelated texts. The first (A) is carved on the left jamb of the doorway leading to the main hall. The other two (B, C) are on the north wall of the main hall. All three are written in vertical columns. Text C has longish lacunae in lines 3-13, because the rock surface had been patched with stones which subsequently fell out.

All three texts are of considerable interest. Text A contains the formal dedication of the temple and the well. It begins with the royal titulary and some traditional phrases; then follows a lively and skilled two-part poem that praises the life-giving well and the king who ordered it dug. Text B narrates how the king, impressed by the hardships of desert travel, planned the digging of the well, an enterprise which the gods blessed with success. Text C is a decree designed to assure a perpetual supply of gold for the king's mortuary temple at Abydos. A troop of gold-washers, newly appointed by the king, is to form part of the endowment of the temple at Abydos, and is not to be employed for other tasks. Such decrees of endowment and exemption, issued since the Old Kingdom, depended for their continuity on the loyalty and piety of successive kings. Hence King Seti's emphatic blessings on those who would maintain his endowment in future days and equally emphatic curses on those who would violate it. In fact, his son and successor, Ramses II, completed the mortuary temple at Abydos and set up its endowment, as he reports in a long inscription carved on a wall at the rear of the first court of that magnificent sanctuary.

Publication: V. S. Golenishchev, *RT*, 13 (1890), 76-77 and pls. I-II. S. Schott, *Kanais, der Tempel Sethos I. im Wadi Mia*, Nachrichten der Akademie der Wissenschaften in Göttingen, philologisch-historische Klasse, 1961/6 (Göttingen, 1961)   Kitchen, *Inscriptions*, I, 65-70.

Translation: *BAR*, III, §§162-198.   B. Gunn and A. H. Gardiner, *JEA*, 4 (1917), 241-251.

A. The Dedication

(1) Horus: Strong-Bull-arisen-in-Thebes, Who sustains the Two Lands; the King of Upper and Lower Egypt: [*Menmare*]. He made as his monument for his father Amen-Re together with his Ennead the making for them of a new temple in which the gods are content. He dug a well in front of it, the like of which had never been done by any king, except the beneficent King, the Son of Re: *Seti, Beloved of Ptah*;

the good herdsman who sustains his troops, the father and mother of all. They said from mouth to mouth:

Amun, give him eternity,
　　double him everlastingness;
Gods who are in the well,
　　give him your span of life!
For he opened the way for us to go,
　　that had been blocked before us.
Of which we said, "If we pass it we are safe,"
　　we now say, "If we reach it we live";[1]
The difficult way that troubled us,
　　it has become an excellent way.

He made the transport of the gold to be as the falcon's sight,[2]
All generations yet to be wish him eternity;
May he have jubilees like Atum,
May he be young like Horus of Behdet.
For he made a memorial in desert lands to all the gods,
He drew water from mountains far away from people;
Every foot that treads the desert says, "Life-stability-dominion"
For King *Menmare*, beloved of Amen-Re, King of Gods.

B. The Narration

14 columns

(1) Year 9, third month of summer, day 20, under the Majesty of Horus: Strong-Bull-arisen-in-Thebes, Who sustains the Two Lands; Two Ladies: Renewing birth, Mighty of sword, Smiter of the Nine Bows in all lands; the King of Upper and Lower Egypt: *Menmare*; the Son of Re: *Seti, Beloved of Ptah*, given life forever and ever.

On that day[3] his majesty inspected the desert lands as far as the mountains, for his heart desired to see the mines from which the fine gold is brought. After his majesty had gone up for many miles, he halted on the way in order to take counsel with his heart. He said: "How painful is a way that has no water! What are travelers to do to relieve the parching of their throats? What quenches their thirst, the homeland being far away and the desert wide? Woe to the man who thirsts in the wilderness! Now then[4] I will plan for them. I will make for them the means to sustain them, so that they may bless my name in the future, in years to come; that generations yet to be may come to glory in me for my energy. For I am indeed considerate and com-passionate toward (5) travelers."

Now after his majesty had spoken these words to his own heart, he went about on the desert seeking a place to make a watering station.

And God was guiding him, so as to grant the request of one whom he loved. Stone workers were ordered to dig a well in the mountains, in order that it might uplift the weary and refresh the heart of him who burns in the summer heat. Then this place was built, bearing the great name of *Menmare*. It is full of water in great quantity, like the cavern of the twin sources at Yebu.[5]

His majesty said: "God has granted my wish. He has made water come forth for me from the mountain. A way that was arduous since (the time of) the gods has been made pleasant in my reign.[6] Pasture lands profit the herdsman.[7] The breadth of the land is fortunate when the king is active. A deed that had been unknown, [God] let it [be done] by me. Another good deed has come into my heart by God's command also: to found a town with a sanctuary in it. Noble is the town that has a temple. I will build a sanctuary on this spot, bearing the great name of my fathers, [the gods]. May they make my deeds endure and my name flourish throughout the desert lands."

His majesty commanded (10) to give directions to the leader of the royal workers who were with him as stone cutters. By cutting into this mountain a temple was made for these [gods]. Amun is in it, Re is within it; Ptah and Osiris are in its great hall, and Horus, Isis, and *Menmare*; they are the Ennead in this temple.[8]

When the monument had been finished and its inscriptions completed, his majesty came to adore his fathers, all the [gods], and said: "Hail to you, great gods who founded heaven and earth at your pleasure! May you favor me for all eternity; may you perpetuate my name forever! For I am helpful, for I am good to you; for I watch over your interests. May you speak to those who shall come, kings, officials, and people, who shall confirm[9] for me what I have done as being under the control of my House at Abydos. Happy is he who acts on the word of God, for his plans do not fail. Speak, and your word shall be acted on, for you are the lords. I pass my lifetime in action for you, so as to seek my well-being from you. Make my monuments endure for me, my name lasting upon them!" The Good God, the Lord of the Two Lands, *Menmare*; the Son of Re, lord of crowns, *Seti, Beloved of Ptah*, given life, stability, and dominion.

C. The Decree

19 columns

(1) The King of Upper and Lower Egypt: *Menmare*; the Son of Re: *Seti, Beloved of Ptah*. He speaks before his fathers,[10] all the kings of Upper Egypt, the kings of Lower Egypt, the rulers of people:

> Listen to me, ye leaders of Egypt,
> And may others listen to you!

If you say, "Gladly," as I desire,
Your deeds will also be repaid.
You are like divinities,
A king is counted among the gods.

I speak as follows in assigning my troop of gold-washers to my temple. They are appointed to transport to my House [in Abydos, to furnish gold to] my sanctuary. As to the gold, the flesh of gods, it does not belong to your requirements.[11] Beware of saying what Re said when he began to speak: "My skin is pure gold." For Amun, the lord of my temple, will ------.[12] His eyes are upon his belongings. They (the gods) do not like misuse of their possessions. Beware of injuring their people; for they are indeed like crocodiles.

Do not (5) rejoice ------. He who damages the work of another, the like is done to him in the end. A despoiler's monuments are despoiled. A liar's deed does not endure. A king's [strength] is [*maat*]. [⌈Listen to me, ye kings who shall be after me⌉] --- to let you know; I foretell from afar so as to protect you.

I have appointed a troop of gold-washers anew, in my name, ------ king alone. I appointed them as a new troop in order that they should remain for me. I did not take (them) from another troop in order to [put them to this task. They and their dependents are exempt] as children of my House, as dependents of my temple.

As to any future king who shall make my acts endure, so as to maintain [the appointment of my troop of gold-washers], so that it transports its produce to the House of *Menmare*, to gild all their images[13]—Amun, Re-Harakhti, Ptah (10) Tatenen, Wen[nofer and the other gods of my temple] shall cause them to prosper. They shall rule the lands in happiness. They shall trample on the Red Land and Nubia. Their provisions shall endure; their foods shall last and shall feed those on earth. Re shall hear [their prayers] ---, so that none shall say, "If only I had!"

But as to any future king who shall destroy any of my plans and shall say: "The lands are under my control; they are mine as they were his," the gods judge it an evil deed. He will receive his answer in On.[14] They are the tribunal ---; they shall answer for the sake of their property. They shall be red like a firebrand; they shall burn the flesh of those who will not listen to me. They shall punish him who spoils my plans; they shall deliver him to the slaughterhouse in *dat*![15] [I have said this so as to protect] you. Let him who is free of crime be saved. But woe to one whose heart strays! The Ennead will deal with him!

As to any official who shall turn to the King and shall make him remember to maintain my works in my name, God shall make him revered upon earth, his end being peaceful (15) as one who goes to his *ka*.

But as to any official who, in the manner of an evil witness, shall suggest to his lord to remove the workmen and place them in another service,[16] he is destined for the fire that shall burn his body, for the flame that shall consume his limbs! For his majesty[17] has done all this for the *ka*'s of the lords of my House! God abhors him who interferes with his people. He does not fail to thwart the despoiler.

In particular, the troop of gold-washers that I have appointed for the House of *Menmare* shall be exempted and protected. It shall not be approached by anyone in the whole land, by any controller of gold, by any inspector of the desert. As to anyone who shall interfere with any of them so as to put them in another place, all the gods and goddesses of my House shall be his adversaries. For all my things belong to them[18] by testament for ever and ever.

In particular, the chief of the troop of gold-washers of the House of *Menmare* shall have a free hand in delivering their produce of gold to the House of *Menmare*.

As to anyone who shall be deaf to this decree, Osiris shall be after him, Isis after his wife, Horus after his children; and all the great ones, the lords of the necropolis, will make their reckoning with him!

1. I.e., in the past safety lay in having left the desert road behind and having returned to the Nile Valley; now the desert road is safe because of the life-giving well.

2. I.e., as swift as the falcon's sight.

3. The phrase "on that day" is not clear. The date at the beginning of the text must refer to the completion of the building and its dedication, but after "on that day" there follows the narration of the king's previous planning of the well and temple. Did the scribe omit a date?

4. *Isy-m* is treated as an exhortation by Gunn-Gardiner and as a question by Schott.

5. The Nile was believed to rise from a cavern at Elephantine.

6. *Dr ntrw w3t ksnti sndmti hft nsywt.i* is an interesting construction. The unusual word order with prepositional *dr ntrw* in initial position was noted by Gunn-Gardiner and Schott, the latter quoting the parallel *dr rk ntr* from the dedication inscription of Ramses II at Abydos (*Inscription dédicatoire*, line 59). The chiastic sentence pattern (*dr ntrw* balanced by *hft nsywt.i*) may have been the inducement, though no chiastic order is present in the example from the inscription of Ramses II. In any case, the sentence lends support to my rendering of line I,5 of the *Building Inscription of Sesostris I* as a chiastic period beginning with the preposition *n m-ht* (*Ancient Egyptian Literature* I, Berkeley, 1973, 116).

7. So with Gunn-Gardiner for *3h i3dwt n mniw*. Schott's "ergiebig an Weideplatz für den Hirten," referring back to *w3t*, would require *3hti*.

8. The king is a member of this Ennead of seven whose number is brought up to nine by the king's having three statues in the sanctuary.

9. One expects "to confirm," but the scribe wrote *smnty.sn*, "who shall confirm."

10. The king's "fathers" are his ancestors. They are invoked as witnesses while the speech itself is addressed to the kings of the future.

11. The king insists that gold is exclusively for the use of the gods. The symbolic and sacred value of gold is brought out clearly.

12. A phrase like "punish the transgressor" is called for.

13. The images of the gods in the king's mortuary temple at Abydos.

14. Heliopolis was the place where the gods sat in judgment.

15. *Dat*, the netherworld, contained a place of execution where sinners met their real and final death.

16. Or "foundation," see Schott's note.

17. Faulty for "my majesty."

18. Literally, "are under their feet." A juridical commentary on the sentence is given by A. Théodoridès in *RdE*, 24 (1972), 188-192.

THE KADESH BATTLE INSCRIPTIONS OF RAMSES II

In the fifth year of his reign, Ramses II led a large army to Kadesh-on-Orontes in an attempt to dislodge the Hittites from northern Syria. Subsequently the campaign was told at length in two separate accounts which scholars have called the *Bulletin* (or, the *Record*) and the *Poem*. The two accounts are supplemented by pictorial reliefs with explanatory captions. The whole composition offers a number of striking features. First, the fact that there are two distinct though overlapping accounts. Second, the fact that the two versions were not merely carved once on the walls of a temple but were repeated in multiple copies—the *Bulletin* seven times and the *Poem* eight times. They are inscribed on the walls of the temples of Abydos, Luxor, Karnak, Abu Simbel, and the Ramesseum; and the *Poem* is also found on fragments of two hieratic papyri.

Taken together, the two accounts, supplemented by the pictorial record, offer a vivid and detailed campaign report which is clear in its main features, and which may be summarized as follows. The army that Ramses II led into Syria consisted of four divisions, each composed of infantry and chariotry, and named after the four great gods: Amun, Re (called Pre with definite article), Ptah, and Seth (= Sutekh). As the king, who led the division of Amun, approached the city of Kadesh, he was met by two spies from the Hittite army who feigned to be deserters and gave the king the false information that the Hittite army stood in the vicinity of Khaleb (Aleppo), some hundred and twenty miles north of Kadesh. Not suspecting a ruse, Pharaoh continued forward until he reached high ground to the northwest of Kadesh, where he went into camp to await the arrival of the main body of his army. While he waited, his troops captured two Hittite scouts who, after being beaten, revealed the true position of the Hittite army: it was standing to the northeast of Kadesh. After berating his officers for their failure to locate the enemy's position sooner, the king dispatched messengers to hasten the march of his army. Meanwhile a force of Hittite chariotry attacked the flank of the marching Egyptian army, which broke ranks and hurried northward toward the royal camp with the Hittites in pursuit. As the news of the attack reached the king, he found his camp surrounded by Hittite chariots.

At this point the two Egyptian accounts leave the realm of the possible and become entirely fanciful, for they claim that Pharaoh, charging the enemy from his chariot and killing vast numbers, fought his way out of the encirclement by himself alone, having been deserted by all his troops. The likely course of events was that the Egyptian troops rallied, and that the timely arrival of a special force, which had previously been detached from the army and ordered to march by a different route (the troop is shown and described on a relief scene but is not mentioned in the *Poem* and the *Bulletin*), turned the battle from a near-disaster into a partial success. The *Poem* further relates that the king fought another victorious battle on the following day, until the Hittite king sent a letter asking for peace.

Scholars have given much attention to the course of the campaign and its historical implication, and their discussions will be found in the literature cited. My focus is on the literary form of the two accounts, which has not been fully examined and is less understood than the factual content. Breasted had classified the Kadesh Inscriptions under three headings: (1) the *Poem*, (2) the *Record*, and (3) the *Reliefs* with their captions. This classification had usually been adhered to with only minor adjustments, such as substituting the term *Bulletin* for the word *Record*, and placing the *Bulletin* ahead of the *Poem*, thus viewing it as the basic factual account and the *Poem*, which is three times as long as the *Bulletin*, as a poetic elaboration. Though accepting the term *Poem* for the long text, most scholars, however, translated it as a prose narration. Only R. O. Faulkner emphasized that the central portion of the *Poem*—not the entire text—is in fact a poem, and he rendered it accordingly in metrical lines.

Sir Alan Gardiner, in the most recent study of the Kadesh Inscriptions, denied that the *Poem* showed poetic form and insisted that the *Bulletin* and the *Poem* were written in one and the same prose style. But what then was the reason for composing two separate prose accounts? To explain this, Gardiner claimed that the *Bulletin* was not the official report but was merely a part of the pictorial record with which it shares space on the same walls, while the long *Poem* occupies other walls. He therefore proposed a new bipartite classification of all the material in place of the former tripartite one: (1) the *Pictorial Record* which includes the "Bulletin" as its most important item, and (2) the *Literary Record* which is "the so-called Poem."

Gardiner's diverging interpretation illustrates how tentative, uncertain, and incomplete is our grasp of ancient Egyptian styles and literary forms. Personally I am convinced that the central portion of the *Poem* is indeed a poem, and that the old tripartite division of the Kadesh texts and scenes is correct. I see in the poetic centerpiece of the *Poem* a variant, or subspecies, of poetry invented in the New Kingdom. In the earlier periods, poetry had been employed for laudation, reflection, and instruction; in the Kadesh Battle Poem we encounter poetry in the service of narration.

Egyptian poetry as well as the intermediate style which I call "symmetrically structured speech" rely heavily on parallelism of members and related devices that make for symmetry. The resulting repetitive elaboration is perfectly suited to reflective and didactic contents, but it is unsuited to narration. Hence the author of the Kadesh Battle Poem trimmed the use of parallelisms and repetitions so as to allow the narrative to move forward at an adequate pace. As a result, we who study the metrical form of this new type of poem are here and there left without the firm guideposts provided by parallelistically structured sentences. We can therefore not be sure in all cases that our division into metrical lines is correct. But I have no doubt that the text is to be read as a metrical composition. The demonstration that this is so would require a sentence-by-sentence analysis which cannot be done here. It would reveal the stylistic differences between the initial and concluding *prose* sections of the *Poem* on the one hand and the central metrical portion on the other.

The combination, in historical inscriptions, of prose narratives with poems extolling the royal victories is of course not new. What is new is that the poem should be more than a brief song of triumph that sums up the narration and should itself be narrative. That is to say, in the Kadesh Battle Poem we encounter a genre not hitherto found in Egypt: the epic poem.

King Ramses II must have been pleased with the whole composition and ordered it reproduced in multiple copies. We may also assume that the *Bulletin* and the *Poem* were written by the same author. The epic poem required a setting and hence received a prose introduction and a prose ending. These contained enough factual detail to set off the heroic role of the king, which was the poem's real topic. There was no need to relate all the pertinent facts, in particular the humiliation of the king's being deceived by a Hittite ruse, which were told in the *Bulletin*. Thus the *Bulletin* and the *Poem* each had a purpose and complemented each other.

Since the beginning, Egyptian monumental art depicted a victory in battle by showing the king towering over all men and slaying the enemy. The New Kingdom enlarged the concept by adding the fighting armies and creating detailed battle scenes but always with the king in central position. These large-scale battle scenes, an innovation of Ramesside art, are the pictorial equivalent of the narrative battle poem, of which the Kadesh Battle Poem is the first known example, in that they both focus on the central heroic role of Pharaoh. This stylization necessarily distorts the facts, but the facts themselves are nevertheless presented in the details of the relief scenes, their captions, and the prose narratives.

In Ch. Kuentz's synoptic edition of the Kadesh Inscriptions the texts of the *Poem* and of the *Bulletin* were divided into paragraphs, and by this numbering the *Poem* consists of 343 paragraphs and the *Bulletin* of 119. Kuentz placed the *Poem* ahead of the *Bulletin*, but I have followed Faulkner's order in which the *Bulletin* comes first. The metrical, or poetic, part of the *Poem* occupies §§88-294. In addition there is a short poetic encomium of the king in §§7-23.

Publication: Ch. Kuentz, *La Bataille de Qadech*, Mémoires de l'Institut Français d'Archéologie Orientale, vol. 55 (Cairo, 1928-1934).   S. Hassan, *Le Poème dit de Pentaour et le rapport officiel sur la bataille de Qadesh* (Cairo, 1929)   Kitchen, *Inscriptions*, II, 2-124.

Translation: B*AR*, III, §§298-327 (excerpts).   J. A. Wilson, *AJSL*,

43 (1927), 266-287.   R. O. Faulkner, *MDIK*, 16 (1958), 93-111. A. H. Gardiner, *The Kadesh Inscriptions of Ramses II* (Oxford, 1960). Comments on the campaign: A. H. Burne, *JEA*, 7 (1921), 191-195. A. Alt, *ZDPV*, 55 (1932), 1-25; and *ZDPV*, 66 (1943), 1-20.   E. Edel, *ZA*, n.s., 15 (1949), 195-212.   *AEO*, I, 188*-189*.   A. R. Schulman, *JARCE*, 1 (1962), 47-53.   H. Goedicke, *JEA*, 52 (1966), 71-80.   Additional references will be found in the articles by Schulman and Goedicke.

The Bulletin

(1) Year 5, third month of summer, day 9, under the majesty of Re-Harakhti: The Strong-Bull-beloved-of-Maat; the King of Upper and Lower Egypt: *Usermare-sotpenre*; the Son of Re: *Ramesse, Beloved of Amun*, given life eternally. Now his majesty was in Djahi[1] on his second campaign of victory. A good awakening in life, prosperity, and health, in the tent of his majesty in the hill country south of Kadesh. Thereafter, in the morning, his majesty appeared like the rising of Re, clad in the panoply of his father Mont. The Lord proceeded northward and arrived in the region south of the town of Shabtuna. Then came two Shosu of the tribes of Shosu[2] to say to his majesty: "Our brothers who are chiefs of tribes with the Foe from Khatti (10) have sent us to his majesty to say that we will be servants of Pharaoh and will abandon the Chief of Khatti." His majesty said to them: "Where are they, your brothers who sent you to tell this matter to his majesty?" They said to his majesty: "They are where the vile Chief of Khatti is; for the Foe from Khatti is in the land of Khaleb[3] to the north of Tunip. He was too fearful of Pharaoh to come southward when he heard that Pharaoh had come northward."

Now the two Shosu who said these words to his majesty said them falsely, for it was the Foe from Khatti who had sent them to observe where his majesty was, (20) in order to prevent his majesty's army from making ready to fight with the Foe from Khatti. For the Foe from Khatti had come with his infantry and his chariotry, and with the chiefs of every land that was in the territory of the land of Khatti, and their infantry and their chariotry, whom he had brought with him as allies to fight against the army of his majesty, he standing equipped and ready behind Kadesh the Old, and his majesty did not know that they were there.

When the two Shosu who were in the Presence[4] had been ⌈released⌉,[5] his majesty proceeded northward and reached the northwest of Kadesh. (30) The camp of his majesty's army was pitched there, and his majesty took his seat on a throne of fine gold to the north of Kadesh on the west side of the Orontes. Then came a scout who was in his majesty's retinue bringing two scouts of the Foe from Khatti.

When they had been brought into the Presence, his majesty said to them: "What are you?" They said: "We belong to the Chief of Khatti. It is he who sent us to observe where his majesty is." His majesty said to them: "Where is he, the Foe from Khatti? I have heard he is in the land of Khaleb to the north of Tunip."

(40) They said to his majesty: "Look, the vile Chief of Khatti has come together with the many countries who are with him, whom he has brought with him as allies, the land of Dardany, the land of Nahrin, that of Keshkesh, those of Masa, those of Pidasa, the land of Karkisha and Luka, the land of Carchemish, the land of Arzawa, the land of Ugarit, that of Irun, the land of Inesa, Mushanet, Kadesh, Khaleb, and the entire land of Kedy. They are equipped with their infantry and their chariotry, and with their weapons of war. (50) They are more numerous than the sands of the shores. Look, they stand equipped and ready to fight behind Kadesh the Old."

Thereupon his majesty summoned the leaders into the Presence, to let them hear all the words which the two scouts of the Foe from Khatti who were in the Presence had spoken. Then his majesty said to them: "Observe the situation in which the governors of foreign countries and the chiefs of the lands of Pharaoh are. Every day they stood up to tell Pharaoh: 'The vile Chief of Khatti is in the land of Khaleb north of Tunip, having fled before his majesty when he heard that Pharaoh had come.' So they said daily to his majesty. (60) But now, this very moment, I have heard from these two scouts of the Foe from Khatti that the vile Foe from Khatti has come with the many countries that are with him, men and horses as numerous as the sand. Look, they stand concealed behind Kadesh the Old, while my governors of foreign countries and my chiefs of the land of Pharaoh were unable to tell us that they had come."

Then spoke the chiefs who were in the Presence in answer to the Good [God]: "It is a great crime that the governors of foreign countries and the chiefs of Pharaoh have committed (70) in failing to discover for themselves the Foe from Khatti wherever he was, and to report him to Pharaoh daily." Then the vizier was commanded to hasten the army of Pharaoh as it marched on the way to the south of the town of Shabtuna, so as to bring it to where his majesty was.

Now while his majesty sat speaking with the chiefs, the vile Foe from Khatti came with his infantry and his chariotry and the many countries that were with him. Crossing the ford to the south of Kadesh they charged into his majesty's army (80) as it marched unaware. Then the infantry and chariotry of his majesty weakened before them on their way northward to where his majesty was. Thereupon the forces of the Foe from Khatti surrounded the followers of his majesty who were by his side. When his majesty caught sight of them he rose quickly, enraged at them like his father Mont. Taking up weapons and donning his armor he was like Seth in the moment of his power. He mounted 'Victory-in-Thebes,' his great horse,[6] and started out quickly alone by himself. (90) His majesty was mighty, his heart stout, one could not stand before him.

All his ground was ablaze with fire; he burned all the countries with his blast. His eyes were savage as he beheld them; his power flared like fire against them. He heeded not the foreign multitude; he regarded them as chaff. His majesty charged into the force of the Foe from Khatti and the many countries with him. His majesty was like Seth, great-of-strength, like Sakhmet in the moment of her rage. His majesty slew the entire force of the Foe from Khatti, together with his great chiefs and all his brothers, as well as all the chiefs of all the countries that had come with him, (100) their infantry and their chariotry falling on their faces one upon the other. His majesty slaughtered them in their places; they sprawled before his horses; and his majesty was alone, none other with him.

My majesty[7] caused the forces of the foes from Khatti to fall on their faces, one upon the other, as crocodiles fall, into the water of the Orontes. I was after them like a griffin; I attacked all the countries, I alone. For my infantry and my chariotry had deserted me; not one of them stood looking back. As I live, as Re loves me, as my father Atum favors me, (110) everything that my majesty has told I did it in truth, in the presence of my infantry and my chariotry.[8]

The Poem

(1) Beginning of the victory[9] of the King of Upper and Lower Egypt: *Usermare-sotpenre*; the Son of Re: *Ramesse, Beloved of Amun*, given life forever, which he won over the land of Khatti, of Nahrin, the land of Arzawa, of Pidasa, that of Dardany, the land of Masa, the land of Karkisha and Luka, Carchemish, Kedy, the land of Kadesh, the land of Ugarit, and Mushanet.[10]

> His majesty was a youthful lord,
> Active and without his like;
> His arms mighty, his heart stout,
> His strength like Mont in his hour.
> Of perfect form like Atum,
> Hailed when his beauty is seen;
> (10) Victorious over all lands,
> Wily in launching a fight.
> Strong wall around his soldiers,
> Their shield on the day of battle;

A bowman without his equal,
Who prevails over vast numbers.
Head on he charges a multitude,
His heart trusting his strength;
Stout-hearted in the hour of combat,
Like the flame when it consumes.
Firm-hearted like a bull ready for battle,
He heeds not all the lands combined;
A thousand men cannot withstand him,
A hundred thousand fail at his sight.
Lord of fear, great of fame,
In the hearts of all the lands;
Great of awe, rich in glory,
As is Seth upon his mountain;
[Casting fear] in foreigners' hearts,
Like a wild lion in a valley of goats.
(20) Who goes forth in valor, returns in triumph,
Looking straight and free of boasting;
Firm in conduct, good in planning,
Whose first response is ever right.
Who saves his troops on battle day,
Greatly aids his charioteers;
Brings home his followers, rescues his soldiers,
With a heart that is like a mountain of copper:
The King of Upper and Lower Egypt, *Usermare-sotpenre*,
The Son of Re, *Ramesse, Beloved of Amun*,
Given life forever like Re.

Now his majesty had made ready his infantry and his chariotry, and the Sherden in his majesty's captivity whom he had brought back in the victories of his strong arm. They had been supplied with all their weapons, and battle orders had been given to them. His majesty journeyed northward, his infantry and his chariotry with him, having made a good start with the march in year 5, second month of summer, day 9. (30) His majesty passed the fortress of Sile, being mighty like Mont in his going forth, all foreign lands trembling before him, their chiefs bringing their gifts, and all rebels coming bowed down through fear of his majesty's might. His majesty's army traveled on the narrow paths as if on the roads of Egypt.

Now when days had passed over this, his majesty was in Ramesse-meramun, the town which is in the Valley of the Pine,[11] and his majesty proceeded northward. And when his majesty reached the hill country of Kadesh, his majesty went ahead like Mont, the lord of Thebes. He crossed the ford of the Orontes with the first army,

"Amun-gives-victory-to-Usermare-sotpenre," (40) and his majesty arrived at the town of Kadesh.

Now the vile Foe from Khatti had come and brought together all the foreign lands as far as the end of the sea. The entire land of Khatti had come, that of Nahrin also, that of Arzawa and Dardany, that of Keshkesh, those of Masa, those of Pidasa, that of Irun, that of Karkisha, that of Luka, Kizzuwadna, Carchemish, Ugarit, Kedy, the entire land of Nuges, Mushanet, and Kadesh. He had not spared a country from being brought, of all those distant lands, and their chiefs were there with him, each one with his infantry and (50) chariotry, a great number without equal. They covered the mountains and valleys and were like locusts in their multitude. He had left no silver in his land. He had stripped it of all its possessions and had given them to all the foreign countries in order to bring them with him to fight.

Now the vile Foe from Khatti and the many foreign countries with him stood concealed and ready to the northeast of the town of Kadesh, while his majesty was alone by himself with his attendants, the army of Amun marching behind him, the army of Pre crossing the ford in the neighborhood south of the town of Shabtuna (60) at a distance of 1 *iter* from where his majesty was, the army of Ptah being to the south of the town of Ironama, and the army of Seth marching on the road. And his majesty had made a first battle force from the best of his army, and it was on the shore of the land of Amor. Now the vile Chief of Khatti stood in the midst of the army that was with him and did not come out to fight for fear of his majesty, though he had caused men and horses to come in very great numbers like the sand— they were three men to a chariot and equipped with all weapons of warfare—(70) and they had been made to stand concealed behind the town of Kadesh.

Then they came forth from the south side of Kadesh and attacked the army of Pre in its middle, as they were marching unaware and not prepared to fight. Then the infantry and chariotry of his majesty weakened before them, while his majesty was stationed to the north of the town of Kadesh, on the west bank of the Orontes. They came to tell it to his majesty, and his majesty rose like his father Mont. He seized his weapons of war; he girded his coat of mail; he was like Baal in his hour. The great horse that bore his majesty was "Victory-in-Thebes" of the great stable of *Usermare-sotpenre*, beloved of Amun.

(80) Then his majesty drove at a gallop and charged the forces of the Foe from Khatti, being alone by himself, none other with him. His majesty proceeded to look about him and found 2,500 chariots ringing him on his way out, of all the fast troops of the Foe from Khatti and the many countries with him—Arzawa, Masa, Pidasa,

Keshkesh, Irun, Kizzuwadna, Khaleb, Ugarit, Kadesh and Luka, three men to a team acting together.

No officer was with me, no charioteer,[12]
No soldier of the army, no shield-bearer;
(90) My infantry, my chariotry yielded[13] before them,
Not one of them stood firm to fight with them.
His majesty spoke: "What is this, father Amun?
Is it right for a father to ignore his son?
Are my deeds a matter for you to ignore?
Do I not walk and stand at your word?
I have not neglected an order you gave.
Too great is he, the great lord of Egypt,
To allow aliens to step on his path!
What are these Asiatics to you, O Amun,
The wretches ignorant of god?
Have I not made for you many great monuments,
Filled your temple with my booty,
(100) Built for you my mansion of Millions-of-Years,
Given you all my wealth as endowment?
I brought you all lands to supply your altars,
I sacrificed to you ten thousands of cattle,
And all kinds of sweet-scented herbs.
I did not abstain from any good deed,
So as not to perform it in your court.
I built great pylons for you,
Myself I erected their flagstaffs;
I brought you obelisks from Yebu,
It was I who fetched their stones.
I conveyed to you ships from the sea,
To haul the lands' produce to you.
Shall it be said: 'The gain is small
For him who entrusts himself to your will'?[14]
Do good to him who counts on you,
Then one will serve you with loving heart.
(110) I call to you, my father Amun,
I am among a host of strangers;
All countries are arrayed against me,
I am alone, there's none with me!
My numerous troops have deserted me,
Not one of my chariotry looks for me;
I keep on shouting for them,
But none of them heeds my call.
I know Amun helps me more than a million troops,

More than a hundred thousand charioteers,
More than ten thousand brothers and sons
Who are united as one heart.
The labors of many people are nothing,
Amun is more helpful than they;
(120) I came here by the command of your mouth,
O Amun, I have not transgressed your command!"

Now though I prayed in the distant land,
My voice resounded in Southern On.[15]
I found Amun came when I called to him,
He gave me his hand and I rejoiced.
He called from behind as if near by:[16]
"Forward, I am with you,
I, your father, my hand is with you,
I prevail over a hundred thousand men,
I am lord of victory, lover of valor!"
I found my heart stout, my breast in joy,
All I did succeeded, I was like Mont.
(130) I shot on my right, grasped with my left,
I was before them like Seth in his moment.
I found the mass[17] of chariots in whose midst I was
Scattering before my horses;
Not one of them found his hand to fight,
Their hearts failed in their bodies through fear of me.
Their arms all slackened, they could not shoot,
They had no heart to grasp their spears;
I made them plunge into the water as crocodiles plunge,
They fell on their faces one on the other.
(140) I slaughtered among them at my will,
Not one looked behind him,
Not one turned around,
Whoever fell down did not rise.

And the wretched Chief of Khatti stood among his troops and
    chariots,
Watching his majesty fight all alone,
Without his soldiers and charioteers,
Stood turning, shrinking, afraid.
Then he caused many chiefs to come,
Each of them with his chariotry,
Equipped with their weapons of warfare:
The chief of Arzawa and he of Masa,
The chief of Irun (150) and he of Luka,

He of Dardany, the chief of Carchemish,
The chief of Karkisha, he of Khaleb,
The brothers of him of Khatti all together,
Their total of a thousand chariots came straight into the fire.
I charged toward them, being like Mont,
In a moment I gave them a taste of my hand,
I slaughtered among them, they were slain on the spot,
One called out to the other saying:
"No man is he who is among us,
It is Seth great-of-strength, Baal in person;
Not deeds of man are these his doings,
They are of one who is unique,
(160) Who fights a hundred thousand without soldiers and
    chariots,
Come quick, flee before him,
To seek life and breathe air;
For he who attempts to get close to him,
His hands, all his limbs grow limp.
One cannot hold either bow or spears,
When one sees him come racing along!"
My majesty hunted them like a griffin,
I slaughtered among them unceasingly.

I raised my voice to shout to my army:
"Steady, steady your hearts, my soldiers;
(170) Behold me victorious, me alone,
For Amun is my helper, his hand is with me.
How faint are your hearts, O my charioteers,
None among you is worthy of trust!
Is there none among you whom I helped in my land?
Did I not rise as lord when you were lowly,
And made you into chiefs by my will every day?
I have placed a son on his father's portion,
I have banished all evil from the land.
I released your servants to you,
Gave you things that were taken from you.
(180) Whosoever made a petition,
'I will do it,' said I to him daily.
No lord has done for his soldiers
What my majesty did for your sakes.
I let you dwell in your villages
Without doing a soldier's service;
So with my chariotry also,
I released them to their towns;

Saying, 'I shall find them just as today
In the hour of joining battle.'
But behold, you have all been cowards,
Not one among you stood fast,
To lend me a hand while I fought!
As the *ka* of my father Amun endures,
I wish I were in Egypt,
Like my fathers who did not see Syrians,
(190) And did not fight them ⌐abroad⌐!
For not one among you has come,
That he might speak of his service in Egypt!
What a good deed to him who raised monuments
In Thebes, the city of Amun;
This crime of my soldiers and charioteers,
That is too great to tell!"

Behold, Amun gave me his strength,
When I had no soldiers, no chariotry;
He caused every distant land to see
My victory through my strong arm,
I being alone, no captain behind me,
No charioteer, foot soldier, officer.
(200) The lands that beheld me will tell my name,
As far as distant lands unknown.
Whoever among them escaped from my hand,
They stood turned back to see my deeds.
When I attacked their multitudes,
Their feet were infirm and they fled;
All those who shot in my direction,
Their arrows veered as they attacked me.

Now when Menena my shield-bearer saw
That a large number of chariots surrounded me,
He became weak and faint-hearted,
Great fear invading his body.
He said to his majesty: "My good lord,
Strong ruler, great savior of Egypt in wartime,
(210) We stand alone in the midst of battle,
Abandoned by soldiers and chariotry,
What for do you stand to protect them?
Let us get clear, save us, Usermare-sotpenre!"
His majesty said to his shield-bearer:
"Stand firm, steady your heart, my shield-bearer!
I will charge them as a falcon pounces,
I will slaughter, butcher, fling to the ground;
Why do you fear these weaklings
Whose multitudes I disregard?"

His majesty then rushed forward,
At a gallop he charged the midst of the foe,
For the sixth time he charged them.
I was after them like Baal in his moment of power,
I slew them without pause.

Now when my soldiers and chariotry saw
That I was like Mont, strong-armed,
That my father Amun was with me,
Making the foreign lands into chaff before me,
They started coming one by one,
(230) To enter the camp at time of night.
They found all the foreign lands I had charged
Lying fallen in their blood;
All the good warriors of Khatti,
The sons and brothers of their chiefs.
For I had wrecked[18] the plain of Kadesh,
It could not be trodden because of their mass.
Thereupon my soldiers came to praise me,
Their faces [bright] at the sight of my deeds;
My captains came to extol my strong arm,
My charioteers likewise exalted my name:
"Hail, O good warrior, firm of heart,
(240) You have saved your soldiers, your chariotry;
You are Amun's son who acts with his arms,
You have felled Khatti by your valiant strength.
You are the perfect fighter, there's none like you,
A king who battles for his army on battle day;
You are great-hearted, first in the ranks,
You heed not all the lands combined.
You are greatly victorious before your army,
Before the whole land, it is no boast;
Protector of Egypt, curber of foreign lands,
(250) You have broken the back of Khatti forever!"

Said his majesty to his infantry,
His captains and his chariotry:
"What about you, my captains, soldiers,
My charioteers, who shirked the fight?
Does a man not act to be acclaimed in his town,
When he returns as one brave before his lord?
A name made through combat is truly good,
A man is ever respected for valor.
Have I not done good to any of you,
That you should leave me alone in the midst of battle?
(260) You are lucky to be alive at all,

You who took the air while I was alone!
Did you not know it in your hearts:
I am your rampart of iron!
What will men say when they hear of it,
That you left me alone without a comrade,
That no chief, charioteer, or soldier came,
To lend me a hand while I was fighting?
I crushed a million countries by myself
On Victory-in-Thebes, Mut-is-content, my great horses;
It was they whom I found supporting me,
When I alone fought many lands.
(270) They shall henceforth be fed in my presence,
Whenever I reside in my palace;
It was they whom I found in the midst of battle,
And charioteer Menena, my shield-bearer,
And my household butlers who were at my side,
My witnesses in combat, behold, I found them!"
My majesty paused in valor and victory,
Having felled hundred thousands by my strong arm.

At dawn I marshaled the ranks for battle,
I was ready to fight like an eager bull;
I arose against them in the likeness of Mont,
Equipped with my weapons of victory.
(280) I charged their ranks fighting as a falcon pounces,
The serpent on my brow felled my foes,
Cast her fiery breath in my enemies' faces,
I was like Re when he rises at dawn.
My rays, they burned the rebels' bodies,
They called out to one another:
"Beware, take care, don't approach him,
Sakhmet the Great is she who is with him,
She's with him on his horses, her hand is with him;
Anyone who goes to approach him,
Fire's breath comes to burn his body!"
(290) Thereupon they stood at a distance,
Touching the ground with their hands before me.
My majesty overpowered them,
I slew them without sparing them;
They sprawled before my horses,
And lay slain in heaps in their blood.

Then the vile Chief of Khatti wrote and worshiped my name like that of Re, saying: "You are Seth, Baal in person; the dread of you is a fire in the land of Khatti." (300) He sent his envoy with a letter in his hand (addressed) to the great name of my majesty, greeting the Majesty of the Palace: "Re-Harakhti, The Strong-Bull-beloved-of-Maat, the Sovereign who protects his army, mighty on account of his strong arm, rampart of his soldiers on the day of battle, King of Upper and Lower Egypt: *Usermare-sotpenre*, the Son of Re, the lion lord of strength: *Ramesse, Beloved of Amun*, given life forever":

"Your servant speaks to let it be known that you are the Son of Re who came from his body. He has given you all the lands together. As for the land of Egypt and the land of Khatti, they are your servants, under your feet. (310) Pre, your august father, has given them to you. Do not overwhelm us. Lo, your might is great, your strength is heavy upon the land of Khatti. Is it good that you slay your servants, your face savage toward them and without pity? Look, you spent yesterday killing a hundred thousand, and today you came back and left no heirs. Be not hard in your dealings, victorious king! (320) Peace is better than fighting. Give us breath!"

Then my majesty relented in life and dominion, being like Mont at his moment when his attack is done. My majesty ordered brought to me all the leaders of my infantry and my chariotry, all my officers assembled together, to let them hear the matter about which he had written. My majesty let them hear these words which the vile Chief of Khatti had written to me. Then they said with one voice: "Very excellent is peace, O Sovereign our Lord! There is no blame in peace when you make it. (330) Who could resist you on the day of your wrath?" My majesty commanded to hearken to his words, and I moved in peace southward.

His majesty returned in peace to Egypt with his infantry and his chariotry, all life, stability, and dominion being with him, and the gods and goddesses protecting his body. He had crushed all lands through fear of him; his majesty's strength had protected his army; all foreign lands gave praise to his fair face.

Arrival in peace in Egypt, in Per-Ramesse-meramun-great-of-victories.[19] Resting in his palace of life and dominion like Re in his horizon, (340) the gods of this land hailing him and saying: "Welcome, our beloved son, King *Usermare-sotpenre*, the Son of Re, *Ramesse, Beloved of Amun*, given life!" They granted him millions of jubilees forever on the throne of Re, all lowlands and all highlands lying prostrate under his feet for ever and all time.

Colophon of Papyrus Sallier III

This writing [was written] in year 9, second month of summer, of the King of Upper and Lower Egypt, *Usermare-sotpenre*, the Son of Re, *Ramesse, Beloved of Amun*, given life for all eternity like his father Re.

[It has been brought to a successful conclusion] through the agency of the Chief Archivist of the Royal Treasury, Amenemone, the Scribe of the Royal Treasury, Amenemwia, and the Scribe of the Royal Treasury, ---.

Made by the Scribe Pentwere.[20]

NOTES

1. On Djahi see p. 38 n. 3.

2. The term "Shosu" was applied to a group of nomads in Palestine and Syria. The Egyptian evidence on the Shosu has been assembled by R. Giveon, *Les bédouins Shosou des documents égyptiens* (Leiden, 1971).

3. Modern Aleppo.

4. Circumlocution for Pharaoh.

5. A verb written *mšd* in one version and *wšd* in another, in both with the walking legs determinative.

6. I.e., he mounted his chariot drawn by two horses whose names were "Victory-in-Thebes" and "Mut-is-content," as we are told in §267 of the *Poem*.

7. The mixture of first-person and third-person narrative is common in royal inscriptions of the New Kingdom.

8. The concluding sentences, in §§111-119, are almost entirely destroyed.

9. I.e., the recital of the victory.

10. On the Egyptian names of the foreign countries consult Gardiner, *The Kadesh Inscriptions of Ramses II*, Appendix.

11. A town in Lebanon to which Ramses II had given his name. The Valley of the Pine (or Valley of the Cedar) is familiar from the *Tale of Two Brothers*.

12. Here begins the metrical composition.

13. The precise meaning of *mrḫt*, written with walking-legs determinative, is unknown.

14. The sentence has been variously rendered; see Gardiner, *op. cit.*, pp. 9 and 20.

15. I.e., Thebes.

16. Literally, "as face to face."

17. Literally, "the 2,500 chariots."

18. Despite the sun determinative, I assume that the verb is *ḥḏi*, "to destroy."

19. The Delta residence of Ramses II.

20. The colophon of the papyrus copy indicates that the work was written down in the ninth year of the reign of Ramses II, and that this particular copy was the work of the scribe Pentwere. This scribe is known to have lived under King Merneptah; hence the text copy of Papyrus Sallier III is considerably later than the composition itself.

THE POETICAL STELA OF MERNEPTAH (ISRAEL STELA)

Cairo Museum 34025 (Verso)

The stela had belonged to Amenhotep III, who had inscribed its *recto* with an account of his building activities (see p. 43). It was appropriated by Merneptah, who placed it in his mortuary temple and had the *verso* inscribed with a poetic account of his victory over the Libyans who had invaded Egypt in the fifth year of his reign. A duplicate copy of this text was written on a stela erected in the temple of Karnak. Furthermore, a long prose account of the Libyan war (not translated here) was inscribed on the inside of the eastern wall that connects the central part of the Karnak temple with Pylon No. VII.

As regards literary composition, the situation is parallel to that of the Kadesh Battle Inscriptions of Ramses II. Again we have two major accounts covering the same campaign: a prose report of a more or less factual nature and a poetic version abounding in hyperbole. But here the poetic version is much shorter than the prose text. Also as in the case of the Kadesh Battle Poem, Merneptah's victory poem contains narration and is thus a second example of epic poetry in New Kingdom literature. Here too the use of parallelism is attenuated. Yet the stylistic devices that create roughly symmetrical sentences are sufficiently strong to serve as guideposts for the metrical reading of the text. Only in a few instances does the metrical division appear uncertain.

The text begins with the royal titulary and a formal encomium, strictly composed in eight symmetrical distichs. Then comes the narrative poem whose freer form makes for liveliness and variety. It begins with a graphic description of the Libyan defeat: the rout of the troops, the flight of the chief, and the desolation at home. Next is a court session of the gods at Heliopolis in which Merneptah is declared victor and presented with the sword of victory. Then follows a vivid and joyful description of the return of peace.

The final portion of the text is a twelve-line poem of praise which complements the initial encomium. Where in the beginning the king had been lauded as the victor who freed Egypt from the Libyan menace, the concluding poem extols him as victor over all of Egypt's neighbors, especially the peoples of Palestine and Syria. At the present time, scholars are wary of seeking historically accurate information in such triumphal poetry; hence one would hesitate to treat the poem as firm evidence for an Asiatic campaign of Merneptah. But the poem has a special significance owing to its mentioning Israel among the conquered peoples and places; for this is the only occurrence of the name of Israel in Egyptian texts.

Publication: W. M. F. Petrie, *Six Temples at Thebes* (London, 1897), pls. xiii-xiv.   W. Spiegelberg, *ZÄS*, 34 (1896), 1-25.   P. Lacau, *Stèles du nouvel empire*, I, pp. 52-59 and pls. xvii-xix. Catalogue général . . . du Musée du Caire (Cairo, 1909).   Ch. Kuentz, *BIFAO*, 21 (1922/ 23), 113-117 and 1 plate (the Karnak duplicate).   Kitchen, *Inscriptions*, IV, 12-19.

Translation: *BAR* III, §§602-617.   Erman, *Literature*, pp. 274-278. J. A. Wilson in *ANET*, pp. 376-378.

(1) Year 5, 3d month of summer, day 3, under the Majesty of Horus: Mighty Bull, Rejoicing in Maat; the King of Upper and Lower Egypt: *Banere-meramun*; the Son of Re: *Merneptah, Content with Maat*, magnified by the power, exalted by the strength of Horus; strong bull who smites the Nine Bows, whose name is given to eternity forever.

Recital of his victories in all lands, to let all lands together know, to let the glory of his deeds be seen: the King of Upper and Lower Egypt: *Banere-meramun*; the Son of Re: *Merneptah, Content with Maat*; the Bull, lord of strength who slays his foes, splendid on the field of valor when his attack is made:

> Shu who dispelled the cloud that was over Egypt,
>   letting Egypt see the rays of the sun disk.
> Who removed the mountain of copper from the people's neck,
>   that he might give breath to the imprisoned folk.
> Who let Hut-ka-Ptah[1] exult over its foes,
>   letting Tjenen[2] triumph over his opponents.
> Opener of Memphis' gates that were barred,
>   who allowed the temples to receive their foods.
> The King of Upper and Lower Egypt, *Banere-meramun*,
>   the Son of Re, *Merneptah, Content with Maat*.
> The Sole One who steadied the hearts of hundred thousands,
>   breath entered their nostrils at the sight of him.
> Who destroyed the land of the Tjemeh in his lifetime,
>   cast abiding terror (5) in the heart of the Meshwesh.
> He turned back the Libyans who trod Egypt,
>   great is dread of Egypt in their hearts.
>
> Their leading troops were left behind,[3]
> Their legs made no stand except to flee,
> Their archers abandoned their bows,
> The hearts of their runners grew weak as they sped,
> They loosened their waterskins, cast them down,
> Their packs were untied, thrown away.
> The vile chief, the Libyan foe,
> Fled in the deep of night alone,
> No plume on his head, his feet unshod,
> His wives were carried off from his presence,
> His food supplies were snatched away,
> He had no drinking water to sustain him.
> The gaze of his brothers was fierce to slay him,
> His officers fought among each other,
> Their tents were fired, burnt to ashes,
> All his goods were food for the troops.[4]

When he reached his country he was in mourning,
Those left in his land were loath to receive him,
"A chief, ill-fated, evil-plumed,"
All said of him, those of his town.
"He is in the power of the gods, the lords of Memphis,
The Lord of Egypt has made his name accursed;
Merey[5] is the abomination of Memphis,
So is son after son of his kin forever.
Banere-meramun will be after his children,
Merneptah, Content with Maat is given him as fate.
He has become a ⌈proverbial (10) saying⌉ for Libya,
Generation says to generation of his victories:
It was never done to us since the time of Re;"[6]
So says every old man speaking to his son.

Woe to Libyans, they have ceased to live
In the good manner of roaming the field;
In a single day their stride was halted,
In a single year were the Tjehenu burned!
Seth[7] turned his back upon their chief,
By his word their villages were ruined;
There's no work of carrying ⌈loads⌉ these days,
Hiding is useful, it's safe in the cave.
The great Lord of Egypt, might and strength are his,
Who will combat, knowing how he strides?
A witless fool is he who takes him on,
He knows no tomorrow who attacks his border!
As for Egypt, "Since the gods," they say,
"She is the only daughter of Pre;
His son is he who's on the throne of Shu,[8]
None who attacks her people will succeed.
The eye of every god is after her despoiler,
It will make an end of all its foes,"
So say they who gaze toward their stars,
And know all their spells by looking to the winds.

A great wonder has occurred for Egypt,
Her attacker was placed captive ⟨in⟩ her hand,
Through the counsels of the godly king,
Who prevailed against his foes before Pre.
Merey who stealthily did evil
To all the gods who are in Memphis,
He was contended (15) with in On,
The Ennead found him guilty of his crimes.

Said the Lord-of-all: "Give the sword to my son,
The right-hearted, kind, gracious *Banere-meramun*,
Who cared for Memphis, who avenged On,
Who opened the quarters that were barred.
He has freed the many shut up in all districts,
He has given the offerings to the temples,
He has let incense be brought to the gods,
He has let the nobles retain their possessions,
He has let the humble frequent their towns."
Then spoke the lords of On in behalf of their son,
Merneptah, Content with Maat:
"Grant him a lifetime like that of Re,
To avenge those injured by any land;
Egypt has been assigned him as portion,
He owns it forever to protect its people."
Lo, when one dwells in the time of the mighty,
The breath of life comes readily.
The brave bestows wealth on the just,
The cheat cannot retain his plunder;
⌐What a man has of ill-gotten wealth
Falls to others, not⟨his⟩ children.¬

This (too) shall be said:
Merey the vile foe, the Libyan foe
Had come to attack the walls of Ta-tenen,
Whose lord had made his son arise in his place,
The King of Upper and Lower Egypt, *Banere-meramun*,
Son of Re, *Merneptah, Content with Maat.*
Then said Ptah concerning the vile Libyan foe:
"His crimes (20) are all gathered upon his head.
Give him into the hand of *Merneptah, Content with Maat,*
He shall make him spew what he gorged like a crocodile.
Lo, the swift will catch the swift,
The lord who knows his strength will snare him;
It is Amun who curbs him with his hand,
He will deliver him to his *ka* in Southern On,[9]
The King of Upper and Lower Egypt, *Banere-meramun*,
Son of Re, *Merneptah, Content with Maat.*"

Great joy has arisen in Egypt,
Shouts go up from Egypt's towns;
They relate the Libyan victories
Of *Merneptah, Content with Maat*:

"How beloved is he, the victorious ruler!
How exalted is he, the King among the gods!
How splendid is he, the lord of command!
O how sweet it is to sit and babble!"
One walks free-striding on the road,
For there's no fear in people's hearts;
Fortresses are left to themselves,
Wells are open for the messengers' use.
Bastioned ramparts are becalmed,
Sunlight only wakes the watchmen;
Medjai are stretched out asleep,
Nau and Tekten are in the fields they love.[10]
The cattle of the field are left to roam,
No herdsmen cross the river's flood;
There's no calling out at night:
"Wait, I come," in a stranger's voice.
Going and coming are with song,
People don't ⌐ lament ⌐ and mourn;
Towns are settled once again,
He who tends his crop will eat it.
Re has turned around to Egypt,
The Son is ordained as her protector,
The King of Upper and Lower Egypt, *Banere-meramun*,
Son of Re, *Merneptah, Content with Maat.*

The princes are prostrate saying: "Shalom!"
Not one of the Nine Bows lifts his head:
Tjehenu is vanquished, Khatti at peace,
Canaan is captive with all woe.
Ashkelon is conquered, Gezer seized,
Yanoam made nonexistent;
Israel is wasted, bare of seed,
Khor is become a widow for Egypt.
All who roamed have been subdued
By the King of Upper and Lower Egypt, *Banere-meramun*,
Son of Re, *Merneptah, Content with Maat,*
Given life like Re every day.

NOTES

1. A name for Memphis.

2. Tjenen is a writing of Ta-tjenen or Ta-tenen, the Memphite earth god who was identified with Ptah, the chief god of Memphis.

3. Here begins the narrative poem.

4. The Egyptian troops.

5. Name of the Libyan chief.

6. Since primordial times when the gods lived on earth.

7. The god Seth was viewed as the protector of the foreign peoples to the east and west of Egypt. Here the god has turned against Libya.

8. The definite article is here attached to Re as well as to Shu.

9. Thebes.

10. Medjai, Nau, and Tekten were foreign tribes whose members were employed as soldiers and police.

PART TWO

Hymns, Prayers, and a Harper's Song

THE GREAT HYMN TO OSIRIS

On the Stela of Amenmose
Louvre C 286

A round-topped limestone stela, 1.03 × 0.62 m, of fine workmanship, dating from the Eighteenth Dynasty. In the lunette there are two offering scenes showing, on the left, the official Amenmose and his wife Nefertari seated before an offering table, and, on the right, a lady named Baket, whose relationship to Amenmose is not stated. Before Amenmose stands a son with his arms raised in the gesture of offering. Another son stands behind the couple, and more sons and daughters are seated below. A priest also performs offering rites before the lady Baket. Below the scenes is the hymn to Osiris in twenty-eight horizontal lines.

This hymn contains the fullest account of the Osiris myth extant in Egyptian, as distinct from Greek, sources. Allusions to the Osiris myth are very frequent in Egyptian texts, but they are very brief. It seems that the slaying of Osiris at the hands of Seth was too awesome an event to be committed to writing. Other parts of the story could be told more fully, especially the vindication of Osiris and of his son Horus, to whom the gods awarded the kingship of Egypt that had belonged to Osiris. The latter, though resurrected, no longer ruled the living but was king of the dead in the netherworld. The final part of the hymn praises the beneficent rule of Horus, and, since each living Pharaoh represented Horus, the praise is directed to the reigning king as well.

Publication: A. Moret, BIFAO, 30 (1931), 725-750 and 3 plates. Translation: Erman, *Literature*, pp. 140-145.

(1) Adoration of Osiris by the overseer of the cattle of [Amun], [Amen]mose, and the lady Nefertari. He says:

Hail to you, Osiris,
Lord of eternity, king of gods,
Of many names, of holy forms,
Of secret rites in temples!
Noble of *ka* he presides in Djedu,[1]
He is rich in sustenance in Sekhem,[2]
Lord of acclaim in Andjty,[3]
Foremost in offerings in On.[4]
Lord of remembrance in the Hall of Justice,[5]
Secret *ba* of the lord of the cavern,
Holy in White-Wall,[6]
Ba of Re, his very body.
Who reposes in Hnes,[7]
Who is worshiped in the *naret*-tree,
That grew up to bear his *ba*.[8]
Lord of the palace in Khmun,[9]
Much revered in Shashotep,[10]

81

Eternal lord who presides in Abydos,[11]
Who dwells distant in the graveyard
Whose name endures in peoples' mouth.

Oldest in the joined Two Lands,
Nourisher[12] before the Nine Gods,
Potent spirit among spirits.
Nun has given him his waters,
Northwind journeys south to him,
Sky makes wind before his nose,
That his heart be satisfied.
Plants sprout by his wish,
Earth grows its food for him,
Sky and its stars obey him,
The great portals open for him.
Lord of acclaim in the southern sky,
Sanctified in the northern sky,
The imperishable stars are under his rule,
The unwearying stars are his abode.
One offers to him by Geb's command,
The Nine Gods adore him,
Those in *dat* kiss the ground,
Those on high[13] bow down.
The ancestors rejoice to see him,
Those yonder are in awe of him.

The joined Two Lands adore him,
When His Majesty approaches,
Mightiest noble among nobles,
Firm of rank, of lasting rule.
Good leader of the Nine Gods,
Gracious, lovely to behold,
Awe inspiring to all lands,
That his name be foremost.
All make offering to him,
The lord of remembrance in heaven and earth,
Rich in acclaim at the *wag*-feast,
Hailed in unison by the Two Lands.
The foremost of his brothers,
The eldest of the Nine Gods,
Who set Maat throughout the Two Shores,
Placed the son on his father's seat.
Lauded by his father Geb,
Beloved of his mother Nut,

Mighty when he fells the rebel,
Strong-armed when he slays (10) his foe.
Who casts fear of him on his enemy,
Who vanquishes the evil-plotters,
Whose heart is firm when he crushes the rebels.

Geb's heir (in) the kingship of the Two Lands,
Seeing his worth he gave (it) to him,
To lead the lands to good fortune.
He placed this land into his hand,
Its water, its wind,
Its plants, all its cattle.
All that flies, all that alights,
Its reptiles and its desert game,
Were given to the son of Nut,
And the Two Lands are content with it.
Appearing on his father's throne,
Like Re when he rises in lightland,
He places light above the darkness,
He lights the shade with his plumes.[14]
He floods the Two Lands like Aten[15] at dawn,
His crown pierces the sky, mingles with the stars.
He is the leader of all the gods,
Effective in the word of command,
The great Ennead praises him,
The small Ennead loves him.

His sister was his guard,
She who drives off the foes,
Who stops the deeds of the disturber
By the power of her utterance.
The clever-tongued whose speech fails not,
Effective in the word of command,
Mighty Isis who protected her brother,
Who sought him without wearying.
Who roamed the land lamenting,
Not resting till she found him,
Who made a shade with her plumage,
Created breath with her wings.
Who jubilated, joined her brother,
Raised the weary one's inertness,
Received the seed, bore the heir,
Raised the child in solitude,
His abode unknown.

Who brought him when his arm was strong
Into the broad hall of Geb.

The Ennead was jubilant:
"Welcome, Son of Osiris,
Horus, firm-hearted, justified,
Son of Isis, heir of Osiris!"
The Council of Maat assembled for him
The Ennead, the All-Lord himself,
The Lords of Maat, united in her,
Who eschew wrongdoing,
They were seated in the hall of Geb,
To give the office to its lord,
The kingship to its rightful owner.
Horus was found justified,
His father's rank was given him,
He came out crowned by Geb's command,
Received the rule of the two shores.

The crown placed firmly on his head,
He counts the land as his possession,
Sky, earth are under his command,
Mankind is entrusted to him,
Commoners, nobles, sunfolk.[16]
Egypt and the far-off lands,
What Aten (20) encircles is under his care,
Northwind, river, flood,
Tree of life, all plants.
Nepri gives all his herbs,
Field's Bounty[17] brings satiety,
And gives it to all lands.
Everybody jubilates,
Hearts are glad, breasts rejoice,
Everyone exults,
All extol his goodness:
How pleasant is his love for us,
His kindness overwhelms the hearts,
Love of him is great in all.

They gave to Isis' son his foe,
His attack collapsed,
The disturber suffered hurt,
His fate overtook the offender.

The son of Isis who championed his father,
Holy and splendid is his name,
Majesty has taken its seat,
Abundance is established by his laws.
Roads are open, ways are free,
How the two shores prosper!
Evil is fled, crime is gone,
The land has peace under its lord.
Maat is established for her lord,
One turns the back on falsehood.
May you be content, Wennofer![18]
Isis' son has received the crown,
His father's rank was assigned him
In the hall of Geb.
Re spoke, Thoth wrote,
The council assented,
Your father Geb decreed for you,
One did according to his word.

An offering which the king gives (to) Osiris Khentamentiu, lord of
Abydos, that he may grant an offering of bread and beer, oxen and
fowl, ointment and clothing and plants of all kinds, and the making of
transformations: to be powerful as Hapy, to come forth as living *ba*, to
see Aten at dawn, to come and go in Rostau,[19] without one's *ba* being
barred from the necropolis.

May he be supplied among the favored ones before Wennofer,
receiving the offerings that go up on the altar of the great god,
breathing the sweet northwind, drinking from the river's pools: for the
ka of the overseer of the cattle of [Amun], [Amen]mose, justified,
born of the lady Henut, justified, and of his beloved wife, [the lady
Nefertari, justified].

NOTES

1. Busiris.
2. Letopolis.
3. The Ninth Nome of Lower Egypt.
4. Heliopolis.
5. Literally, "the Two Justices" (or, "the Two Truths"), the name of
the hall in the netherworld in which the judgment of the dead takes
place.
6. Memphis and its nome.
7. Heracleopolis Magna.
8. According to the tradition of Heracleopolis the tomb of Osiris was
located in that town, and the sacred *naret*-tree grew over the tomb and
sheltered the *ba* of Osiris.
9. Hermopolis.

10. Hypselis.

11. The hymn enumerates the chief cult centers of Osiris from north to south, beginning with Busiris, his foremost northern center of worship, and ending with Abydos, his main cult center in Upper Egypt.

12. _Df3_ here, and again in line 20, is abundance of food personified as a divinity.

13. I.e., those buried in the high ground of the desert tombs.

14. _Šw_ is written but _šwt_ must have been intended. Note the wordplay on _šw(t)_, "shade," and _šwty_, "plumes."

15. Though written without the divine determinative, the word _itn_ has probably already assumed the connotation of a divinity. The divine determinative is also lacking in the two occurrences of _df3_, "Abundance," where the personification is clear.

16. The population of Egypt and mankind as a whole.

17. See note 12.

18. A name of Osiris.

19. A name for the necropolis and specifically that of Giza.

TWO HYMNS TO THE SUN-GOD

From a Stela of the Brothers Suti and Hor

British Museum 826

In the course of the Eighteenth Dynasty, the rise to prominence of Amun of Thebes resulted in his assimilation to the supreme god, the sun-god Re. Furthermore, the conceptual dominance of sun worship had turned the sun-god into the all-embracing creator-god who manifested himself in many forms and under many names. Thus he absorbed Amun and Horus, and he was Atum, Harakhti, and Khepri. And his visible form, the sun-disk (Aten) became yet another manifestation of the god himself. The hymns to the sun-god of the twin brothers Suti and Hor, who lived in the reign of Amenhotep III, address the god in these various forms, and they accord a prominent place to the Aten, the most recently evolved personification of the god. In the first hymn the sun-god is addressed as Amun, Harakhti, Re, and Khepri; in the second hymn he is Aten, Khepri, and Horus.

The hymns are inscribed on a rectangular stela in door form, of gray granite and measuring 1.44 × 0.88 m. The central portion of the surface is carved to resemble a round-topped stela. In the lunette are the standing figures of Anubis and Osiris who are adored by the brothers Suti and Hor and their wives. The figures of the worshiping couples have been erased. Below the figures are twenty-one horizontal lines of text. The first hymn ends in the middle of line 8. The second runs from the middle of line 8 to near the end of line 14. The remaining lines consist of personal statements and prayers of the two brothers.

Publication: _Hieroglyphic Texts_, Part VIII (1939), pp. 22-25 and plate xxi.   A. Varille, _BIFAO_, 41 (1942), 25-30.   _Urk._ IV, 1943-1947. Fragment of a duplicate text: H. M. Stewart, _JEA_, 43 (1957), 3-5.

Translation: J. Sainte Fare Garnot, _CRAIBL_ 1948, pp. 543-549, and _JEA_, 35 (1949), 63-68.   J. A. Wilson in _ANET_, pp. 367-368.   Helck, _Übersetzung_, pp. 328-331.   G. Fecht, _ZÄS_, 94 (1967), 25-50.   References to older studies will be found in the literature cited.

First hymn

(1) Adoration of Amun when he rises as Harakhti by the overseer of the works of Amun, Suti, (and) the overseer of the works of Amun, Hor. They say:

Hail to you, Re, perfect each day,
Who rises at dawn without failing,
Khepri who wearies himself with toil!
Your rays are on the face, yet unknown,
Fine gold does not match your splendor;
Self-made you fashioned your body,
Creator uncreated.
Sole one, unique one, who traverses eternity,
⌐Remote one⌐,[1] with millions under his care;
Your splendor is like heaven's splendor,
Your color brighter than its hues.
When you cross the sky all faces see you,
When you set you are hidden from their (5) sight;
Daily you give yourself at dawn,
Safe is your sailing under your majesty.
In a brief day you race a course,
Hundred thousands, millions of miles;
A moment is each day to you,
It has passed when you go down.
You also complete the hours of night,
You order it without pause in your labor.
Through you do all eyes see,
They lack aim when your majesty sets.
When you stir to rise at dawn,
Your brightness opens the eyes of the herds;
When you set in the western mountain,
They sleep as in the state of death.

Second hymn

Hail to you, Aten of daytime,
Creator of all, who makes them live!
Great falcon, brightly plumed,
Beetle who raised himself.
Self-creator, uncreated,
Eldest Horus within Nut,
Acclaimed (10) in his rising and setting.
Maker of the earth's yield,
Khnum and Amun of mankind,
Who seized the Two Lands from great to small.
Beneficent mother of gods and men,

Craftsman with a patient heart,
Toiling long to make them countless.
Valiant shepherd who drives his flock,
Their refuge, made to sustain them.
Runner, racer, courser,
Khepri of distinguished birth,
Who raises his beauty in the body of Nut,
Who lights the Two Lands with his disk.
The Two Lands' Oldest who made himself,
Who sees all that he made, he alone.
Who reaches the ends of the lands every day,
In the sight of those who tread on them.
Rising in heaven formed as Re,
He makes the seasons with the months,
Heat as he wishes, cold as he wishes.
He makes bodies slack, he gathers them up,[2]
Every land rejoices at his rising,
Every day gives praise to him.

Prayers

The overseer of works, Suti; the overseer of works, (15) Hor. He says:

I was controller in your sanctuary,
Overseer of works in your very shrine,
Made for you by your beloved son,
The Lord of the Two Lands, *Nebmare*,[3] given life.
My lord made me controller of your monuments,
Because he knew my vigilance.
I was a vigorous controller of your monuments,
One who did right (maat) as you wished.
For I knew you are content with right,
You advance him who does it on earth.
I did it and you advanced me,
You made me favored on earth in Ipet-sut,[4]
One who was in your following when you appeared.[5]
I was a true one who abhors falsehood,
Who does not trust the words of a liar.
But my brother, my likeness, his ways I trust,
He came from the womb with me the same day.

The overseer(s) of Amun's works in Southern Ipet,[6] Suti, Hor.

When I was in charge on the westside,
He was in charge on the eastside.

We controlled great monuments in Ipet-sut,
At the front of Thebes, the city of Amun.
May you give me old age in your city,
My eye ⟨beholding⟩ your beauty;
A burial in the west, the place of heart's content,
As I join the favored ones who went in peace.
May you give me sweet breeze when I land,
And ⌐garlands⌐ 7 on the day of the *wag*-feast.

NOTES

1. What is written is *ḥry w3wt*, "who is above the ways," but perhaps *ḥryw*, "remote," was intended.
2. Or, "when he embraces them"? But a contrast with slackness is more plausible.
3. Amenhotep III. The two brothers were architects in the service of this king.
4. Karnak.
5. When the statue of Amun appeared in a festival procession.
6. Luxor.
7. The *sšdw* received on a feast day must be decorative ribbons, scarves, or garlands rather than wrappings.

HYMNS AND PRAYERS FROM EL-AMARNA

As early as the Old Kingdom, Egyptian religion had tended to attribute supreme power to one god, and to subordinate the other gods to him. But while increasingly heaping attributes of universal power on the sun-god Re, the religion remained essentially polytheistic. The worship of the sun-disk (Aten) as a manifestation of the sun-god Re had been growing since the beginning of the Eighteenth Dynasty and reached prominence in the reign of Amenhotep III, as shown, for example, by the hymns to the Sun of the brothers Suti and Hor (pp. 86-89). In these hymns, the Aten, merged with Re, is the supreme creator-god, supreme but not sole god.

It was Amenhotep IV who converted the supreme god into the sole god by denying the reality of all other gods. Thus the king eliminated the clash between the claims of the "one" and the "many." But this was a radical break with the past. His doctrine was profoundly uncongenial and gave great offense. The nation was not willing to jettison its long-held beliefs and, after the king's death, the heretical teaching was wiped out. The "many" had overpowered the "one."

The Great Hymn to the Aten is an eloquent and beautiful statement of the doctrine of the one god. He alone has created the world and all it contains. He alone gives life to man and beast. He alone watches over his creations. He alone inhabits the sky. Heretofore the sun-god had appeared in three major forms: as Harakhti in the morning, as Khepri in midday, and as Atum in the evening. His daily journey across the sky had been done in the company of many gods. It had involved the ever-recurring combat against the primordial serpent Apopis. In traversing the night sky the god had been acclaimed by the multitudes of the dead who rest there; and each hour of the night had marked a specific stage in his journey. Thus the daily circuit of the sky was a drama with a large supporting cast. In the new doctrine of the Aten as sole god all these facets were eliminated. The Aten rises and sets in lonely majesty in an empty sky. Only the earth is peopled by his creatures, and only they adore his rising and setting.

As we know from the *Boundary Stelae* (pp. 48-51), Amenhotep IV Akhenaten had dedicated his new city to the Aten, and the public worship of the god must have been the central feature in the daily life of the court. The principal surviving sources for the reconstruction of this worship are the reliefs and inscriptions in the rock-tombs of the courtiers. The doctrine of the Aten as taught by the king was undoubtedly recorded in many writings. But it has survived in only two forms: in the statements of the king on the boundary stelae, and in the hymns and prayers inscribed in the tombs of the courtiers.

The tombs contain numerous short prayers and hymns addressed to the Aten, or jointly to the Aten and the king. These brief compositions resemble one another closely and thereby show that they were derived from a common stock of formulations assembled by the royal scribes. One such text is found in nearly identical versions in five tombs: the tombs of Apy, Any, Meryre, Mahu, and Tutu. N. de Garis Davies, the excavator of the Amarna tombs, called it "the shorter hymn to the Aten," and it is now usually referred to as *The Short Hymn to the Aten*.

The texts in the tomb of the courtier Ay have yielded the most extensive statements of Aten worship. Here we have not only several short hymns and prayers but, above all, the long text which has come to be known as *The Great Hymn to the Aten*. The east wall of the tomb is inscribed with three hymns and prayers to the Aten and to the king, and the west wall contains the great hymn.

The five texts translated here are: (1) *The Short Hymn to the Aten*; (2) *Two Hymns and a Prayer* from the east wall of the tomb of Ay; (3) *The Great Hymn to the Aten* from the west wall of the tomb of Ay.

THE SHORT HYMN TO THE ATEN

As already said, the hymn occurs in five Amarna tombs. The five copies fall into two groups. One consists of the text as given in the tombs of Any and Meryre; the other is the version of the other three tombs. Apart from minor textual variations, the principal difference between the two groups is that Any and Meryre are the worshipers who recite the hymn, whereas in the three other tombs the hymn is spoken by the king.

The hymn gives the impression of consisting of bits and pieces drawn from the scribal stock of formulations that reflected the royal teaching. Though not without beauty it lacks structural unity. The translation is made from the synoptic text with the version of Apy serving as base. The line count is that of Apy's text.

Publication: Davies, *Amarna*, IV, 26-29 and pls. xxxii-xxxiii.   Sandman, *Akhenaten*, pp. 10-15.

Translation: A. Scharff, *Aegyptische Sonnenlieder* (Berlin, 1922), pp. 67-69.

(1) Adoration of *Re-Harakhti-who-rejoices-in-lightland In-his-name-Shu-who-is-Aten*, who gives life forever, by the King who lives by Maat, the Lord of the Two Lands: *Neferkheprure, Sole-one-of-Re*; the Son of Re who lives by Maat, the Lord of crowns: *Akhenaten*, great in his lifetime, given life forever.[1]

> Splendid you rise, O living Aten, eternal lord!
> You are radiant, beauteous, mighty,
> Your love is great, immense.
> Your rays light up all faces,
> Your bright hue gives life to hearts,
> When you fill the Two Lands with your love.
> August God who fashioned himself,
> Who made every land, created what is in it,
> All peoples, herds, and flocks,
> All trees that grow from soil;
> They live when you dawn for them,
> You are mother and father of all that you made.
>
> When you dawn their eyes observe you,
> As your rays light the whole earth;
> Every heart acclaims your sight,
> When you are risen as their lord.
> When you set (5) in sky's western lightland,
> They lie down as if to die,
> Their heads covered, their noses stopped,
> Until you dawn in sky's eastern lightland.
> Their arms adore your *ka*,
> As you nourish the hearts by your beauty;
> One lives when you cast your rays,
> Every land is in festivity.
>
> Singers, musicians, shout with joy,
> In the court of the *benben*-shrine,[2]
> And in all temples in Akhet-Aten,
> The place of truth in which you rejoice.
> Foods are offered in their midst,
> Your holy son performs your praises,
> O Aten living in his risings,
> And all your creatures leap before you.
> Your august son exults in joy,
> O Aten living daily content in the sky,
> Your offspring, your august son, Sole one of Re;[3]
> The Son of Re does not cease to extol his beauty,[4]
> *Neferkheprure, Sole-one-of Re.*

I am your son who serves you, who exalts your name,
Your power, your strength, are firm in my heart;
You are the living Aten whose image endures,
You have made the far sky to shine in it,
To observe all that you made.
You are One (10) yet a million lives are in you,
To make them live ⟨you give⟩ the breath of life to their noses;
By the sight of your rays all flowers exist,
What lives and sprouts from the soil grows when you shine.
Drinking deep of your sight all flocks frisk,[5]
The birds in the nest fly up in joy;
Their folded wings unfold in praise
Of the living Aten, their maker.

NOTES

1. As originally composed, the hymn was recited by the king, hence this introduction. In the final portion of the hymn, the king speaks in the first person. In the tombs of Any and Meryre the hymn was adapted to the use of the courtiers, and the scribe of Meryre was consistent in that he omitted the final portion; but the scribe of Any retained it.

2. A sanctuary of Aten at El Amarna which seems to have been named after the sanctuary of Re at Heliopolis that bore this name.

3. The epithet which forms part of Akhenaten's throne name.

4. One expects "your beauty."

5. The version of Apy ends here. The remainder is the text of Tutu.

TWO HYMNS AND A PRAYER IN THE TOMB OF AY

The east wall of the unfinished tomb of Ay is inscribed with two hymns and a prayer, addressed to the Aten and to the king. The texts occupy the lower half of the wall and are accompanied by the kneeling figures of Ay and his wife. The upper half of the wall, now much destroyed, showed the royal family at worship.

The theme of both hymns is the close association of the Aten with King Akhenaten, as reiterated by the king on his monuments. The hymns are followed by a biographical statement and a prayer of Ay in which the courtier asks for the king's continuing favor which is to protect him in life as well as after death.

The prayer shows clearly the effect which the Aten cult had on the expectations and practices of the courtiers. They could no longer pray to Anubis for protection; nor could they look toward passing the judgment before Osiris and being welcomed by the gods. All that a courtier of Akhenaten could hope for was to be granted a tomb and that his *ka* would survive by virtue of his association with the king. It is no wonder that after the death of Akhenaten his followers hastily abandoned his teaching and returned to the comforting beliefs in the many gods who offered help to man in life and beyond death.

Publication: Davies, *Amarna*, VI, 17-19, 28-29, and pls. xxv and xxxviii-xxxix.   Sandman, *Akhenaten*, pp. 90-93.
Translation: B*AR*, II, §§991-996.

1. Hymn to the Aten and the King

East Wall, columns 1-5

(1) Adoration of *Re-Harakhti-who-rejoices-in-lightland In-his-name-Shu-who-is-Aten*, who gives life forever; (and of) the King of Upper and Lower Egypt: *Neferkheprure, Sole-one-of-Re*, the Son of Re: *Akhenaten*, great in his lifetime; (and) the great Queen, *Nefer-nefru-Aten Nefertiti*, living forever.

Praises to you when you dawn in lightland,
O living Aten, lord of eternity!
Kissing the ground when you dawn in heaven,
To light all lands with your beauty.
Your rays are on your son, your beloved,
Your hands hold millions of jubilees
For the King, *Neferkheprure, Sole-one-of-Re*,
Your child who came from your rays.
You grant him your lifetime, your years,
You hearken to the wish of his heart,
You love him, you make him like Aten.
You dawn to give him eternity,
When you set you give him infinity.
You create him daily like your forms,
You build him in your image (5) like Aten.
The Ruler of Maat who came from eternity,
The Son of Re who exalts his beauty,
Who offers him the product of his rays,
The King who lives by Maat,
The Lord of the Two Lands, *Neferkheprure, Sole-one-of-Re*,
(And) the great Queen, *Nefer-nefru-Aten Nefertiti*.

2. Hymn to the Aten and the King

East Wall, columns 6-10

(6) The God's Father,[1] the favorite of the Good God, the Vizier and Fanbearer to the right of the King, the Master of all the horses of his majesty, the true, beloved royal scribe, Ay. He says:

Hail to you, O living Aten!
Dawning in heaven he floods the hearts,
Every land is in feast at his rising;
Their hearts rejoice in acclamations,

When their lord, their maker,[2] shines upon them.
Your son offers Maat to your fair face,
You delight in seeing him who came from you;
The son of eternity who came from Aten,
Who benefits his benefactor,[3] pleases the heart of Aten.

When he dawns in heaven he rejoices in his son,
He enfolds him in his rays;
He gives him eternity as king like the (9) Aten:
Neferkheprure, Sole-one-of-Re, my God,
Who made me, who fosters my *ka*.
Grant me to be sated with seeing you always,
My Lord, built like Aten, abounding in wealth;
Hapy flowing daily who nourishes Egypt,
Silver and gold are like the sands of the shores.
The land wakes to hail the power of his *ka*,
O Son of Aten, you are eternal,
Neferkheprure, Sole-one-of-Re,
You live and thrive for he made you.

3. Self-Justification and Prayer to the King
Columns 11-30

(11) the God's Father, the Vizier and Fanbearer on the right of the King, the Master of all the horses of his majesty, the true, beloved Royal Scribe, Ay. He says:

I am one truthful to the King who fostered him,
One who is straight to the Ruler and helps his Lord:
A *ka*-attendant of his majesty, his favorite,
Who sees his beauty when he appears in his palace.
I am leader of the nobles, the royal companions,
Chief of all those who follow his majesty;
He set Maat in my body, I abhor falsehood,
I know what pleases the Sole one of Re, my Lord,
Who is knowing like Aten, truly wise.
He heaps my rewards of silver and gold,
I being chief of the nobles, leader of the people;
My nature, my good character made my position,
My Lord has taught me, I do his teaching.
I live by worshiping his *ka*,
I am sated by attending him;
My breath, by which I live, is this northwind,
This thousandfold Hapy who flows every day,
Neferkheprure, Sole-one-of-Re.

(15) Grant me a lifetime high in your favor!
How happy is your favorite, O Son of the Aten!
All his deeds will endure and be firm,
When the *ka* of the Ruler is with him forever,
He will be sated with life when he reaches old age.
My Lord who makes people and fosters a lifetime,
Give a happy fate to him whom you favor,
Whose heart rests on Maat, who abhors falsehood.
How happy is he who hears your teaching of life!
He is sated by seeing you constantly,
His eyes beholding the Aten each day.
Grant me a good old age as you favor me,
Grant me a good burial by the wish of your *ka*
In the tomb you assigned me to rest in,
In the mountain of Akhet-Aten, the blessed place.
May I hear your sweet voice in the *benben*-temple,
As you do what your father praises, the living Aten;
He will assign you to everlastingness,
He will reward you with jubilee feasts.

Like a counting of shore-⟨sands⟩ by the *oipe*,
Like reckoning the sea by the *dja*,[4]
The sum total of mountains weighed in the balance,
The feathers of birds, (20) the leaves of trees—
Such are the jubilees of the Sole one of Re, king forever,
And of the great Queen, his beloved, rich in beauty,
Who contents the Aten with a sweet voice,
With her beautiful hands on the sistra,
The Lady of the Two Lands, *Nefer-nefru-Aten Nefertiti*,
    everliving
Who is at the side of the Sole one of Re for all time.

As heaven will endure (25) with what it contains,
Your father, the Aten, will dawn in the sky,
To protect you every day for he made you.
Grant me to kiss the holy ground,
To come before you with offerings
To Aten, your father, as gifts of your *ka*.
Grant that my *ka* abide and flourish for me,
As when on earth I followed your *ka*,
So as to rise in my name to the blessed place,
In which you grant me to rest, my word being true.
May my name be pronounced in it by your will,
I being your favorite who follows your *ka*,

That I may go with your favor when old age has come:
For the *ka* of the Vizier, Fanbearer on the right of the King,
True, beloved Royal Scribe, God's Father, Ay, living anew.

NOTES

1. The title "god's father" was often borne by priests but sometimes by courtiers who did not have priestly functions. Its meaning has been discussed a number of times, notably by A. H. Gardiner, *AEO*, I, 47*-52*; C. Aldred, *JEA*, 43 (1957), 35-37; H. Brunner, *ZÄS*, 86 (1961), 90-100; H. Kees, *ZÄS*, 86 (1961), 115-125.

2. The scribe wrote "his maker."

3. The king is *3ḫ n 3ḫ n.f*, "one who benefits his benefactor," an allusion to the name *Akhenaten* ("He who benefits Aten") which he had assumed when he discarded the name *Amenhotep*.

4. The *oipe* and the *dja* are measures of capacity.

THE GREAT HYMN TO THE ATEN

In the Tomb of Ay

West Wall, 13 columns

The long text columns begin at the top of the wall. Below the text are the kneeling relief figures of Ay and his wife.

Publication: Davies, *Amarna*, VI, 29-31 and pls. xxvii and xli. Sandman, *Akhenaten*, pp. 93-96.

Translation: J. A. Wilson in *ANET*, pp. 369-371.   Gardiner, *Egypt*, pp. 225-227.   Simpson, *Literature*, pp. 289-295. (There exist countless translations of the hymn)

(1) Adoration of *Re-Harakhti-who-rejoices-in-lightland In-his-name-Shu-who-is-Aten*, living forever; the great living Aten who is in jubilee, the lord of all that the Disk encircles, lord of sky, lord of earth, lord of the house-of-Aten in Akhet-Aten; (and of) the King of Upper and Lower Egypt, who lives by Maat, the Lord of the Two Lands, *Neferkheprure, Sole-one-of-Re*; the Son of Re who lives by Maat, the Lord of Crowns, *Akhenaten*, great in his lifetime; (and) his beloved great Queen, the Lady of the Two Lands, *Nefer-nefru-Aten Nefertiti*, who lives in health and youth forever. The Vizier, the Fanbearer on the right of the King, ----- [Ay]; he says:[1]

Splendid you rise in heaven's lightland,
O living Aten, creator of life!
When you have dawned in eastern lightland,
You fill every land with your beauty.
You are beauteous, great, radiant,
High over every land;
Your rays embrace the lands,

To the limit of all that you made.
Being Re, you reach their limits,[2]
You bend them ⟨for⟩ the son whom you love;
Though you are far, your rays are on earth,
Though one sees you, your strides are unseen.

When you set in western lightland,
Earth is in darkness as if in death;
One sleeps in chambers, heads covered,
One eye does not see another.
Were they robbed of their goods,
That are under their heads,
People would not remark it.
Every lion comes from its den,
All the serpents bite;[3]
Darkness hovers, earth is silent,
As their maker rests in lightland.

Earth brightens when you dawn in lightland,
When you shine as Aten of daytime;
As you dispel the dark,
As you cast your rays,
The Two Lands are in festivity.
Awake they stand on their feet,
You have roused them;
Bodies cleansed, (5) clothed,
Their arms adore your appearance.
The entire land sets out to work,
All beasts browse on their herbs;
Trees, herbs are sprouting,
Birds fly from their nests,
Their wings greeting your *ka*.
All flocks frisk on their feet,
All that fly up and alight,
They live when you dawn for them.
Ships fare north, fare south as well,
Roads lie open when you rise;
The fish in the river dart before you,
Your rays are in the midst of the sea.

Who makes seed grow in women,
Who creates people from sperm;
Who feeds the son in his mother's womb,
Who soothes him to still his tears.

Nurse in the womb,
Giver of breath,
To nourish all that he made.
When he comes from the womb to breathe,
On the day of his birth,
You open wide his mouth,
You supply his needs.
When the chick in the egg speaks in the shell,
You give him breath within to sustain him;
When you have made him complete,
To break out from the egg,
He comes out from the egg,
To announce his completion,
Walking on his legs he comes from it.

How many are your deeds,
Though hidden from sight,
O Sole God beside whom there is none!
You made the earth as you wished, you alone,
All peoples, herds, and flocks;
All upon earth that walk on legs,
All on high that fly on wings,
The lands of Khor and Kush,
The land of Egypt.
You set every man in his place,
You supply their needs;
Everyone has his food,
His lifetime is counted.
Their tongues differ in speech,
Their characters likewise;
Their skins are distinct,
For you distinguished the peoples.[4]

You made Hapy in *dat*,[5]
You bring him when you will,
To nourish the people,
For you made them for yourself.
Lord of all who toils for them,
Lord of all lands who shines for them,
Aten of daytime, great in glory!
All distant lands, you make them live,
You made a heavenly Hapy descend for them;

(10) He makes waves on the mountains like the sea,
To drench their fields and their towns.
How excellent are your ways, O Lord of eternity!
A Hapy from heaven for foreign peoples,
And all lands' creatures that walk on legs,
For Egypt the Hapy who comes from *dat.*[6]

Your rays nurse all fields,
When you shine they live, they grow for you;
You made the seasons to foster all that you made,
Winter to cool them, heat that they taste you.
You made the far sky to shine therein,
To behold all that you made;
You alone, shining in your form of living Aten,
Risen, radiant, distant, near.
You made millions of forms from yourself alone,
Towns, villages, fields, the river's course;
All eyes observe you upon them,
For you are the Aten of daytime on high.
. . . .――― . . .[7]

You are in my heart,
There is no other who knows you,
Only your son, *Neferkheprure, Sole-one-of-Re,*
Whom you have taught your ways and your might.
⟨Those on⟩ earth come from your hand as you made them,
When you have dawned they live,
When you set they die;
You yourself are lifetime, one lives by you.
All eyes are on ⟨your⟩ beauty until you set,
All labor ceases when you rest in the west;
When you rise you stir [everyone] for the King,
Every leg is on the move since you founded the earth.
You rouse them for your son who came from your body,
The King who lives by Maat, the Lord of the Two Lands,
Neferkheprure, Sole-one-of-Re,
The Son of Re who lives by Maat, the Lord of crowns,
Akhenaten, great in his lifetime;
(And) the great Queen whom he loves, the Lady of the Two
    Lands,
Nefer-nefru-Aten Nefertiti, living forever.

NOTES

1. Though the hymn was undoubtedly composed for recitation by the king, inscribed in the tomb of Ay, it was adapted to recitation by the courtier.

2. The sentence consists of a wordplay on r', "Sun," and r', "end," "limit."

3. This is one of several passages that recall similar formulations in the 104th Psalm and have led to speculations about possible interconnections between the Hymn to the Aten and the 104th Psalm. The resemblances are, however, more likely to be the result of the generic similarity between Egyptian hymns and biblical psalms. A specific literary interdependence is not probable.

4. The Hymn to the Aten expresses the cosmopolitan and humanist outlook of the New Kingdom at its purest and most sympathetic. All peoples are seen as the creatures of the sun-god, who has made them diverse in skin color, speech, and character. Their diversity is described objectively, without a claim of Egyptian superiority. On the theme of the differentiation of languages see S. Sauneron, *BIFAO*, 60 (1960), 31-41.

5. The netherworld.

6. Hapy, the inundating Nile, emerges from the netherworld to nourish Egypt, while foreign peoples are sustained by a "Nile from heaven" who descends as rain.

7. Several obscure sentences containing corruptions and a lacuna.

A PRAYER AND A HYMN OF GENERAL HAREMHAB

On his Statue in the Metropolitan Museum of Art, New York

The beautiful life-size granite statue of Haremhab shows him seated in the scribal posture with a papyrus scroll on his lap. The statue dates from the reign of Tutankhamun, when Haremhab commanded the army and was stationed in the Memphite area; it may have stood in the precinct of the temple of Ptah in Memphis. The two-part prayer is inscribed on the base, and the hymn is carved on the scroll which Haremhab holds unrolled in his lap.

The prayer is addressed to Thoth, Ptah, and Osiris, and the hymn is in praise of Thoth. The texts illustrate the quick reappearance of the traditional beliefs that had been suppressed by Akhenaten. The hymn to Thoth brings out the specific roles of the god: he is chief judge, counselor, mediator, and record keeper for gods and men. He is also the close companion of the sun-god, and this role includes steering the sun-bark and slaying the Apopis serpent, though the latter function is often assigned to other gods.

Publication: H. E. Winlock, *JEA*, 10 (1924), 1-5 and pls. i-iv. *Urk. IV*, 2089-2094.

Translation: Helck, *Übersetzung*, pp. 393-395.

The Prayer

Left side of base

A royal offering to Thoth, lord of writing, lord of Khmun,
Who determines *maat*, who embarks Re in the night-bark,
May you let the speech be answered for its rightness.
I am a righteous one toward the courtiers,[1]
   If a wrong is told me,
   (My) tongue is skilled to set it right.
I am the recorder of royal laws,
   Who gives directions to the courtiers,
   Wise in speech, there's nothing I ignore.
I am the adviser of everyone,
   Who teaches each man his course,
   Without forgetting my charge.
I am one who reports to the Lord of the Two Lands,
   Who speaks of whatever was forgotten,[2]
   Who does not ignore the words of the Lord.
I am the herald of the council,
   Who does not ignore the plans of his majesty;
   For the *ka* of the Prince, Royal Scribe, Haremhab, justified.

Right side of base

A royal offering to Ptah South-of-his-Wall,
Sakhmet, the beloved of Ptah,
Ptah-Sokar, lord of Shetit,[3]
Osiris, lord of Rostau:[4]
May you let the *ba* come forth by day to see Aten,[5]
And listen to his daily prayer as a spirit whom you made spirit.
May you command me to follow you always as one of your
   favorites,
For I am a just one of God since being on earth,
I satisfy him with *maat* every day.
I have shunned wrongdoing before him,
I never [did evil] since my birth;
Indeed I am a gentle one before God,
One wise, one calm, who listens to *maat*.
May you let me be in the crew of the *neshmet*-bark,[6]
At its feast in the region of Peqer;
For the *ka* of the Prince, Sole Companion,
King's Deputy before the Two Lands,
Royal Scribe, Haremhab, justified.

The Hymn to Thoth

On the scroll, in 22 columns

(1) Adoration of Thoth, Son of Re, Moon,
Of beautiful rising, lord of appearings, light of the gods,
By the Prince, Count, Fan-bearer on the King's right,
Great Troop-commander, Royal Scribe, Haremhab, justified,
    he says:
Hail to you, Moon, Thoth,
Bull in Khmun, dweller in Hesret,
Who makes way for the gods![7]
Who knows the secrets,
Who records their expression,
Who distinguishes one speech from another,
Who is judge of everyone.
Keen-faced in the Ship-of-millions,[8]
Courier of mankind,
Who knows a man by (5) his utterance,
Who makes the deed rise against the doer.
Who contents Re,
Advises the Sole Lord,
Lets[9] him know whatever happens;
At dawn he summons in heaven,
And forgets not yesterday's report.

Who makes safe the night-bark,
Makes tranquil the day-bark,
With arms outstretched in the bow of the ship.
Pure-faced when he takes the stern-rope,
As the day-bark rejoices in the night-bark's joy,[10]
At the feast of crossing the sky.
Who fells the fiend,[11]
Sunders western lightland.
The Ennead in the night-bark worships Thoth,
They say (10) to him: "Hail, [Son of] Re,
Praised of Re, whom the gods applaud!"
They repeat what your *ka* wishes,
As you make way for the place of the bark,
As you act against that fiend:
You cut off his head, you break his *ba*,
You cast (15) his corpse in the fire,
You are the god who slaughters him.
Nothing is done without your knowing,
Great one, son of a Great one, who came from her limbs,
Champion of Harakhti,

Wise friend in On,
Who makes the place of the gods,
Who knows the secrets,
Expounds their words.

Let us give praise[12] to Thoth,
Straight plummet in the scales,
Who repulses evil,
Who accepts him who leans not on crime.
The vizier who settles cases,
Who changes turmoil to peace;
The scribe of the mat who keeps the book,
Who punishes crime,
Who accepts the ⌜submissive.⌝
Who is sound of (20) arm,
Wise among the Ennead,
Who relates what was forgotten.
Counselor to him who errs,
Who remembers the fleeting moment,
Who reports the hour of night,
Whose words endure forever,
Who enters *dat*, knows those in it,
And records them in the list.

NOTES

1. The text on the left side of the base consists of tristichs. After the introduction, each tristich is composed of a tripartite period introduced by the phrase "I am." The same device is employed in the biographical stela of Intef son of Sent (British Museum 581; see my *Ancient Egyptian Literature*, I, 120-123.)

2. Or: "Who speaks to him who is forgetful"?

3. Name of the sanctuary of Ptah at Giza.

4. Word for the necropolis and often specifically that of Giza.

5. Though written without the divine determinative, the sun-disk, *itn*, has probably retained its personified meaning. In the sun-hymn of Haremhab on his stela in the British Museum (No. 551), which also dates from the reign of Tutankhamun, the word *itn* has the divine determinative (see *Urk. IV*, 2095.7)

6. The bark of Osiris.

7. Literally, "opens a place for the gods."

8. The sun-bark.

9. The scribe reverted to the second person and wrote "you let him know."

10. The sentence division is problematical. My rendering differs from that of Winlock and Helck.

11. The serpent Apopis.

12. The form "let us" in the invitation to praise god, so common in biblical psalms, is rare in Egyptian hymns, where the usual forms are "I will" or "ye shall."

THREE PENITENTIAL HYMNS FROM DEIR EL-MEDINA

With Thebes the capital of the state since the beginning of the Eighteenth Dynasty, the ever growing number of royal and private tombs on the city's westbank required the continuous labors of numerous workmen, artisans, scribes, and others. Thus a workmen's village was laid out in a narrow valley on the fringe of the western desert, in the area now known as Deir el-Medina. Unusually well preserved and systematically excavated, the village has yielded an immensely rich documentation on the life and thoughts of this New Kingdom community of average people who ranged from poor to moderately wealthy, from simple laborers to skilled artists.

At the beginning of the nineteenth century the site was plundered on a large scale, and many of the stelae then removed reached the museums of Europe. While the plundering blotted out their exact provenience, it gradually became clear that many of the stelae came not from tombs but rather from several small temples in which the villagers had offered their devotions.

Among these many votive stelae a number stand out by virtue of their unusual texts. They consist of hymns and prayers whose themes are crime and punishment, contrition and forgiveness. It is often said that Egyptian biographical and religious texts show much pride and little humility. On the votive stelae of Deir el-Medina, however, contrition and humility are the central concerns. To the scholars who first studied these hymns they seemed to offer so great a contrast to the usual complacency of Egyptian religiosity that they saw in them either the emergence of a new type of religious feeling in the Ramesside period ("personal piety," Breasted), or the particular religious attitude of poor people ("the religion of the poor," Gunn). Both terms describe valid insights, but they require some modification; for at the present time we see these hymns not as something quite new but rather as the end product of a long evolution.

What comes to fruition in the New Kingdon is the self-awareness of the individual person, an awareness that makes itself felt on many levels. The proliferation of Book of the Dead copies is as much a part of it as are the personal prayers from Deir el-Medina. Moreover, many personal prayers are found among the short compositions written on papyrus which were used as model texts in the training of scribes. Yet another aspect of conscious individualism is found in the love poems preserved on papyri of the Ramesside age. Thus the personal piety of the prayers from Deir el-Medina stems from the evolved individualism of the New Kingdom. And as regards their humility, this too is not an isolated phenomenon. The virtue of humility was already taught in the Instructions of the Old Kingdom and it plays a prominent part in the New Kingdom Instructions of Any and Amenemope.

The prayers on the votive stelae of Deir el-Medina are penitential hymns akin to biblical penitential psalms. Hymn and prayer are here merged into one: the deity is praised and adored in the traditional manner of the hymn and also prayed to in specific and personal terms. The votaries of Deir el-Medina give thanks for the recovery from illness, and they view their illness as divine punishment for sins they have committed.

The contrite admission of guilt has induced the god to show mercy and grant the return of health.

The three most important hymns of this group are translated here. Additional examples will be found in the literature cited.

I. VOTIVE STELA OF NEBRE WITH HYMN TO AMEN-RE

From Deir el-Medina

Berlin Museum 20377

A round-topped limestone stela, 0.67 × 0.39 m. At the top the god Amun is enthroned before a tall pylon. Before him kneels Nebre with arms raised in prayer. Below the scene is the hymn in sixteen text columns. In the lower right corner four men are kneeling in prayer.

Publication: Erman, *Denksteine*, pp. 1087-1097 and pl. xvi. *Aegyptische Inschriften aus den staatlichen Museen zu Berlin*, Vol. II (Leipzig, 1924), pp. 158-162.

Translation: J. H. Breasted, *Development of Religion and Thought in Ancient Egypt* (New York, 1912), pp. 350-352 (in chap. 10, "The Age of Personal Piety"). B. Gunn, "The Religion of the Poor in Ancient Egypt," *JEA*, 3 (1916), 83-85. J. A. Wilson in *ANET*, pp. 380-381.

Text above and behind the god

Amen-Re, Lord of Thrones-of-the-Two-Lands,
The great god who presides over Ipet-sut,
The august god who hears prayer,
Who comes at the voice of the poor in distress,
Who gives breath to him who is wretched.

Above Nebre

Giving praise to Amen-Re,
Lord of Thrones-of-the-Two-Lands,
Who presides over Ipet-sut;
Kissing the ground to Amun of Thebes, the great god,
The lord of this sanctuary, great and fair,
That he may let my eyes see his beauty;
For the *ka* of the draftsman of Amun, Nebre, justified.

The hymn

(1) Praisegiving to Amun.
I make for him adorations to his name,
I give him praises to the height of heaven,
And over the breadth of the earth,
I tell his might to travelers north and south:

Beware ye of him!
Declare him to son and daughter,
   To the great and small,
Herald him to generations,
   Not yet born;
Herald him to fishes in the deep,
   To birds in the sky,
Declare him to fool and wise,
Beware ye of him![1]

You are Amun, the Lord of the silent,
Who comes at the voice of the poor;
When I call to you in my distress,
You (5) come to rescue me,
To give breath to him who is wretched,
To rescue me from bondage.

You are Amen-Re, Lord of Thebes,
Who rescues him who is in *dat*;
For you are he who is [merciful],
When one appeals to you,
You are he who comes from afar.

Made by the draftsman of Amun in the Place-of-Truth,[2] Nebre,
justified, son of the draftsman in the Place-of-Truth, Pay, [justified],
to the name of his Lord Amun, Lord of Thebes, who comes at the
voice of the poor.

I made[3] for him praises to his name,
For his might is great;
I made supplications before him,
In the presence of the whole land,
On behalf of the draftsman Nakhtamun, justified,
Who lay sick unto death,
⟨In⟩ the power of Amun, through his ⌐sin⌐.[4]
I found the Lord of Gods coming as northwind,
Gentle breezes before him;
He saved Amun's draftsman Nakhtamun, justified,
Son of Amun's draftsman in the Place-of-Truth, Nebre,
   justified,
(10) Born of the Lady Peshed, justified.

He says:
Though the servant was disposed to do evil,

The Lord is disposed to forgive.
The Lord of Thebes spends not a whole day in anger,
His wrath passes in a moment, none remains.
His breath comes back to us in mercy,
Amun returns upon his breeze.
May your *ka* be kind,[5] may you forgive,
It shall not happen again.
Says the draftsman in the Place-of-Truth, Nebre, justified.

He says:
"I will make this stela to your name,
And record this praise on it in writing,
For you saved for me the draftsman Nakhtamun,"
(15) So I said to you and you listened to me.
Now behold, I do what I have said,
You are the Lord to him who calls to you,
Content with *maat*, O Lord of Thebes!
Made by the draftsman Nebre and his son, the scribe Khay.

NOTES

1. These nine lines form a stanza composed by means of an inversion or, ascending and descending pattern: the verbs, *beware, declare, herald,* are repeated in inverse order. The form was studied by H. Grapow, *ZÄS*, 79 (1954), 19-21; see also my *Ancient Egyptian Literature*, I, 202-203.

2. A name for the Theban necropolis.

3. The writing is faulty; the sense requires "I made."

4. Erman read the damaged group as *ist* and emended it to *isft*, "sin," "crime." The determinative, however, looks more like a cow than a bird; hence the word has been read as *iḥt*, "cow." But it is not very plausible that the word "cow" was intended.

5. *W3ḥ k3.k* is probably not the oath formula but rather the verb *w3ḥ* in the sense of "be kind," "overlook," "forgive," as in line 4 of Neferabu's Hymn to Ptah; see p. 110 n. 3.

II. VOTIVE STELA OF NEFERABU WITH HYMN TO MERTSEGER

From Deir el-Medina

Turin Museum 102 (= 50058)

The draftsman Neferabu was an artist of some prominence and wealth. He raised a large family and built himself a fine tomb. In addition to the votive stela in Turin, three other stelae of his and an offering table are in the British Museum. One of these (no. 589) also has a penitential hymn, this one addressed to Ptah. Both hymns are translated below.

The Turin stela is a rectangular limestone slab, 0.20 × 0.54 m. It is dedicated to the serpent-goddess Mertseger, a guardian goddess of the Theban necropolis who was viewed as dwelling in, or being identical with, a mountain peak of the western desert. Hence she was also worshiped under the name of "Peak of the West."

The goddess is depicted on the right side of the stela as a serpent with one human head and two serpent heads. Before her is an offering stand, and above her is the legend: "Mertseger, Lady of heaven, Mistress of the Two Lands, whose good name is Peak of the West." To the left of the goddess and filling the entire surface is the hymn in seventeen columns.

Publication: Erman, *Denksteine*, pp. 1098-1100.   M. Tosi and A. Roccati, *Stele e altre epigrafi di Deir El Medina, n. 50001-n. 50262* (Turin, 1972), pp. 94-96 and 286.

Translation: B. Gunn, *JEA*, 3 (1916), 86-87.   J. A. Wilson in *ANET*, p. 381.

(1) Giving praise to the Peak of the West,
Kissing the ground to her *ka*.
I give praise, hear (my) call,
I was a truthful man on earth!
Made by the servant in the Place-of-Truth, Neferabu, justified.

⟨I was⟩ an ignorant man and foolish,
Who knew not good from evil;[1]
I did the transgression[2] against the Peak,
And she taught a lesson to me.
I was in her hand (5) by night as by day,
I sat on bricks like the woman in labor,
I called to the wind, it came not to me,
I libated[3] to the Peak of the West, great of strength,
And to every god and goddess.

Behold, I will say to the great and small,
Who are in the troop:
Beware of the Peak!
For there is a lion within her!
The (10) Peak strikes with the stroke of a savage lion,
She is after him who offends her!

I called upon my Mistress,
I found her coming to me as sweet breeze;
She was merciful to me,
Having made me see her hand.
She returned to me appeased,
She made my malady forgotten;
For the Peak of the West is appeased,
If one calls upon her.

So says Neferabu, justified.
He says:
Behold, let hear every ear,
That lives upon earth:
Beware the Peak of the West!

NOTES

1. *Nfr r bin* is written.
2. *P3 sp n h3i* is an unusual term for "transgression," "sin."
3. Despite the wrong determinative, *kb*, "to libate" seems intended.

III. VOTIVE STELA OF NEFERABU WITH HYMN TO PTAH

From Deir el-Medina

British Museum 589

A round-topped limestone stela, 0.39 × 0.28 m, inscribed on both sides. The obverse is divided into two registers. In the upper register Ptah is shown seated in a kiosk and facing an offering table. In front of his head is the legend: "Ptah, Lord of *maat*, King of the Two Lands, the fair-faced on his sacred seat." On the right side of the lower register is the kneeling figure of Neferabu. The left side is filled with the first portion of the hymn, written in vertical columns. The text continues on the reverse in ten columns which occupy the entire surface.

In this hymn to Ptah, the draftsman Neferabu relates that he had sworn a false oath, and the god had punished him by making him blind.

Publication: Erman, *Denksteine*, pp. 1100-1102.   *Hieroglyphic Texts*, Part 9 (1970), p. 36 and pl. xxxi.

Translation: B. Gunn, *JEA*, 3 (1916), 88-89.

(1) Praisegiving to Ptah, Lord of Maat,
King of the Two Lands,
Fair of face on his great seat,
The One God[1] among the Ennead,
Beloved as King of the Two Lands.
May he give life, prosperity, health,
Alertness, favors, and affection,
And that my eyes may see Amun (5) every day,
As is done for a righteous man,
Who has set Amun in his heart!
So says the servant in the Place-of-Truth, Neferabu,
    justified.

(*Reverse*) Beginning of the recital of the might of Ptah, South-of-his-Wall, by the servant in the Place-of-Truth on the West of Thebes, Neferabu, justified. He says:

I am a man who swore falsely by Ptah, Lord of Maat,
And he made me see darkness by day.
I will declare his might to the fool and the wise,[2]
To the small and great:
Beware of Ptah, Lord of Maat!
Behold, he does not overlook[3] (5) anyone's deed!
Refrain from uttering Ptah's name falsely,
Lo, he who utters it falsely, lo he falls!

He caused me to be as the dogs of the street,
I being in his hand;
He made men and gods observe me,
I being as a man who has sinned against his Lord.
Righteous was Ptah, Lord of Maat, toward me,
When he taught a lesson to me!
Be merciful to me, look on me in mercy!

So says the servant in the Place-of-Truth on the West of Thebes,
Neferabu, justified before the great god.

NOTES

1. Calling Ptah the "one" god is designed to set him above the Ennead. In the post-Amarna period the epithet "one" was often applied to one or another of the great gods.

2. Literally, "to him who ignores him and him who knows him," as in the hymn of Nebre, line 3.

3. *W3ḥ* in the sense of "overlook," "forgive;" see p. 107 n. 5.

PRAYERS USED AS SCHOOL TEXTS

As already noted, the short prayers found in papyri of the Ramesside age express the individual piety which is characteristic of the New Kingdom. These prayers are less specific and personal than the penitential hymns from Deir el-Medina; and their more general character turned them into model compositions that were copied as exercises. Because they were used as school texts, the same prayer is often found in more than one copy.

Ramesside scribes often employed punctuation marks, consisting of black or red dots placed at intervals above the lines. They occur primarily in texts that have a metrical structure; hence scholars have termed them "verse-points." They do, however, also occur in some prose texts. Thus their purpose is somewhat ambiguous and the term "verse-points" is not entirely correct. Basically, they are indications of natural pauses between sentences and parts of sentences. Since such sentences and clauses also underly the metrical schemes, the presence of verse-points serves as corroborative evidence for the scanning of metrical lines.

Praise of Amen-Re

P. Bologna 1094.2, 3-7 and P. Anastasi II.6, 5-7

Publication: Gardiner, *LEM*, pp. 2 and 16.
Translation: Caminos, *LEM*, pp. 9-10 and 50.   Fecht, *Zeugnisse*, pp. 39-41.

Amen-Re who first was king,[1]
The god of earliest time,
The vizier of the poor.
He does not take bribes from the guilty,
He does not speak to the witness,
He does not look at him who promises,[2]
Amun judges the land with his fingers.
He speaks to the heart,
He judges the guilty,
He assigns him to the East,
The righteous to the West.[3]

NOTES

1. This portion of Papyrus Anastasi II is written with verse-points, and the sentence division indicated by the verse-points is followed here.
2. In the version of P. Anastasi II this sentence is lacking.
3. The judgment of the dead is meant.

Prayer to Amun

P. Anastasi II.8,5-9,1

Publication: Gardiner, *LEM*, p. 17.
Translation: Caminos, *LEM*, pp. 44-45.   J. A. Wilson in *ANET*, p. 380.   Fecht, *Zeugnisse*, pp. 44-45.   M. Lichtheim, *JARCE*, 9 (1971/72), 108-110.

Amun, lend your ear to the lonely in court,
He is poor, he is not rich;
For the court extorts from him:
"Silver and gold for the clerks,
Clothes for the attendants!"
Might Amun appear as the vizier,
To let the poor go free;
Might the poor appear as the justified,
And want surpass wealth![1]

NOTES

1. This portion of P. Anastasi II is written without verse-points. As usual in metrically structured texts, the sentences form loose groups by virtue of parallelism and related devices. Here the lines make a distich, a tristich, and a quatrain, hence a pattern of 2-3-4. As I pointed out in *JARCE*, 9, 110, the quatrain employs alternate parallelism, i.e., the first and third and the second and fourth lines are parallel.

Prayer to Amun

P. Anastasi II.9,2-10,1

Publication: Gardiner, *LEM*, pp. 17-18.
Translation: Caminos, *LEM*, pp. 58-59. Fecht, *Zeugnisse*, pp. 46-47.

Pilot who knows the water,[1]
Helmsman[2] of [ʳthe weakꜗ];[3]
Who gives bread to him who has none,
Who nourishes the servant of his house.
I take not a noble as protector,
I associate not with a man of wealth,
I place not my share in another's care,[4]
⟨My⟩ wealth is in the house of my [lord].
My lord is my protector,
I know his might, to wit:
A helper strong of arm,
None but he is strong.
Amun who knows compassion,
Who hearkens to him who calls him,
Amen-Re, the King of Gods,
The Bull great of strength, who loves strength.

NOTES

1. There are no verse-points. By their structure the sentences form four quatrains.
2. *Ḥmyt*, "rudder," is written, but *ḥmy*, "helmsman," is more plausible.
3. For the short lacuna ending with the letter *m*, a word such as "weak," "poor," "helpless," is indicated. Fecht suggested to restore it as *sḏm*, "the hearer."
4. Literally, "under the strong arm of a man." The sentence ends here; *wnw* belongs to the next sentence.

Prayer to Thoth

P. Anastasi V.9,2-10,2

Publication: Gardiner, *LEM*, p. 60.
Translation: Caminos, *LEM*, pp. 232-233.   Fecht, *Zeugnisse*, pp.
65-66.

Come to me, Thoth, O noble Ibis,
O god who loves Khmun;
O letter-writer of the Ennead,
Great one who dwells in Un![1]
Come to me and give me counsel,
Make me skillful in your calling;
Better is your calling than all callings,
It makes (men) great.
He who masters it is found fit to hold office,
I have seen many whom you have helped;[2]
They are (now) among the Thirty,[3]
They are strong and rich through your help.
You are he who offers counsel,[4]
Fate and Fortune are with you,
Come to me and give me counsel,
I am a servant of your house.
Let me tell of your valiant deeds,
Wheresoever I may be;
Then the multitudes will say:
"Great are they, the deeds of Thoth!"
Then they'll come and bring their children,
To assign them ⟨to⟩ your calling,
A calling that pleases the lord of strength,
Happy is he who performs it![5]

NOTES

1. *Ḥmnw* and *Wnw*, the two names of Hermopolis, make a rhyme.
2. Literally, "for whom you have acted."
3. The Council of Thirty, an often mentioned tribunal.
4. The sentence, "You are he who offers counsel to the orphan," which follows here, is undoubtedly a dittography, as was suggested by Gardiner.
5. There are no verse-points. The sentences form quatrains throughout.

Prayer to Thoth

P. Sallier I.8,2-7

Publication: Gardiner, *LEM*, pp. 85-86.
    Translation: Caminos, *LEM*, p. 321.   J. A. Wilson in *ANET*, p. 379.
Fecht, *Zeugnisse*, pp. 73-75.

The chief archivist of the Treasury of Pharaoh, Amenemone, speaks to the scribe Pentwere. This letter is brought to you to say:[1]

O Thoth, convey me to Khmun,
Your town where life is pleasing;
Supply my needs of bread and beer,
And guard my mouth ⟨in⟩ speaking!
If only I had Thoth behind me tomorrow,
"Come!" They would say;
I enter in before the lords,
I leave as one who is justified.[2]
You great dum-palm of sixty cubits,
On which there are nuts;
There are kernels in the nuts,
There is water in the kernels.
You who bring water ⟨from⟩ afar,
Come, rescue me, the silent;
O Thoth, you well that is sweet
To a man who thirsts in the desert!
It is sealed to him who finds words,
It is open to the silent;
Comes the silent, he finds the well,
⟨To⟩ the heated man you are [ʳhiddenʰ].[3]

NOTES

1. Texts used in the training of scribes were often cast in the form of letters even when the content did not warrant it.
2. The judgment of the dead seems to be meant. The various interpretations of the passage that have been offered are reviewed by Fecht, *op. cit.*, pp. 76-77.
3. There are no verse-points. By their structure and by their content, the sentences form quatrains.

A HARPER'S SONG FROM THE TOMB OF NEFERHOTEP

Theban Tomb No. 50

Reign of Haremhab

When they first appeared in the Middle Kingdom, the texts known as Harper's Songs were designed to praise death and the life after death. But in the famous *Harper's Song from the Tomb of King Intef*, preserved in a papyrus copy, the praises of the afterlife were replaced by anxious doubts about its reality, and by the advice to make merry while alive and to shun the thought of death. Such a skeptic-hedonistic message may have originated in songs sung at secular feasts; but when transmitted as a funerary text inscribed in a tomb and addressed to the tomb-owner, the message became incongruous and discordant. The incongruity did not pass unnoticed. In the tomb of the priest Neferhotep there are three Harper's Songs, each expressing a particular response. One song continued the skeptic-hedonistic theme but blended it with elements of traditional piety in an attempt to tone down and harmonize the contrary viewpoints. The second song is an outright rejection of skepticism and hedonism, coupled with a praise of the land of the dead. The third is a description of life after death in traditional ritualistic terms. Thus, the three songs in one and the same tomb reflect the Egyptian preoccupation with the nature of death and the varying and conflicting answers and attitudes which continued side by side.

The second and third songs, and the figures of the harpers who recite them, form part of a banquet scene on the left rear wall of the hall. The first song occurs in the context of an offering-table scene, in the passage leading from the hall to the inner shrine. The second song, the one that deliberately rejects the skeptic message, is translated below.

Publication: A. H. Gardiner, *PSBA*, 35 (1913), 165-170.

Translation: Erman, *Literature*, pp. 253-254.   M. Lichtheim, *JNES*, 4 (1945), 197-198.   J. A. Wilson in *ANET*, pp. 33-34.

Study of Harper's Songs: M. Lichtheim, *JNES*, 4 (1945), 178-212 and pls. i-vii.   *Idem, Ancient Egyptian Literature*, I, 193-197.

Says the singer-with-harp of the divine father of Amun, Neferhotep,[1] justified:

> All ye excellent nobles and gods of the graveyard,
> Hearken to the praise-giving for the divine father,
> The worship of the honored noble's excellent *ba*,
> Now that he is a god everliving, exalted in the West;
> May they[2] become a remembrance for posterity,
> For everyone who comes to pass by.

> I have heard those songs that are in the tombs of old,
> What they tell in extolling life on earth,
> In belittling the land of the dead.[3]
> Why is this done to the land of eternity,

The right and just that has no terrors?
Strife is abhorrent to it,
No one girds himself against his fellow;
This land that has no opponent,
All our kinsmen rest in it
Since the time of the first beginning.
Those to be born to millions of millions,
All of them will come to it;
No one may linger in the land of Egypt,
There is none who does not arrive in it.[4]
As to the time of deeds on earth,
It is the occurrence of a dream;[5]
One says: "Welcome safe and sound,"
To him who reaches the West.

NOTES

1. The name and priestly title of the tomb-owner. The harpist remains unnamed.

2. The praises.

3. In these lines the singer explicitly refers to harper's songs that express skepticism.

4. The thought expressed in this quatrain occurs in almost identical terms in hymns to Osiris, where it is the god, rather than the land of the dead, to whom all must come; see Louvre Stela C 218 (Pierret, *Recueil*, II, 134-138) and British Museum Stela 164 (*Hieroglyphic Texts*, 9, pp. 25-26 and pls. xxi-xxiA).

5. Note the appearance of the thought that life is a dream.

PART THREE

From the Book of the Dead

The Book of the Dead, or, "the coming forth by day," as the Egyptians called it, was a large compilation of spells designed to bring about the resurrection of the dead person and his safety in the afterlife. It is the direct successor of the Middle Kingdom Coffin Texts. Like the Pyramid Texts and the Coffin Texts, the Book of the Dead reflects ritual acts performed during and after the burial. Gathered into a collection and inscribed on papyrus scrolls, the spells acquired the form of a mass-produced book that could be purchased by anyone. The prospective owner merely had to have his name and titles inserted in a ready-made scroll, or he could have a copy made to order. The finished scroll was buried with its owner, either placed on the sarcophagus, or on the body itself, or in a special container.

At the beginning of the New Kingdom, the Book of the Dead was still in the process of formation. It achieved its final form in the Saite period (the Twenty-Sixth Dynasty), when all its spells were put into a fixed sequence of chapters. Modern scholarship has added numbers to the chapters; the total number of chapters presently known is 192. No individual scroll contains all the chapters. In their fixed sequence the chapters offer a certain degree of order but no precise plan or progression.

The texts are written in cursive hieroglyphs and are accompanied by illustrations, or vignettes, drawn in ink of various colors. Like those of the Pyramid Texts and Coffin Texts, the spells of the Book of Dead vary greatly in length. One of the longest, and the most famous, is Chapter 125, the Judgment of the Dead. The chapter's principal illustration is the scene that shows the weighing of the dead person's heart on the scales before an assembly of gods who are presided over by Osiris. The selection of Book of the Dead texts given here is designed to lead up to Chapter 125 through a small sampling of a few major themes in a number of short spells selected to serve as background against which to view the climactic judgment scene.

It is evident that the Book of the Dead is a book of magic. In all periods of ancient Egyptian culture magic was considered a legitimate tool; and in the confrontation with death the magical approach attained its most luxuriant growth. That is to say, magical means were not felt to be inimical to piety. If not inimical, the reliance on magical means was nevertheless distinct from the humble approach to the gods which informs the prayers.

No other nation of the ancient world made so determined an effort to vanquish death and win eternal life. Individual thinkers might increasingly lose faith in the promise of eternal life, and might adopt attitudes of resignation and even skepticism. But the majority appear to have clung to the hope of a bodily afterlife and to a reliance on magic as the means to achieve it. Eternal life had come to be conceived in the most grandiose terms: the dead were to become godlike and join the company of the gods. Yet when combined with the ethical concept of a judgment in the hereafter, the magical approach could not but be contrary to morality and piety. It is thus no accident that the positive virtues taught in the *Instructions* and affirmed in the *Autobiographies* are almost all given the form of negative statements in Chapter 125: the dead delivers a long recitation of sins not committed in order to pass the judgment of the gods. Magic and morality are here yoked together, but they remain incompatible.

The translations given here are made from the text versions used as basic texts in Naville's edition of the Book of the Dead. Other versions have not been utilized except to complete a few short lacunae of the main texts.

Publication: E. Naville, *Das ägyptische Totenbuch der XVIII. bis XX. Dynastie* (3 vols.; Berlin, 1886).

Translation: P. Barguet, *Le livre des morts des anciens Égyptiens* (Paris, 1967).   On Chapter 125 see also: C. Maystre, *Les déclarations d'innocence (Livre des Morts, chapitre 125)*. Institut Français d'Archéologie Orientale, Recherches d'archéologie, de philologie et d'histoire, v. 8 (Cairo, 1937).   J. A. Wilson in *ANET*, pp. 34-36.   For further bibliography of the Book of the Dead see P. Barguet, *op. cit.*

Chapter 23

The Opening of the Mouth

Formula for opening N's mouth[1] for him in the necropolis. He shall say:

My mouth is opened by Ptah,
My mouth's bonds are loosed by my city-god.
Thoth has come fully equipped with spells,
He looses the bonds of Seth from my mouth.
Atum has given me my hands,
They are placed as guardians.

My mouth is given to me,
My mouth is opened by Ptah
With that chisel of metal
With which he opened the mouth of the gods.
I am Sakhmet-Wadjet who dwells in the west of heaven,
I am Sahyt among the souls of On.

As for any spells, any spells spoken against me,
The gods shall rise up against them,
The entire Ennead, the entire Ennead!

NOTES

1. The name and title of the deceased are given. The opening of the mouth was an important ritual that was performed before statues and before mummies prior to their burial. It has been studied by E. Otto, *Das altägyptische Mundöffnungsritual*, Ägyptologische Abhandlungen, 3 (Wiesbaden, 1960).

Chapter 30B

The heart as witness

Formula for not letting the heart of N oppose him in the necropolis. He shall say:

O my heart of my mother,[1]
O my heart of my mother,
O my heart of my being!
Do not rise up against me as witness,
Do not oppose me in the tribunal,
Do not rebel against me before the guardian of the scales!

You are my *ka* within my body,
The Khnum who prospers my limbs.
Go to the good place prepared for us,
Do not make my name stink before them,
The magistrates who put people in their places!
If it's good for us it's good for the judge,
It pleases him who renders judgment.
Do not invent lies before the god,
Before the great god, the lord of the west,
Lo, your uprightness brings vindication!

NOTES

1. I.e., the person's very own heart which he had since birth.

Chapter 43

To retain one's head

Formula for not letting the head of N be cut off in the necropolis.

I am the Great one, son of the Great one,
The Fiery one, son of the Fiery one,
To whom his head was given after having been cut off.[1]
The head of Osiris shall not be taken from him,
My head shall not be taken from me!
I am risen, renewed, refreshed,
I am Osiris!

NOTES

1. The deceased identifies himself with Osiris who was resurrected despite having been slain and dismembered by Seth.

Chapter 59

To have air and water

Formula for breathing air and obtaining water in the necropolis for the Osiris N. He shall say:

O you Sycamore of Nut,
Give me the water and air in you![1]
I am he who holds that seat in the center of Un,[2]
I have guarded that egg of the Great Honker.[3]
As it is sound, I am sound,
As it lives, I live,
As it breathes air, I breathe air!

NOTES

1. The vignettes to this chapter and many reliefs in the private tombs show the goddess Nut emerging from the branches of a sycamore to pour water for the dead.
2. Hermopolis Magna, the home of Thoth and of the primordial Ogdoad with whom the process of creation began.
3. The creator-god viewed as a goose and variously identified with Geb, Amun, or Ptah.

Chapter 77

Transformation into a falcon

Formula for appearing as a falcon of gold.
I am a great falcon who is come from his egg,
I fly, I alight as a falcon of four cubits,[1]
My wings are of greenstone.
I have come from the cabin of the nightbark,
And my heart was brought me from the eastern mountain.
I alight in the daybark that came for me,
And the Oldest ones are brought to me bowed down.
They kiss the ground as I rise whole
As a falcon of gold, ⌜heron-headed⌝,
Whose words Re enters to hear every day.
I dwell among those ancient gods of heaven,
The Field of Offerings is laid before me.
I eat of it, I thrive on it,
I revel in it to my heart's content.
Nepri[2] gave me my throat,
I possess my head.

NOTES

1. Literally, "four cubits on his back," which means "across," i.e., a wing spread of four cubits.
2. The god of grain.

Chapter 105

An address to the ka

Formula to appease the *ka* to be said by N.
Hail to you, my *ka*, my helper!
Behold, I have come before you,
Risen, animated, mighty, healthy!
I have brought incense to you,
To purify you with it,
To purify your sweat with it.

Whatever evil speech I made,
Whatever evil deed I did,
Be it removed from me!
For mine is that green amulet,
Fastened to the neck of Re,
That makes the lightlanders green.
My *ka* greens like theirs,
My *ka*'s food is as theirs.

O Weigher on the scales,
May *maat* rise to the nose of Re that day!
Do not let my head be removed from me!
For mine is an eye that sees,
An ear that hears;
For I am not an ox for slaughter,
I shall not be an offering for those above!
Let me pass by you, I am pure,
Osiris has vanquished his foes!

Chapter 109

Knowing the Souls of the East

Formula for knowing the Souls of the East for N. He shall say:
I know this eastern gate of heaven,
Whose south is the pool of *khar*-geese,
Whose north is the pond of *ro*-geese,

The place whence Re sails with sail and oar.
I am chief announcer in the ship of the god,
A tireless rower in the bark of Re.
I know those two turquoise sycamores,
Between which Re comes forth,
That grow on the elevation of Shu,
At the gate of the lord whence Re comes forth.

I know the Field of Rushes:
Its wall is of metal;
Its barley is five cubits tall—
Ears two cubits, stalks three cubits.
Its emmer is six cubits tall—
Ears three cubits, stalks three cubits.[1]
Noble spirits, each nine cubits tall,
Reap it by the side of the Souls of the East.[2]
I know it is Harakhti and the *khurer*-calf,[3]
I praise Re every day.[4]

NOTES

1. The heights of the barley and emmer that grow in the celestial field are given differently in different versions of the chapter. In this version the scribe has garbled the figures.

2. Reaping the tall grain is counted among the pleasurable activities of the afterlife.

3. I.e., Harakhti and the *khurer*-calf are the gods called "Souls of the East." What is meant by the *khurer*-calf is not known.

4. The name and title of the deceased are repeated here and are followed by the reaffirmation of knowing the celestial field: "I know it, I know its name; Field of Rushes is its name."

Chapter 125

The Judgment of the Dead

The declaration of innocence

(1) To be said on reaching the Hall of the Two Truths[1] so as to purge N of any sins committed and to see the face of every god:

Hail to you, great God, Lord of the Two Truths!
I have come to you, my Lord,
I was brought to see your beauty.
I know you, I know the names of the forty-two gods,[2]
Who are with you in the Hall of the Two Truths,

Who live by warding off evildoers,
Who drink of their blood,
On that day (5) of judging characters before Wennofer.[3]
Lo, your name is "He-of-Two-Daughters,"
(And) "He-of-Maat's-Two-Eyes."
Lo, I come before you,
Bringing Maat to you,
Having repelled evil for you.

I have not done crimes against people,
I have not mistreated cattle,
I have not sinned in the Place of Truth.[4]
I have not known what should not be known,[5]
I have not done any harm.
I did not begin a day by exacting more than my due,
My name did not reach the bark of the mighty ruler.
I have not blasphemed (10) a god,
I have not robbed the poor.
I have not done what the god abhors,
I have not maligned a servant to his master.
I have not caused pain,
I have not caused tears.
I have not killed,
I have not ordered to kill,
I have not made anyone suffer.
I have not damaged the offerings in the temples,
I have not depleted the loaves of the gods,
I have not stolen (15) the cakes of the dead.
I have not copulated nor defiled myself.
I have not increased nor reduced the measure,
I have not diminished the arura,
I have not cheated in the fields.
I have not added to the weight of the balance,
I have not falsified the plummet of the scales.
I have not taken milk from the mouth of children,
I have not deprived cattle of their pasture.
I have not snared birds in the reeds of the gods,
I have not caught fish in their ponds.
I have not held back water in its season,
I have not dammed a flowing stream,
I have not quenched a needed (20) fire.
I have not neglected the days of meat offerings,
I have not detained cattle belonging to the god,
I have not stopped a god in his procession.

I am pure, I am pure, I am pure, I am pure!
I am pure as is pure that great heron in Hnes.
I am truly the nose of the Lord of Breath,
Who sustains all the people,
On the day of completing the Eye[6] in On,
In the second month of winter, last day,
In the presence of the lord of this land.
I have seen the completion of the Eye in On!
No evil shall befall me in this land,
In this Hall of the Two Truths;
For I know the names of the gods in it,
The followers of the great God!

The Declaration to the Forty-two Gods[7]

O Wide-of-stride who comes from On: I have not done evil.
O Flame-grasper who comes from Kheraha: I have not robbed.
O Long-nosed who comes from Khmun:[8] I have not coveted.
O Shadow-eater who comes from the cave: I have not stolen.
O Savage-faced who comes from Rostau: I have not killed people.
O Lion-Twins who come from heaven: I have not trimmed the measure.
O Flint-eyed who comes from Khem: I have not cheated.
O Fiery-one who comes backward: I have not stolen a god's property.
O Bone-smasher who comes from Hnes: I have not told lies.
O Flame-thrower who comes from Memphis: I have not seized food.
O Cave-dweller who comes from the west: I have not sulked.
O White-toothed who comes from Lakeland:[9] I have not trespassed.
O Blood-eater who comes from slaughterplace: I have not slain sacred cattle.
O Entrail-eater who comes from the tribunal: I have not extorted.
O Lord of Maat who comes from Maaty: I have not stolen bread rations.
O Wanderer who comes from Bubastis: I have not spied.
O Pale-one who comes from On: I have not prattled.
O Villain who comes from Anjdty: I have contended only for my goods.

O Fiend who comes from slaughterhouse: I have not committed adultery.

O Examiner who comes from Min's temple: I have not defiled myself.

O Chief of the nobles who comes from Imu: I have not caused fear.

O Wrecker who comes from Huy: I have not trespassed.

O Disturber who comes from the sanctuary: I have not been violent.

O Child who comes from the nome of On: I have not been deaf to Maat.

O Foreteller who comes from Wensi: I have not quarreled.

O Bastet who comes from the shrine: I have not winked.

O Backward-faced who comes from the pit: I have not copulated with a boy.

O Flame-footed who comes from the dusk: I have not been false.

O Dark-one who comes from darkness: I have not reviled.

O Peace-bringer who comes from Sais: I have not been aggressive.

O Many-faced who comes from Djefet: I have not had a hasty heart.

O Accuser who comes from Utjen: I have not attacked and reviled a god.

O Horned-one who comes from Siut: I have not made many words.

O Nefertem who comes from Memphis: I have not sinned, I have not done wrong.

O Timeless-one who comes from Djedu: I have not made trouble.

O Willful-one who comes from Tjebu: I have not ⌐waded⌐ in water.

O Flowing-one who comes from Nun: I have not raised my voice.

O Commander of people who comes from his shrine: I have not cursed a god.

O Benefactor who comes from Huy: I have not been boastful.

O Nehebkau who comes from the city: I have not been haughty.

O High-of-head who comes from the cave: I have not wanted more than I had.

O Captor who comes from the graveyard: I have not cursed god in my town.

The Address to the Gods

Hail to you, gods!
I know you, I know your names.
I shall not fall in fear of you,
You shall not acccuse me of crime to this god whom you
    follow!
(5) No misfortune shall befall me on your account!
You shall speak rightly about me before the All-Lord,
For I have acted rightly in Egypt.
I have not cursed a god,
I have not been faulted.
Hail to you, gods in the Hall of the Two Truths,
Who have no lies in their bodies,
Who live on *maat* in On,
Who feed on their rightness before Horus in his disk.
Rescue me from Babi, who feeds on the entrails of nobles,
On that day of the great reckoning.
Behold me, I have come to you,
Without sin, without guilt, without evil,
Without a witness against me,
Without one whom I have wronged.
I live (10) on *maat*, I feed on *maat*,
I have done what people speak of,
What the gods are pleased with,
I have contented a god with what he wishes.
I have given bread to the hungry,
Water to the thirsty,
Clothes to the naked,
A ferryboat to the boatless.
I have given divine offerings to the gods,
Invocation-offerings to the dead.
Rescue me, protect me,
Do not accuse me before the great god!

I am one pure of mouth, pure of hands,
One to whom "welcome" is said by those who see him;
For I have heard the words spoken by the Donkey and the
    Cat,
In the house of the Open-mouthed;
I was a witness before him when he cried out,
I saw the splitting of the *ished*-tree in (15) Rostau.
I am one who is acquainted with the gods,
One who knows what concerns them.
I have come here to bear witness to *maat*,

To set the balance in right position among the dead.
O you who are high upon your standard,
Lord of the *atef*-crown,
Who is given the name "Lord of Breath":[10]
Rescue me from your messengers,
Who inflict wounds,
Who mete out punishment,
Who have no compassion,
For I have done *maat* for the Lord of *maat*!
I am pure,
My front is pure,
My rear is pure,
My middle has been in the well of *maat*,
No limb of mine is unclean.
I have washed in the well of the South,
I have halted at the town of the North,
(20) In the meadow of the grasshoppers,
Where the crew of Re bathes by day and by night,
Where the gods enjoy passing by day and by night.

The First Interrogation

"Let him come," they say to me,
"Who are you?" they say to me,
"What is your name?" they say to me.
"I am the stalk of the papyrus,
He-who-is-in-the-moringa[11] is my name."
"Where have you passed by?" they say to me,
"I have passed by the town north of the moringa."
"What have you seen there?"
"The Leg and the Thigh."
"What did you say to them?"
"I have witnessed the acclaim in the land of the Fenkhu."
"What did they give you?"
A firebrand and a faience column."
"What did you do with them?"
"I buried them on the shore of the pool Maaty,
At the time of the evening meal."
"What (25) did you find there on the shore of the pool
   Maaty?"
"A scepter of flint whose name is 'Breath-giver'."
"What did you do to the firebrand and the faience column,
When you had buried them?"
"I lamented over them,
I took them up,

I extinguished the fire,
I broke the column,
Threw it in the pool."[12]
"Come then, enter the gate of this Hall of the Two Truths,
For you know us."

The Second Interrogation

"I shall not let you enter through me,"
Says the beam of this gate,
(30) "Unless you tell my name."
"'Plummet-of-the-Place-of-Truth' is your name."
"I shall not let you enter through me,"
Says the right leaf of this gate,
"Unless you tell my name."
"'Scale-pan-that-carries-maat' is your name."
"I shall not let you enter through me,"
Says the left leaf of this gate,
"Unless you tell my name."
"'Scale-pan-of-wine' is your name."
"I shall not let you pass over me,"
Says the threshold of this gate,
(35) "Unless you tell my name."
"'Ox-of-Geb' is your name."
"I shall not open for you,"
Says the bolt of this gate,
"Unless you tell my name."
"'Toe-of-his-mother' is your name."
"I shall not open for you,"
Says the bolt-clasp of this gate,
"Unless you tell my name."
"'Eye-of-Sobk-Lord-of-Bakhu' is your name."
"I shall not open for you,
I shall not let you enter by me,"
Says the keeper of this gate,
"Unless you tell my name."
"'Breast-of-Shu-given-him-to-guard-Osiris' is your name."
"We shall not let you pass over us,"
Say the cross-timbers,
"Unless you tell our name."
"'Offspring-of-Renenutet' is your name."
"You (40) know us, pass over us."

"You shall not tread upon me,"
Says the floor of this hall.

"Why not, since I am pure?"
"Because we do not know your feet,
With which you tread on us;
Tell them to me."
"'Who-enters-before-Min' is the name of my right foot,
"'Wnpt¹³-of-Nephthys' is the name of my left foot."
"Tread upon us, since you know us."
"I shall not announce you,"
Says the guard of the Hall,
"Unless you tell my name."
"'Knower-of-hearts Examiner-of-bellies' is your name."
"To which god present shall I announce you?"
"Tell it to the Interpreter of the Two Lands."
"Who is the Interpreter of the Two Lands?"
"It is Thoth."

"Come," says Thoth,
"Why have you come?"
"I have come here to report."
"What is your condition?"
"I am free of (45) all wrongdoing,
I avoided the strife of those in their day,
I am not one of them."
"To whom shall I announce you?"
"To him whose roof is of fire,
Whose walls are living cobras,
The floor of whose house is in the flood."
"Who is he?"
"He is Osiris."
"Proceed, you are announced,
The Eye is your bread,
The Eye is your beer,
The Eye is your offering on earth,"
So says he to me.

Instructions for use

(1) This is the way to act toward the Hall of the Two Truths. A man says this speech when he is pure, clean, dressed in fresh clothes, shod in white sandals, painted with eye-paint, anointed with the finest oil of myrrh. One shall offer to him beef, fowl, incense, bread, beer, and herbs. And you make this image in drawing on a clean surface in ⸢red paint⸣ mixed with soil on which pigs and goats have not trodden.

He for whom this scroll is recited will prosper, and his children will prosper. He will be the friend of the king and his courtiers. He will receive bread, beer, and a big chunk of meat from the altar of the great god. He will not be held back at any gate of the west. (10) He will be ushered in with the kings of Upper and Lower Egypt. He will be a follower of Osiris.

Effective a million times.

NOTES

1. *Maat* in dual form.
2. The dead person insists that he knows the names of the gods. Knowing their names meant having power over them.
3. A name of Osiris.
4. A term for temple and necropolis.
5. Literally, "I have not known what is not."
6. The Horus Eye.
7. Most of the forty-two gods are minor demons: only a few are major gods.
8. Thoth of Hermopolis in the shape of the long-nosed Ibis.
9. Sobk, the crocodile-god of the Fayyum.
10. Osiris is meant.
11. Epithet of Osiris.
12. Most of the questions and answers refer to the mysteries of Osiris.
13. An unknown word.

PART FOUR

Instructions

THE INSTRUCTION OF ANY

The Instruction of Any has long been known through a single manuscript: Papyrus Boulaq 4 of the Cairo Museum, which dates from the Twenty-First or Twenty-Second Dynasty. Of the first pages only small fragments have remained, and the copy as a whole abounds in textual corruptions due to incomprehension on the part of the copying scribe. The introductory sentence of the work is preserved on a tablet in the Berlin Museum (No. 8934), and small portions of the text are found in three papyrus fragments in the Musée Guimet, in Papyrus Chester Beatty V of the British Museum, and in four ostraca from Deir el-Medina.

Given the corruption and lacunae of the main text copy and the absence of sizable duplicate copies, the text has presented great difficulties to editors and translators. In the words of Sir Alan Gardiner: "The papyrus known as *P. Boulaq IV*, to the contents of which Chabas gave the name *Les Maximes du scribe Anii*, has long enjoyed the unenviable reputation of being the obscurest of all Egyptian wisdom texts" (*JEA*, 45 [1959], 12).

An incomplete papyrus of eight pages containing about a third of a duplicate copy of the Instruction of Any came to light in the French excavations at Deir el-Medina (see G. Posener, *RdE*, 6 [1949], 42). It has been edited for publication by G. Posener and is scheduled to appear as a volume of the Institut Français d'Archéologie Orientale du Caire. Professor Posener has very kindly allowed me to use a photocopy of his hieroglyphic transcription of the papyrus; and this has enabled me to better understand a number of passages. The precise extent of the help provided by the partial Deir el-Medina copy will be gauged after it has been published.

The work itself was composed in the New Kingdom, almost certainly in the Eighteenth Dynasty. It combines traditional themes with a certain amount of innovation. Two aspects, in particular, distinguish it from most earlier Instructions. One is the fact that the Instruction of Any comes from the sphere of the middle class and is meant for the average man. The author presents himself as a minor official, and the advice he dispenses, in the usual form of a father instructing his son, is suited to the thinking of anyone who possessed a modicum of education and of material comforts. Thus there is nothing specifically aristocratic about the values that are taught. This is of course in keeping with the evolution of Egyptian society and with the growth of the middle class.

The other novel feature appears in the epilogue. In earlier Instructions the epilogue had consisted either in the grateful acceptance of the teaching by the listeners, or in the teacher's conclusion urging compliance. The epilogue of Any, however, is a debate between father and son in which the son makes the objection that the father's teachings are too difficult to be understood and obeyed. By making the son disinclined to learn and obey, the author of the work introduced a new dimension into the concept of didactic literature: the thought that instruction might fail to have an impact. The thought is introduced in order to be refuted. The father has the last word as well as the more telling arguments. Yet the expression of a negative point of view adds a fresh and realistic note to the genre Instruction by showing an awareness that the efficacy of teaching could be questioned and that the teachability of man had its limitations.

Publication: A. Mariette, *Les papyrus égyptiens du musée de Boulaq* (Paris, 1871), pls. 15-28.   E. Suys, *La sagesse d'Ani: Texte traduction et commentaire*, Analecta Orientalia, 2 (Rome, 1935). Includes hieroglyphic transcription of the Berlin and Paris fragments.

Other fragments: A. H. Gardiner, *Hieratic Papyri*, I, 50, and II, 27: P. Chester Beatty V, verso 2,6-11 (= P. Boulaq 4, 3,1-3 and 6,1-4). Posener, *Ostr. hiér.*, nos. 1063, 1257, 1258, 1259.

Study and translation of excerpts: A. Volten, *Studien zum Weisheitsbuch des Anii*, Danske videnskabernes selskab, historisk-filologiske meddelelser, xxiii, 3 (Copenhagen, 1937-38).

Translation: Erman, *Literature*, pp. 234-242.   J. A. Wilson in *ANET*, pp. 420-421 (excerpts).

Translation of individual maxims: A. Volten, "Ägyptische Nemesis-Gedanken," *Miscellanea Gregoriana* (Rome, 1941), pp. 373-374: lines 8, 14-16.   A. H. Gardiner, *JEA*, 45 (1959), 12-15: lines 3,4-9.

Note: The page and line numbering used here is that of Suys's publication which was also employed by Volten. My translation begins with page 3,1 preceded by the title of the work found on the Berlin tablet.

Beginning of the educational instruction made by the Scribe Any of the Palace of Queen Nefertari.[1]

(3,1) Take a wife while you're young,
That she make a son for you;
She should bear for you while you're youthful,
It is proper to make people.[2]
Happy the man whose people are many,
He is saluted on account of his progeny.

Observe the feast of your god,[3]
And repeat its season,
God is angry if it is neglected.
Put up witnesses (5) when you offer,
The first time that you do it.
When one comes to seek your record,
Have them enter you in the roll;
When time comes to seek your purchase,[4]
It will extol the might of the god.
Song, dance, incense are his foods,
Receiving prostrations is his wealth;
The god does it to magnify his name,
But man it is who is inebriated.

Do not (10) enter the house of anyone,
Until he admits you and greets you;
Do not snoop around in his house,
Let your eye observe in silence.
Do not speak of him to another outside,

Who was not with you;
A great deadly crime

. . . . . .

Beware of a woman who is a stranger,
One not known in her town;
Don't stare at her when she goes by,
Do not know her carnally.
A deep water whose course is unknown,
Such is a woman away from her husband.
"I am pretty," she tells you daily,
When she has no witnesses;
She is ready to ensnare you,
A great deadly crime when it is heard.
. . . . . .[5]

Do not leave when the chiefs enter,
Lest your name stink;
In a quarrel (4,1) do not speak,
Your silence will serve you well.

Do not raise your voice in the house of god,
He abhors shouting;
Pray by yourself with a loving heart,
Whose every word is hidden.
He will grant your needs,
He will hear your words,
He will accept your offerings.
Libate for your father and mother,
Who are resting in the valley;
When the gods (5) witness your action,
They will say: "Accepted."
Do not forget the one outside,
Your son will act for you likewise.

Don't indulge in drinking beer,
Lest you utter evil speech[6]
And don't know what you're saying.
If you fall and hurt your body,
None holds out a hand to you;
Your companions in the drinking
Stand up saying: "Out with the drunk!"
If one comes to seek you (10) and talk with you,
One finds you lying on the ground,
As if you were a little child.

Do not go out of your house,
Without knowing your place of rest.
Let your chosen place be known,
Remember it and know it.
Set it before you as the path to take,
If you are straight you find it.
Furnish your station in the valley,
The grave that shall conceal your corpse;
Set it before you as your concern,
A thing that matters in your eyes.
Emulate the great departed,
Who are at rest within their tombs.
No blame accrues to him who does it,
It is well that you be ready too.
When your envoy[7] (5,1) comes to fetch you,
He shall find you ready to come
To your place of rest and saying:
"Here comes one prepared before you."
Do not say, "I am young to be taken,"
For you do not know your death.
When death comes he steals the infant
Who is in his mother's arms,
Just like him who reached old age.

Behold, I give you these useful counsels,
For you to ponder in your heart;
Do it (5) and you will be happy,
All evils will be far from you.
Guard against the crime of fraud,
Against words that are not ⟨true⟩ ;
Conquer malice in your self,
A quarrelsome man does not rest on the morrow.
Keep away from a hostile man,
Do not let him be your comrade;
Befriend one who is straight and true,
One whose actions you have seen.
If your rightness matches his,
The friendship will be balanced.
Let your hand preserve what is in your house,
Wealth accrues to him who guards it;
Let your hand not scatter it to (10) strangers,
Lest it turn to loss for you.
If wealth is placed where it bears interest,
It comes back to you redoubled;

Make a storehouse for your own wealth,
Your people will find it on your way.
What is given small returns augmented,
⌐What is replaced brings abundance.¬
The wise lives off the house of the fool,
Protect what is yours and you find it;
Keep your eye on what you own,
Lest you end as a beggar.
He who is slack amounts to nothing,
Honored is the man who's active.
. . . . . .⁸

(6,1) Learn about the way of a man
Who undertakes to found his household.
Make a garden, enclose a patch,
In addition to your plowland;
Set out trees within it,
As shelter about your house.
Fill your hand with all the flowers
That your eye can see;
One has need of all of them,
It is good fortune not to lose them.⁹

Do not rely on another's goods,
Guard what you acquire yourself;
Do not depend on another's wealth,
Lest he become master in your house.
Build a house or find and buy one,
Shun ⌐contention¬.
Don't say: "My mother's father has a house,
⌐'A house that lasts,'¬ one calls it;"
When you come to share with your brothers,
Your portion may be a storeroom.
If your god lets you have children,
They'll say: "We are in our father's house."
Be a man hungry or sated in his house,
It is his walls (10) that enclose him.
Do not be a mindless person,
Then your god will give you wealth.

Do not sit when another is standing,
One who is older than you,
Or greater than you in his rank.
No good character is reproached,
An evil character is blamed.

Walk the accustomed path each day,
Stand according to your rank.
"Who's there?" So one always says,
Rank creates its rules;
A woman is asked about (15) her husband,
A man is asked about his rank.

Do not speak rudely to a brawler,
When you are attacked hold yourself back;
You will find this good (7,1) when your relations are friendly,
When trouble has come it will help you bear up,
And the aggressor will desist.
Deeds that are effective toward a stranger
Are very noxious to a brother.[10]
Your people will hail you when you are joyful,
They will weep freely ⌜(when you are sad)⌝;
When you are happy the brave look to you,
When you are lonely you find your relations.

One will do all you say
If you are versed in writings;
Study the writings, put them in your heart,
(5) Then all your words will be effective.
Whatever office a scribe is given,
He should consult the writings;
The head of the treasury has no son,
The master of the seal has no heir.
The scribe is chosen for his hand,
His office has no children;
His pronouncements are his freemen,
His functions are his masters.

Do not reveal your heart to a stranger,
He might use your words against you;
The noxious speech that came from your mouth,
He repeats it and you make enemies.
A man may be ruined by his tongue,
Beware and you will do well.[11]
A man's belly is wider than a granary,
And full of all kinds of answers;
(10) Choose the good one and say it,
While the bad is shut in your belly.
A rude answer brings a beating,
Speak sweetly and you will be loved.
Don't ever talk back to your attacker,

ʿDo not set a trap ⟨for him⟩ʾ;
It is the god who judges the righteous,
His fate comes and takes him away.[12]

Offer to your god,
Beware of offending him.
Do not question his images,
Do not accost him when he appears.
Do not jostle him in order to carry him,
Do not disturb the oracles.[13]
Be careful, help to protect him,
Let your eye watch out (15) for his wrath,
And kiss the ground in his name.
He gives power in a million forms,
He who magnifies him is magnified.
God of this earth is the sun in the sky,
While his images are on earth;
When incense is given them as daily food,
The lord of risings is satisfied.

Double the food your mother gave you,
Support her as she supported you;
She had a heavy load in you,
But she did not abandon you.
When you were born after your months,
She was yet yoked ⟨to you⟩,
Her breast in your mouth for three years.
As you grew and your excrement disgusted,
She was not disgusted, saying: "What shall I do!"
When she sent you to school,
And you were taught to write,
She kept watching over you daily,
With bread (8,1) and beer in her house.
When as a youth you take a wife,
And you are settled in your house,
Pay attention to your offspring,
Bring him up as did your mother.
Do not give her cause to blame you,
Lest she raise her hands to god,
And he hears her cries.

Do not eat bread while another stands by
Without extending your hand to him.
As to food, it is here always,
It is man (5) who does not last;

One man is rich, another is poor,
But food remains for him ⌜who shares it.⌝
As to him who was rich last year,
He is a vagabond this year;
Don't be greedy to fill your belly,
You don't know your end at all.
Should you come to be in want,
Another may do good to you.
When last year's watercourse is gone,
Another river is here today;
Great lakes become dry places,
Sandbanks turn into depths.
Man does not have a single (10) way,
The lord of life confounds him.[14]

Attend to your position,
Be it low or high;
It is not good to press forward,
Step according to rank.
Do not intrude on a man in his house,
Enter when you have been called;
He may say "Welcome" with his mouth,
Yet deride you in his thoughts.
One gives food to one who is hated,
Supplies to one who enters uninvited.

Don't rush to attack your attacker,
Leave him to the god;
Report him daily to the god,
(15) Tomorrow being like today,
And you will see what the god does,
When he injures him who injured you.

Do not enter into a crowd,
If you find it in an uproar
And about to come to blows.
Don't pass anywhere near by,
Keep away from their tumult,
Lest you be brought before the court,
When an inquiry is made.
Stay away from hostile people,
Keep your heart quiet among fighters;
An outsider is not brought to court,
One who knows nothing is not bound in fetters.

(9,1) It is useful to help one whom one loves,
⌐So as to cleanse him of his faults;¬
⌐You will be safe from his errors.¬
. . . . . .
The first of the herd leads to the field,
. . . . . .[15]

Do not control your wife in her house,
When you know she is efficient;
Don't say to her: "Where is it? Get it!"
When she has put it in the right place.
Let your eye observe in silence,
Then you recognize her (5) skill;
It is joy when your hand is with her,
There are many who don't know this.
If a man desists from strife at home,
He will not encounter its beginning.
Every man who founds a household
Should hold back the hasty heart.
Do not go after a woman,
Let her not steal your heart.[16]

Do not talk back to an angry superior,
Let him have his way;
Speak sweetly when he speaks sourly,
It's the remedy that calms the heart.
Fighting answers carry sticks,
And your strength collapses;
. . . . . .
Do not vex your heart.
He will return to praise you soon,
When his hour of rage has passed.
If your words please the heart,
(10) The heart tends to accept them;
Choose silence for yourself,
Submit to what he does.

Befriend the herald[17] of your quarter,
Do not make him angry with you.
Give him food from your house,
Do not slight his requests;
Say to him, "Welcome, welcome here,"
No blame accrues to him who does it.
. . . . . .[18]

Epilogue

The scribe Khonshotep answered his father, the scribe Any:
I wish I were like (you),
As learned as you!
Then I would carry out your teachings,
And the son would be brought to his father's place.
Each man (15) is led by his nature,
You are a man who is a master,
Whose strivings are exalted,
Whose every word is chosen.
The son, he understands little
When he recites the words in the books.
But when your words please the heart,
The heart tends to accept them with joy.
Don't make your virtues too numerous,
That one may raise one's thoughts to you;
A boy does not follow the moral instructions,
Though the writings are on his tongue!

The scribe Any answered his son, the scribe Khonshotep:
Do not rely on such worthless thoughts,
Beware of what you do to yourself!
I judge your complaints to be wrong,
I shall set you right about them.
There's nothing [superfluous in] our words,
Which you say you wished were reduced.
The fighting (10,1) bull who kills in the stable,
He forgets and abandons the arena;
He conquers his nature,
Remembers what he's learned,
And becomes the like of a fattened ox.
The savage lion abandons his wrath,
And comes to resemble the timid donkey.
The horse slips into its harness,
Obedient it goes outdoors.
The dog obeys the word,
And walks behind its master.
The monkey carries the stick,
Though its mother did not carry it.
(5) The goose returns from the pond,
When one comes to shut it in the yard.
One teaches the Nubian to speak Egyptian,
The Syrian and other strangers too.
Say: "I shall do like all the beasts,"
Listen and learn what they do.

The scribe Khonshotep answered his father, the scribe Any:
Do not proclaim your powers,
So as to force me to your ways;
⌈Does it not happen to a man to slacken his hand⌉
So as to hear an answer in its place?
Man resembles the god in his way
If he listens to a man's answer.
⌈One (man) cannot know his fellow⌉
If the masses are beasts;
⌈One (man) cannot know his teachings⌉
And alone possess a mind,
If the multitudes are foolish.
All your sayings are excellent,
But doing them ⌈requires virtues;⌉
Tell the god who gave you wisdom:
"Set them on your path!"

The scribe Any answered his son, the scribe Khonshotep:
Turn your back to these many words,
That are ⌈not worth⌉ being heard.
The crooked stick left on the ground,
With sun and shade attacking it,
If the carpenter takes it, he straightens it,
Makes of it a noble's staff,
And a straight stick makes a collar.[19]
You foolish heart,
Do you wish us to teach,
Or have you been corrupted?

"Look," said he,[20] "you ⌈my father,⌉
You who are wise and strong of hand:
The infant in his mother's arms,
His wish is for what nurses him."
"Look," said he,[21] "when he finds his speech,
He says: "Give me bread.""

NOTES

1. Queen Ahmes-Nefertari, the wife of King Ahmose. The reading is due to Posener, *RdE*, 6 (1949), 42 n. 2.

2. Or: "Teach him to be a man" (Wilson in *ANET*, 420). There is no doubt that *iri rmṯ* sometimes means "to be a man"; but in this context a term denoting procreation seems more suitable. I can, however, not quote parallels.

3. The understanding of this maxim was much advanced by Gardiner's rendering in *JEA*, 45 (1959), 12-14.

4. In JEA, 21 (1935), 143 n. 10, Gardiner had pointed out that $\check{s}sp$ can have the meaning "purchase." This meaning suits here: the worshiper pays for offerings that are made in his name.

5. Several obscure sentences.

6. *Smi snw*, "evil speech," "noxious remarks," and the like.

7. Death.

8. I do not understand the maxim in lines 5,15-17.

9. The flowers are a metaphor for children.

10. Parts of this maxim were rendered by Posener in *RdE*, 16 (1964), 42-43.

11. Read *ikr*.

12. I.e., the aggressor will be punished.

13. This passage was explained by Posener in *ZÄS*, 90 (1963), 98-102.

14. The theme is the reversal of fortune, a topos that plays a considerable part in Egyptian wisdom literature. Some of its aspects were studied by Volten, "Ägyptische Nemesis-Gedanken," *Miscellanea Gregoriana*, pp. 371-379. A wide-ranging study of the theme in Mesopotamian literature is by G. Buccellati in *Bibbia e Oriente*, 14 (1972), 241-264.

15. Several sentences which I do not understand. The whole maxim, which occupies lines 9,1-3, is obscure to me.

16. If that is the meaning, the two lines are tacked on incongruously. Volten, *op. cit.*, pp. 132 and 136, tried to obtain a different meaning.

17. The policeman.

18. The remainder of the maxim is obscure to me.

19. *Drt*, a horse collar; i.e., the crooked stick is made straight, and the straight one is rounded. On the passage see Posener, *ZÄS*, 99 (1973), 130.

20. The son speaks.

21. The father answers. Any's concluding answer apparently means that when a child is old enough to speak he asks to be nourished materially and spiritually.

THE INSTRUCTION OF AMENEMOPE

With this long work, the genre Instruction reaches its culmination. Its worth lies not in any thematic richness, for its range is much narrower than, for example, that of the *Instruction of Ptahhotep*. Its worth lies in its quality of inwardness. Though it is still assumed that right thinking and right action will find their reward, worldly success, which had meant so much in the past, has receded into the background. Even poverty is no longer viewed as a misfortune.

The shift of emphasis, away from action and success, and toward contemplation and endurance, leads to an overall regrouping of values and a redefinition of the ideal man. As early as *Ptahhotep*, the ideal man lacked all martial values; he was a man of peace who strove for advancement and was generous with his wealth. The new ideal man is content with a humble position and a minimal amount of material possessions. His chief characteristic is modesty. He is self-controlled, quiet, and kind toward people, and he is humble before God. This ideal man is indeed not a perfect man, for perfection is now viewed as belonging only to God.

The style of Amenemope is rich in similes and metaphors which are sustained at length and with skill. The work as a whole is carefully composed and unified, both through the device of thirty numbered chapters and through a concentration on two basic themes: first, the depiction of the ideal man, the "silent man," and his adversary, the "heated man"; second, the exhortation to honesty and warnings against dishonesty. All other themes are subservient to these central ones.

The composition of the work is now usually assigned to the Ramesside period, although all the manuscript copies that have reached us are of later date. It was during the Ramesside age that the tribes of Israel became a nation, and much of Israelite knowledge of things Egyptian, as reflected in the Bible, resulted from contacts during this period. The most tangible literary evidence of these contacts is found in the chips from the Instruction of Amenemope that are embedded in the Book of Proverbs. It can hardly be doubted that the author of Proverbs was acquainted with the Egyptian work and borrowed from it, for in addition to the similarities in thought and expression—especially close and striking in Proverbs xxii and xxiii—the line in xxii, 20: "Have I not written for you thirty sayings of admonition and knowledge" derives its meaning from the author's acquaintance with the "thirty" chapters of Amenemope. Ever since Adolf Erman pointed this out there has been a consensus among scholars on a literary relationship, although some scholars have tried to interpret it in reverse by claiming priority for the Hebrew text, or have proposed to derive both works from a lost Semitic original.

The Instruction of Amenemope is completely preserved in the British Museum Papyrus 10474. Small portions of it are found on a papyrus in Stockholm, three writing tablets in Turin, Paris, and Moscow, respectively, and an ostracon in the Cairo Museum. In the British Museum papyrus and on the Turin and Louvre tablets the text is written stichically, that is to say, in lines that show the metrical scheme. This is unusual and important, for it allows us to *see* the metrical organization rather than having to guess it. And since the work is also divided into thirty numbered chapters, we are here precisely informed about two basic features of Egyptian prosody as applied to a particular work: the organization of the metrical line and the grouping of lines into sections or chapters.

The metrical line turns out to be exactly what one expects it to be. It consists of self-contained sentences or clauses. Through parallelism and related devices the lines are grouped loosely into distichs, tristichs, and quatrains. There is no indication that these groups of lines were further gathered into strophes or stanzas. Nor would such strophes be suited to the nature of instructional works. For the Instructions consist of thoughts developed freely over greater or lesser length, and the natural divisions occur when one topic is concluded and another taken up. In earlier Instructions such divisions were not marked by graphic or verbal devices; in Amenemope they are brought out clearly through the use of numbered chapters.

Amenemope is a difficult text. It abounds in rare words, elliptic phrases, and allusions whose meaning escapes us. Furthermore, the copying scribes introduced numerous errors. But we are fortunate to have the complete text preserved in the British Museum Papyrus, where it occupies all twenty-seven pages of the *recto* and the first line of the *verso*.

Publication: E. A. W. Budge, *Facsimiles of Egyptian Hieratic Papyri in the British Museum, Second Series* (London, 1923), pp. 9-18 and 41-51 and pls. 1-14.   H. O. Lange, *Das Weisheitsbuch des Amenemope*, Danske videnskabernes selskab, historisk-filologiske meddelelser, xi,2 (Copenhagen, 1925).

Translation: A. Erman, *OLZ*, 27 (1924), columns 241-252.   E. A. W. Budge, *The Teaching of Amen-em-apt, Son of Kanekht* (London, 1924), pp. 93-234.   F. Ll. Griffith, *JEA*, 12 (1926), 191-231.   F. Lexa, *Archiv Orientalni*, 1 (1929), 14-49.   Fr. W. von Bissing, *Altägyptische Lebensweisheit* (Zurich, 1955), pp. 80-90.   J. A. Wilson in *ANET*, pp. 421-424 (excerpts).   Simpson, *Literature*, pp. 241-265.   I. Grumach, *Untersuchungen zur Lebenslehre des Amenope*, Münchner ägyptologische Studien, Heft 23 (Munich, 1972). Translation and commentary.

Studies, comments, and publication of fragments: A. Erman, *Sitzungsberichte der Berliner Akademie der Wissenschaften*, Philosophisch-historische Klasse, 1924, no. 15 (Berlin, 1924).   D. C. Simpson, *JEA*, 12 (1926), 232-239.   P. Humbert, *Recherches sur les sources égyptiennes de la littérature sapientiale d'Israël* (Neuchatel, 1929), ch. 2.   R. J. Williams, *JEA*, 47 (1961), 100-106.   B. J. Peterson, *JEA*, 52 (1966), 120-128 and pls. xxxi-xxxiA (the Stockholm fragment).   G. Posener, *RdE*, 18 (1966), 45-62 and pls. 1-2 (the three tablets).   R. Anthes in *Galling Festschrift*, pp. 9-18.   G. Posener, *ZÄS*, 99 (1973), 129-135.

Prologue

I,1   Beginning of the teaching for life,
       The instructions for well-being,
       Every rule for relations with elders,
       For conduct toward magistrates;
5   Knowing how to answer one who speaks,
       To reply to one who sends a message.
       So as to direct him on the paths of life,
       To make him prosper upon earth;
       To let his heart enter its shrine,[1]
10   Steering clear of evil;
       To save him from the mouth of strangers,
       To let (him) be praised in the mouth of people.
       Made by the overseer of fields, experienced in his
           office,
       The offspring of a scribe of Egypt,
15   The overseer of grains who controls the measure,
       Who sets the harvest-dues for his lord,
       Who registers the islands of new land,
       In the great name of his majesty,

Who records the markers on the borders of fields,
II,1   Who acts for the king in his listing of taxes,
Who makes the land-register of Egypt;
The scribe who determines the offerings for all
    the gods.
Who gives land-leases to the people,
5   The overseer of grains, [provider of] foods,
Who supplies the granary with grains;
The truly silent in This of Ta-wer,
The justified in Ipu,
Who owns a tomb on the west of Senu,
10   Who has a chapel at Abydos,
Amenemope, the son of Kanakht,
The justified in Ta-wer.²
⟨For⟩ his son, the youngest of his children,
The smallest of his family,
15   The devotee of Min-Kamutef,
The water-pourer of Wennofer,
Who places Horus on his father's throne,
Who guards him in his noble shrine,
Who––––––
III,1   The guardian of the mother of god,
Inspector of the black cattle of the terrace of Min,
Who protects Min in his shrine:
Hor-em-maakher is his true name,
5   The child of a nobleman of Ipu,
The son of the sistrum-player of Shu and Tefnut,
And chief songstress of Horus, Tawosre.

He says: Chapter 1
Give your ears, hear the sayings,
10   Give your heart to understand them;
It profits to put them in your heart,
Woe to him who neglects them!
Let them rest in the casket of your belly,
May they be bolted in your heart;
15   When there rises a whirlwind of words,
They'll be a mooring post for your tongue.
If you make your life with these in your heart,
You will find it a success;
IV,1   You will find my words a storehouse for life,
Your being will prosper upon earth.

Chapter 2

       Beware of robbing a wretch,
5   Of attacking a cripple;
       Don't stretch out your hand to touch an old man,
       Nor ⌐open your mouth¬[3] to an elder.
       Don't let yourself be sent on a mischievous errand,
       Nor be friends with him who does it.
10   Don't raise an outcry against one who attacks you,
       Nor answer him yourself.
       He who does evil, the shore rejects him,
       Its floodwater carries him away.
       The northwind descends to end his hour,
15   It mingles with the thunderstorm.
       The storm cloud is tall, the crocodiles are vicious,
       You heated man, how are you now?
       He cries out, his voice reaches heaven,
       It is the Moon[4] who declares his crime.
V,1   Steer, we will ferry the wicked,
       We do not act like his kind;
       Lift him up, give him your hand,
       Leave him ⟨in⟩ the hands of the god;
5   Fill his belly with bread of your own,
       That he be sated and weep.
       Another thing good in the·heart of the god:
       To pause before speaking.

Chapter 3

10   Don't start a quarrel with a hot-mouthed man,
       Nor needle him with words.
       Pause before a foe, bend before an attacker,
       Sleep (on it) before speaking.
       A storm that bursts like fire in straw,
15   Such is the heated man in his hour.
       Withdraw from him, leave him alone,
       The god knows how to answer him.
       If you make your life with these (words) in
          your heart,
       Your children will observe them.

Chapter 4

VI,1   As for the heated man in the temple,[5]
       He is like a tree growing ⌐indoors¬;

A moment lasts its growth of ⌈shoots⌉,
Its end comes about in the ⌈woodshed⌉;
5   It is floated far from its place,
The flame is its burial shroud.
The truly silent, who keeps apart,
He is like a tree grown in a meadow.
It greens, it doubles its yield,
10   It stands in front of its lord.
Its fruit is sweet, its shade delightful,
Its end comes in the garden.

Chapter 5

Do not falsify[6] the temple rations,
15   Do not grasp and you'll find profit.
Do not remove a servant of the god,
So as to do favors to another.
Do not say: "Today is like tomorrow,"
How will this end?
VII,1   Comes tomorrow, today has vanished,
The deep has become the water's edge.
Crocodiles are bared, hippopotami stranded,
The fish crowded together.[7]
5   Jackals are sated, birds are in feast,
The fishnets have been drained.[8]
But all the silent in the temple,
They say: "Re's blessing is great."
Cling to the silent, then you find life,
10   Your being will prosper upon earth.

Chapter 6

Do not move the markers on the borders of
    fields,
Nor shift the position of the measuring-cord.
Do not be greedy for a cubit of land,
15   Nor encroach on the boundaries of a widow.
The trodden furrow worn down by time,
He who disguises it in the fields,
When he has snared (it) by false oaths,
He will be caught by the might of the Moon.
VIII,1 Recognize him who does this on earth:
He is an oppressor of the weak,
A foe bent on destroying your being,
The taking of life is in his eye.

5   His house is an enemy to the town,
   His storage bins will be destroyed;
   His wealth will be seized from his children's
      hands,
   His possessions will be given to another.
   Beware of destroying the borders of fields,
10   Lest a terror carry you away;
   One pleases god with the might of the lord
   When one discerns the borders of fields.[9]
   Desire your being to be sound,
   Beware of the Lord of All;
15   Do not erase another's furrow,
   It profits you to keep it sound.
   Plow your fields and you'll find what you need,
   You'll receive bread from your threshing-floor.
   Better is a bushel given you by the god,
20   Than five thousand through wrongdoing.
IX,1   They stay not a day in bin and barn,
   They make no food for the beer jar;
   A moment is their stay in the granary,
   Comes morning they have vanished.
5   Better is poverty in the hand of the god,
   Than wealth in the storehouse;
   Better is bread with a happy heart
   Than wealth with vexation.

Chapter 7

10   Do not set your heart on wealth,
   There is no ignoring Fate and Destiny;
   Do not let your heart go straying,
   Every man comes to his hour.
   Do not strain to seek increase,
15   What you have, let it suffice you.
   If riches come to you by theft,
   They will not stay the night with you.
   Comes day they are not in your house,
   Their place is seen but they're not there;
20   Earth opened its mouth, leveled them, swallowed
      them,
X,1   And made them sink into *dat.*
   They made a hole as big as their size,
   And sank into the netherworld;
   They made themselves wings like geese,
5   And flew away to the sky.

Do not rejoice in wealth from theft,
Nor complain of being poor.
If the leading archer presses forward,
His company abandons him;
10   The boat of the greedy is left ⟨in⟩ the mud,
While the bark of the silent sails with the wind.
You shall pray to the Aten when he rises,
Saying: "Grant me well-being and health";
He will give you your needs for this life,
15   And you will be safe from fear.

Chapter 8

Set your goodness before people,
Then you are greeted by all;
One welcomes the Uraeus,
20   One spits upon Apopis.
Guard your tongue from harmful speech,
XI,1   Then you will be loved by others.
You will find your place in the house of god,
You will share in the offerings of your lord.
When you're revered and your coffin conceals
    you,
5   You will be safe from the power of god.[10]
Do not shout "crime" against a man,
When the cause of (his) flight is hidden.
Whether you hear something good or evil,
Do it outside where it is not heard.
10   Put the good remark on your tongue,
While the bad is concealed in your belly.

Chapter 9

Do not befriend the heated man,
Nor approach him for conversation.
15   Keep your tongue from answering your superior,
And take care not to insult him.
Let him not cast his speech to catch you,
Nor give free rein to your answer.
Converse with a man of your own measure,
20   And take care not to ⌜offend⌝ him.
XII,1   Swift is the speech of one who is angered,
More than wind ⌜over⌝ water.
He tears down, he builds up with his tongue,
When he makes his hurtful speech.

5 He gives an answer worthy of a beating,
  For its weight is harm.
  He hauls freight like all the world,
  But his load is falsehood.
  He is the ferryman of snaring words,
10 He goes and comes with quarrels.
  When he eats and drinks inside,
  His answer is (heard) outside.
  The day he is charged with his crime
  Is misfortune for his chilren.
15 If only Khnum came to him,
  The Potter to the heated man,
  So as to knead the ⌈faulty⌉ heart.
  He is like a young wolf in the farmyard,
  He turns one eye against the other,
XIII,1 He causes brothers to quarrel.
  He runs before every wind like clouds,
  He dims the radiance of the sun;
  He flips his tail like the crocodile's young,
5 ⌈He draws himself up so as to strike.⌉
  His lips are sweet, his tongue is bitter,
  A fire burns in his belly.
  Don't leap to join such a one,
  Lest a terror carry you away.

10   Chapter 10

  Don't force yourself to greet the heated man,
  For then you injure your own heart;
  Do not say "greetings" to him falsely,
  While there is terror in your belly.
15 Do not speak falsely to a man,
  The god abhors it;
  Do not sever your heart from your tongue,
  That all your strivings may succeed.
  You will be weighty before the others,
XIV,1 And secure in the hand of the god.
  God hates the falsifier of words,
  He greatly abhors the dissembler.

    Chapter 11

5 Do not covet a poor man's goods,
  Nor hunger for his bread;
  A poor man's goods are a block in the throat,

It makes the gullet vomit.
He who makes gain by lying oaths,
His heart is misled by his belly;
Where there is fraud success is feeble,
The bad spoils the good.[11]
You will be guilty before your superior,
And confused in your account;
Your pleas will be answered by a curse,
Your prostrations by a beating.
The big mouthful of bread—you swallow, you
    vomit it,
And you are emptied of your gain.
Observe the overseer[12] of the poor,
When the stick attains him;
All his people are bound in chains,
And he is led to the executioner.
If you are released before your superior,
You are yet hateful to your subordinates;
Steer away from the poor man on the road,
Look at him and keep clear of his goods.

Chapter 12

Do not desire a noble's wealth,
Nor make free with a big mouthful of bread;
If he sets you to manage his property,
Shun his, and yours will prosper.
Do not converse[13] with a heated man,
So as to befriend a hostile man.
If you are sent to transport straw,
Stay away from its container.
If a man is observed on a fraudulent errand,
He will not be sent on another occasion.

Chapter 13

Do not cheat a man ⟨through⟩ pen on scroll,
The god abhors it;
Do not bear witness with false words,
So as to brush aside a man by your tongue.
Do not assess a man who has nothing,
And thus falsify your pen.
If you find a large debt against a poor man,
Make it into three parts;
Forgive two, let one stand,

You will find it a path of life.
After sleep, when you wake in the morning,
10 You will find it as good news.
Better is praise with the love of men
Than wealth in the storehouse;
Better is bread with a happy heart
Than wealth with vexation.

Chapter 14

15

Do not recall yourself to a man,
Nor strain to seek his hand.
If he says to you: "Here is a gift,
⌐No have-not¬ will refuse it,"[14]
20 Don't blink at him, nor bow your head,
Nor turn aside your gaze.
Salute him with your mouth, say, "Greetings,"
XVII,1 He will desist, and you succeed.
Do not rebuff him in his approach,
⌐Another time he'll be taken away.¬

Chapter 15

5 Do the good and you will prosper,
Do not dip your pen to injure a man.
The finger of the scribe is the beak of the Ibis,
Beware of brushing it aside.
The Ape dwells in the House of Khmun,[15]
10 His eye encircles the Two Lands;
When he sees one who cheats with his finger,
He carries his livelihood off in the flood.
The scribe who cheats with his finger,
His son will not be enrolled.
15 If you make your life with these (words) in your
heart,
Your children will observe them.

Chapter 16

Do not move the scales nor alter the weights,
Nor diminish the fractions of the measure;
20 Do not desire a measure of the fields,
Nor neglect those of the treasury.
The Ape sits by the balance,
XVIII,1 His heart is in the plummet;
Where is a god as great as Thoth,

Who invented these things and made them?
Do not make for yourself deficient weights,
5   They are rich in grief through the might of god.
If you see someone who cheats,
Keep your distance from him.
Do not covet copper,
Disdain beautiful linen;
10   What good is one dressed in finery,
If he cheats before the god?
Faience disguised as gold,
Comes day, it turns to lead.

Chapter 17

15   Beware of disguising the measure,
So as to falsify its fractions;
Do not force it to overflow,
Nor let its belly be empty.
Measure according to its true size,
20   Your hand clearing exactly.
Do not make a bushel of twice its size,
For then you are headed for the abyss.
The bushel is the Eye of Re,
XIX,1   It abhors him who trims;
A measurer who indulges in cheating,
His Eye seals (the verdict) against him.
Do not accept a farmer's dues
5   And then assess him so as to injure him;
Do not conspire with the measurer,
So as to defraud the share of the Residence.
Greater is the might of the threshing floor
Than an oath by the great throne.

10   ## Chapter 18

Do not lie down in fear of tomorrow:
"Comes day, how will tomorrow be?"
Man ignores how tomorrow will be;
God is ever in his perfection,
15   Man is ever in his failure.[16]
The words men say are one thing,
The deeds of the god are another.
Do not say: "I have done no wrong,"
And then strain to seek a quarrel;
20   The wrong belongs to the god,

He seals (the verdict) with his finger.
There is no perfection before the god,
But there is failure before him;[17]

XX,1   If one strains to seek perfection,
In a moment he has marred it.
Keep firm your heart, steady your heart,
Do not steer with your tongue;

5   If a man's tongue is the boat's rudder,
The Lord of All is yet its pilot.

Chapter 19

Do not go to court before an official
In order to falsify your words;

10   Do not vacillate in your answers,
When your witnesses accuse.
Do not strain ⟨with⟩ oaths by your lord,
⟨With⟩ speeches at the hearing;
Tell the truth before the official,

15   Lest he lay a hand on you.
If another day you come before him,
He will incline to all you say;
He will relate your speech to the Council of
    Thirty,
It will be observed on another occasion.

20   ## Chapter 20

Do not confound a man in the law court,
In order to brush aside one who is right.

XXI,1   Do not incline to the well-dressed man,
And rebuff the one in rags.
Don't accept the gift of a powerful man,
And deprive the weak for his sake.

5   *Maat* is a great gift of god,
He gives it to whom he wishes.
The might of him who resembles him,
It saves the poor from his tormentor.
Do not make for yourself false documents,

10   They are a deadly provocation;
They (mean) the great restraining oath,[18]
They (mean) a hearing by the herald.
Don't falsify the oracles in the scrolls,[19]
And thus disturb the plans of god;

15   Don't use for yourself the might of god,
As if there were no Fate and Destiny.
Hand over property to its owners,
Thus do you seek life for yourself;
Don't raise your desire in their house,
20   Or your bones belong to the execution-block.

Chapter 21

XXII,1   Do not say: "Find me a strong superior,
For a man in your town has injured me";
Do not say: "Find me a protector,
For one who hates me has injured me."
5   Indeed you do not know the plans of god,
And should not weep for tomorrow;
Settle in the arms of the god,
Your silence will overthrow them.[20]
The crocodile that makes no sound,[21]
10   Dread of it is ancient.
Do not empty your belly to everyone,
And thus destroy respect of you;
Broadcast not your words to others,
Nor join with one who bares his heart.
15   Better is one whose speech is in his belly
Than he who tells it to cause harm.
One does not run to reach success,
One does not move to spoil it.

Chapter 22

20   Do not provoke your adversary,
So as to ⟨make⟩ him tell his thoughts;
Do not leap to come before him,
XXIII,1   When you do not see his doings.
First gain insight from his answer,
Then keep still and you'll succeed.
Leave it to him to empty his belly,
5   Know how to sleep, he'll be found out.
ˤGrasp his legsˀ,[22] do not harm him,
Be wary of him, do not ignore him.
Indeed you do not know the plans of god,
And should not weep for tomorrow;
10   Settle in the arms of the god,
Your silence will overthrow them.

Chapter 23

Do not eat in the presence of an official
And then set your mouth before ⟨him⟩;
15   If you are sated pretend to chew,
Content yourself with your saliva.[23]
Look at the bowl that is before you,
And let it serve your needs.
An official is great in his office,
20   As a well is rich in drawings of water.

Chapter 24

Do not listen to an official's reply indoors
XXIV,1   In order to repeat it to another outside.
Do not let your word be carried outside,
Lest your heart be aggrieved.
The heart of man is a gift[24] of god,
5   Beware of neglecting it.
The man at the side of an official,
His name should not be known.

Chapter 25

Do not laugh at a blind man,
Nor tease a dwarf,[25]
10   Nor cause hardship for the lame.
Don't tease a man who is in the hand of the god,[26]
Nor be angry with him for his failings.
Man is clay and straw,
The god is his builder.
15   He tears down, he builds up daily,
He makes a thousand poor by his will,
He makes a thousand men into chiefs,
When he is in his hour of life.[27]
Happy is he who reaches the west,
20   When he is safe in the hand of the god.

Chapter 26

Do not sit down in the beer-house
XXV,1   In order to join one greater than you,
Be he a youth great through his office,
Or be he an elder through birth.
Befriend a man of your own measure,
5   Re is helpful from afar.

If you see one greater than you outdoors,
Walk behind him respectfully;
Give a hand to an elder sated with beer,
Respect him as his children would.

10   The arm is not hurt by being bared,[28]
The back is not broken by bending it.
A man does not lose by speaking sweetly,
Nor does he gain if his speech bristles.
The pilot who sees from afar,

15   He will not wreck his boat.

Chapter 27

Do not revile one older than you,
He has seen Re before you;
Let ⟨him⟩ not report you to the Aten at his rising,

20   Saying: "A youth has reviled an old man."
Very painful before Pre

XXVI,1   Is a youth who reviles an elder.
Let him beat you while your hand is on your chest,
Let him revile you while you are silent;
If next day you come before him,

5   He will give you food in plenty.
A dog's food is from its master,
It barks to him who gives it.

Chapter 28

Do not pounce on a widow when you find her in
    the fields[29]

10   And then fail to be patient with her reply.
Do not refuse your oil jar to a stranger,
Double it before your brothers.
God prefers him who honors the poor
To him who worships the wealthy.

15   ## Chapter 29

Do not prevent people from crossing the river,
If you stride freely in the ferry.[30]
When you are given an oar in the midst of the
    deep,
Bend your arms and take it.

20   It is no crime before the god,

XXVII,1   ⌐If the passenger is not passed up¬³¹
           Don't make yourself a ferry on the river
           And then strain to seek its fare;
           Take the fare from him who is wealthy,
    5   And let pass him who is poor.

Chapter 30

           Look to these thirty chapters,
           They inform, they educate;
           They are the foremost of all books,
    10   They make the ignorant wise.
           If they are read to the ignorant,
           He is cleansed through them.
           Be filled with them, put them in your heart,
           And become a man who expounds them,
    15   One who expounds as a teacher.
           The scribe who is skilled in his office,
           He is found worthy to be a courtier.

Colophon

           That is its end.
XXVIII,1   Written by Senu, son of the divine father Pemu.

NOTES

1. The heart is viewed as the god who dwells in man. On this concept see Bonnet, *RÄRG*, pp. 225-228.

2. Ipu and Senu are names for Akhmim (Panopolis); Ta-wer is the nome of Abydos. Amenemope identifies himself as a citizen of Akhmim who has built his tomb there and also owns a funerary monument at Abydos.

3. The meaning of *t3i-r*, which recurs in 15,13, is not clear and it has been variously rendered. See I. Grumach, *op. cit.*, p. 31.

4. The god Thoth.

5. On this chapter see now Posener, *ZÄS*, 99 (1973), 129-135.

6. The verb *'šg* recurs in 7,17, 18,12, and 18,15. I follow Griffith in taking it to mean "overlay," "falsify," "disguise."

7. So with I. Grumach, *op. cit.*, p. 50.

8. The theme is the reversal of fortune; see the *Instruction of Any*, p. 146 n. 14.

9. Some translators take *wpt* as a participle referring to god: "He who determines the borders of fields." But then the meaning of the couplet is poor. I have followed Griffith.

10. "Power" here in the sense of "wrath."

11. Assuming *wh3* to be transitive. The usual rendering, "good and bad fail," is not satisfactory.

12. The meaning of *ḥy* is not well established; the word recurs in 24, 17 where the meaning "overseer," or "superior," is suitable. But here a negative connotation such as "oppressor" seems called for.

13. See note 3.

14. The verb *b'ꜣ* (or *b'*) recurs in 21,2, 27,1, and 27,5. The meaning assigned in *Wb*. I, 446 "beachten, berücksichtigen," does not appear suitable here. The four occurrences in Amenemope suggest "rebuff," "refuse," as well as "pass up," "let pass."

15. The ibis and the ape are the images of Thoth.

16. Literally, "the god," and "the man." Amenemope says "god" and "the god," interchangeably. The presence or absence of the definite article seems to be a matter of style.

17. I emend *mn* to *wn*; otherwise the sentence contradicts all that has gone before.

18. On the oath *sḏfꜣ tr* see K. Baer, *JEA*, 50 (1964), 179-180.

19. The passage was explained by Posener, *ZÄS*, 90 (1963), 98-102.

20. The adversaries.

21. On this passage see Posener in *Schott Festschrift*, pp. 106-111.

22. This meaning does not suit; I suspect a corruption.

23. So following H. J. Polotsky in *Textes et langages de l'Égypte Pharaonique: Hommage à Jean-François Champollion, I*, Bibliothèque d'étude, 64/1 (Cairo [1973]), p. 140 n. 3.

24. The Turin tablet has "gift" instead of the "nose" of the British Museum papyrus; see Posener, *RdE*, 18 (1966), 61-62.

25. In the British Museum papyrus the two sentences are written as a single line but on the Turin tablet as two lines.

26. Here in the special meaning of one who is ill or insane.

27. In *Sagesses*, p. 88, A. Volten explained this to mean that the sun-god acts through the gods who are assigned to each hour of the day.

28. I.e., stretching the arm out of the sleeve in a gesture of greeting. The same remark occurs in *Ptahhotep*, line 445/448.

29. I.e., when you find her gleaning in fields not her own.

30. I.e., when there is ample room in the ferry.

31. It is not clear whether *ḥwty* means "passenger" or "sailor"; in any case, the meaning is that the passenger should help with the rowing if asked to do so.

PART FIVE

Be a Scribe

Numerous papyri and ostraca of Ramesside date testify to the existence of a school system that taught young boys to become professional scribes and hence civil servants. Not all instruction took place in schools. Many of the texts suggest a personal form of teaching in which a senior official guided a young man who had completed his basic schooling and was already a member of the bureaucracy.

Writing was taught by making the pupils copy a variety of compositions: literary works that were highly esteemed, and basic genres such as letters, hymns, prayers, and of course, instructions in wisdom. Through copying, taking down dictation, and memorizing the students acquired the basic skills of reading and writing and the more advanced knowledge of grammar, orthography, vocabulary, and composition. Furthermore, it could be hoped that the moral teachings propounded in the didactic texts would help to form the characters of the young scribes.

Through being used as teaching materials, all literary works, as well as actual letters and documents dealing with business and legal matters, became school texts. But the school system also gave rise to a specific genre of texts which reflected the educational process and the relation between teacher and pupil. These were works composed by teachers and pupils which in turn became models to be copied. Their contents revolved around three main themes: 1. The teacher's advice to the student, exhorting him to diligence and warning against dissipation. 2. The praise of the scribe's profession as one superior to all others. 3. The grateful replies of the student who lauds his teacher and wishes him wealth and happiness.

Letter-writing was an important feature of scribal activity. Hence the copying of real letters and the composition of model letters played a large part in the instruction. Even the texts devoted to the teacher-pupil theme were often cast in the form of letters.

In the papyri that have survived, different kinds of texts, used in the schools, were often copied out one after another regardless of their content. Thus works that had originated in specific situations of life, such as business letters, came to be side by side with model compositions invented by teachers and students. But now and then a scribe made a "book" by selecting compositions on related themes and putting them in a meaningful order. Such a book is *Papyrus Lansing*. It is a schoolbook in the specific sense, for it is devoted to the theme "Be a scribe."

The book treats the typical topics of the teacher-pupil relation in a sequence of eleven sections: 1. Address. 2-4. Praise of the scribal profession and exhortations to the pupil. 5-6. The miseries of other professions. 7. Additional advice and exhortations. 8. The special hardships of the soldier's life. 9-11. The pupil praises his teacher. The final section of Papyrus Lansing contains a letter which is not connected with the "book."

Papyrus Chester Beatty IV is a typical scribal miscellany. The *recto* contains religious hymns; the *verso* consists of several short pieces relating to the scribal profession. Among these, one piece is of uncommon interest. It is a praise of the writer's profession which goes beyond the usual cliches and propounds the remarkable idea that the only immortality man can achieve is the fame of his name as transmitted by his books. Man becomes dust; only the written word endures.

PAPYRUS LANSING: A SCHOOLBOOK

P. British Museum 9994

Twentieth Dynasty

The papyrus is written with verse-points and paragraph signs. The writing is rather careless; there are many spelling mistakes and other errors. The first page is marred by lacunae.

Publication: E. A. W. Budge, *Facsimiles of Egyptian Hieratic Papyri in the British Museum, Second Series* (London, 1923), pls. 15-30.   A. Erman and H. O. Lange, *Papyrus Lansing; eine ägyptische Schulhandschrift der 20. Dynastie.* Danske videnskabernes selskab, historisk-filologiske meddelelser, X, 3 (Copenhagen, 1925).   Gardiner, *LEM*, pp. 99-116.

Translation: A. M. Blackman and T. E. Peet, *JEA*, 11 (1925), 284-298. Caminos, *LEM*, pp. 373-428.

1. Title

(1,1) [Beginning of the instruction in letter-writing made by the royal scribe and chief overseer of the cattle of Amen-Re, King of Gods, Nebmare-nakht] for his apprentice, the scribe Wenemdiamun.

2. Praise of the scribe's profession

[The royal scribe] and chief overseer of the cattle of Amen-[Re, King of Gods, Nebmare-nakht speaks to the scribe Wenemdiamun].[Apply yourself to this] noble profession. "Follower of Thoth" is the good name of him who exercises it. ------. He makes friends with those greater than he. Joyful ------. Write with your hand, read with your mouth. Act according to my words. (1,5) ------, my heart is not disgusted. ------. ------ to my instructing you. You will find it useful. ------ [with bread and] beer. You will be advanced by your superiors. You will be sent on a mission ------. Love writing, shun dancing; then you become (2,1) a worthy official. Do not long for the marsh thicket.[1] Turn your back on throw stick and chase. By day write with your fingers; recite by night. Befriend the scroll, the palette. It pleases more than wine. Writing for him who knows it is better than all other professions. It pleases more than bread and beer, more than clothing and ointment. It is worth more than an inheritance in Egypt, than a tomb in the west.

3. Advice to the unwilling pupil

Young fellow, how conceited you are! You do not listen when I speak. Your heart is denser than a great obelisk, a hundred cubits high, ten cubits thick. When it is finished and ready for loading, (2,5) many work gangs draw it. It hears the words of men; it is loaded on a barge. Departing from Yebu it is conveyed, until it comes to rest on its place in Thebes.[2]

So also a cow is bought this year, and it plows the following year. It learns to listen to the herdsman; it only lacks words. Horses brought from the field, they forget their mothers. Yoked they go up and down on all his majesty's errands. They become like those that bore them, that stand in the stable. They do their utmost for fear of a beating.

But though I beat you with every kind of stick, you do not listen. If I knew another way of doing it, I would do it for you, that you might listen. You are a person fit for writing, though you have not yet known a woman. Your heart discerns, (3,1) your fingers are skilled, your mouth is apt for reciting.

Writing is more enjoyable than enjoying a basket of *b3y* and beans; more enjoyable than a mother's giving birth, when her heart knows no distaste. She is constant in nursing her son; her breast is in his mouth every day. Happy is the heart ⟨of⟩ him who writes; he is young each day.

4. The idle scribe is worthless

The royal scribe and chief overseer of the cattle of Amen-Re, King of Gods, Nebmare-nakht, speaks to the scribe Wenemdiamun, as follows. You are busy coming and going, and don't think of writing. You resist listening to me; (3,5) you neglect my teachings.

You are worse than the goose of the shore, that is busy with mischief. It spends the summer destroying the dates, the winter destroying the seed-grain. It spends the balance of the year in pursuit of the cultivators. It does not let seed be cast to the ground without snatching it ⸢in its fall.⸣ One cannot catch it by snaring. One does not offer it in the temple. The evil, sharpeyed bird that does no work!

You are worse than the desert antelope that lives by running. It spends no day in plowing. Never at all does it tread on the threshing-floor. It lives on the oxen's labor, without entering among them. But though I spend the day telling you "Write," it seems like a plague to you. Writing is very (4,1) pleasant! ------.

5. All occupations are bad except that of the scribe

See for yourself with your own eye. The occupations lie before you.[3]

The washerman's day is going up, going down. All his limbs are weak, ⟨from⟩ whitening his neighbors' clothes every day, from washing their linen.

The maker of pots is smeared with soil, like one whose relations have died. His hands, (4,5) his feet are full of clay; he is like one who lives in the bog.

The cobbler mingles with vats.[4] His odor is penetrating. His hands are red with madder, like one who is smeared with blood. He looks behind him for the kite, like one whose flesh is exposed.

The watchman[5] prepares garlands and polishes vase-stands. He spends a night of toil just as one on whom the sun shines.

The merchants travel downstream and upstream. They are as busy as can be, carrying goods from one town to another. They supply him who has wants. But the tax collectors carry off the gold, that most precious of metals.

The ships' crews from every house (of commerce), they receive their loads. (5,1) They depart from Egypt for Syria, and each man's god is with him. (But) not one of them says: "We shall see Egypt again!"

The carpenter who is in the shipyard carries the timber and stacks it. If he gives today the output of yesterday, woe to his limbs! The shipwright stands behind him to tell him evil things.

His outworker who is in the fields, his is the toughest of all the jobs. He spends the day loaded (5,5) with his tools, tied to his tool-box. When he returns home at night, he is loaded with the tool-box and the timbers, his drinking mug, and his whetstones.

The scribe, he alone, records the output of all of them. Take note of it!

6. The misfortunes of the peasant

Let me also expound to you the situation of the peasant, that other tough occupation. [Comes] the inundation and soaks him ---, he attends to his equipment. By day he cuts his farming tools; (6,1) by night he twists rope. Even his midday hour he spends on farm labor. He equips himself to go to the field as if he were a warrior. The dried field lies before him; he goes out to get his team. When he has been after the herdsman for many days, he gets his team and comes back with it. He makes for it a place in the field. (6,5) Comes dawn, he goes to make a start and does not find it in its place. He spends three days searching for it; he finds it in the bog. He finds no hides on them; the jackals have chewed them. He comes out, his garment in his hand, to beg for himself a team.

When he reaches his field he finds ⟨it⟩ ⌐broken up⌐. He spends time cultivating, and the snake is after him. It finishes off the seed as it is cast to the ground. He does not see a green blade. He does three plowings with borrowed grain. His wife (7,1) has gone down to the merchants and found nothing for⌐barter.⌐Now the scribe lands on the shore. He surveys the harvest. Attendants are behind him with staffs, Nubians with clubs. One says (to him): "Give grain." "There is none." He is beaten savagely. He is bound, thrown in the well, submerged head down. His wife is bound in his presence. His children are in fetters. His neighbors (7,5) abandon them and flee. When it's over, there's no grain.

If you have any sense, be a scribe. If you have learned about the peasant, you will not be able to be one. Take note of it!

7. Be a scribe

The scribe of the army and commander[6] of the cattle of the house of Amun, Nebmare-nakht, speaks to the scribe Wenemdiamun, as follows. Be a scribe! Your body will be sleek; your hand will be soft. You will not flicker like a flame, like one whose body is feeble. For there is not the bone of a man in you. You are tall and thin. If you lifted a load to carry it, you would stagger, your legs would tremble. You are lacking in strength; (8,1) you are weak in all your limbs; you are poor in body.

Set your sight on being a scribe; a fine profession that suits you. You call for one; a thousand answer you. You stride freely on the road. You will not be like a hired ox. You are in front of others.

I spend the day instructing you. You do not listen! Your heart is like an ⟨empty⟩ room. My teachings are not in it. Take their ⟨ᵣmeaning⟩ to yourself!

The marsh thicket is before you each day, as a nestling is after its mother. You follow the path of (8,5) pleasure; you make friends with revellers. You have made your home in the brewery, as one who thirsts for beer. You sit in the parlor with an idler.[7] You hold the writings in contempt. You visit the whore. Do not do these things! What are they for? They are of no use. Take note of it!

8. The scribe does not suffer like the soldier

Furthermore. Look, I instruct you to make you sound; to make you hold the palette freely. To make you become one whom the king trusts; to make you gain entrance to treasury and granary. To make you receive the ship-load at the gate of the granary. To make you issue the offerings on feast days. You are dressed in fine clothes; you own horses. Your boat is on (9,1) the river; you are supplied with attendants. You stride about inspecting. A mansion is built in your town. You have a powerful office, given you by the king. Male and female slaves are about you. Those who are in the fields grasp your hand, on plots that you have made. Look, I make you into a staff of life! Put the writings in your heart, and you will be protected from all kinds of toil. You will become a worthy official.

Do you not recall the (fate of) the unskilled man? His name is not known. He is ever burdened ⟨like an ass carrying⟩ in front of the scribe who knows what he is about.

Come, ⟨let me tell⟩ you the woes of (9,5) the soldier, and how many are his superiors: the general, the troop-commander, the officer who leads, the standard-bearer, the lieutenant, the scribe, the commander of fifty, and the garrison-captain. They go in and out in the halls of the palace, saying: "Get laborers!" He is awakened at any hour. One is after him as (after) a donkey. He toils until the Aten sets in his darkness of night. He is hungry, his belly hurts; he is dead while yet alive. When he receives the grain-ration, having been released from duty, it is not good for grinding.

He is called up for Syria. He may not rest. There are no clothes, no sandals. The weapons of war are assembled at the fortress of Sile. (10,1) His march is uphill through mountains. He drinks water every third day; it is smelly and tastes of salt. His body is ravaged by illness. The enemy comes, surrounds him with missiles, and life recedes from him. He is told: "Quick, forward, valiant soldier! Win for yourself a good name!" He does not know what he is about. His body is weak, his legs fail him. When victory is won, the captives are handed over to his majesty, to be taken to Egypt. The foreign woman faints on the march; she hangs herself ⟨on⟩ (10,5) the soldier's neck. His knapsack drops, another grabs it while he is burdened with the woman. His wife and children are in their village; he dies and does not reach it. If he comes out alive, he is worn out from marching. Be he at large, be he detained, the soldier suffers. If he leaps and joins the deserters, all his people are imprisoned. He dies on the edge of the desert, and there is none to perpetuate his name. He suffers in death as in life. A big sack is brought for him; he does not know his resting place.

Be a scribe, and be spared from soldiering! You call and one says: "Here I am." You are safe from torments. Every man seeks to raise himself up. Take note of it!

9. The pupil wishes to build a mansion for his teacher

Furthermore. (To) the royal scribe and chief overseer of the cattle of Amen-Re, King of Gods, Nebmare-nakht. The scribe Wenemdiamun greets his lord: (11,1) In life, prosperity, and health! This letter is to inform my lord. Another message to my lord. I grew into a youth at your side. You beat my back; your teaching entered my ear. I am like a pawing horse. Sleep does not enter my heart by day; nor is it upon me at night. (For I say): I will serve my lord just as a slave serves his master.

I shall build a new mansion for you ⟨on⟩ the ground of your town, with trees (planted) on all its sides. There are stables within it. Its barns are full of barley and emmer, wheat, ⌈cumin,⌉ dates, (11,5) ḥrw-bik, gmnn, beans, lentils, coriander,[8] peas, seed-grain, 'dn, flax, herbs, reeds, rushes, ybr, ištpn, dung for the winter, alfa grass, reeds, rdmtgrass, produced by the basketful. Your herds abound in draft animals, your cows are pregnant. I will make for you five aruras of cucumber beds to the south.

10. The teacher has built a mansion

(12,1) Raia[9] has built a beautiful mansion; it lies opposite Edjo. He has built it on the border. It is ⌐constructed¬ like a work of eternity. It is planted with trees on all sides. A channel was dug in front of it. The lapping of waves sounds in one's sleep. One does not tire of looking at it. One is gay at its door and drunk in its halls. Handsome doorposts of limestone, carved and chiseled. Beautiful doors, freshly carved. Walls inlaid with lapis lazuli.

Its barns are supplied with grain, are bulging with abundance. Fowl yard and aviary are filled with geese; byres filled with cattle. A bird pool full of geese; horses in the stable. Barges, ferryboats, and new cattle boats (12,5) are moored at its quay. Young and old, the poor have come to live around it. Your provisions last; there is abundance for all who come to you.

You walk about on new lands and high lands without limit. Their grain is more abundant than the pond water that was there before. Crews land at the quay to make festive the barns with countless heaps for the Lord of Thebes. Its west side is a pond for snaring geese of all kinds, a resort of hunters from the very beginning. One of its ponds has more fish than a lake. Its 'h-birds are like marsh birds.

Happiness dwells within. No one says, "If only!" Many stables are around it, and grazing fields for cattle. Goats abound, kids caper; the many shorthorns are lowing. There are glens rich in green plants in summer and in winter. Fish abound in their basins: bulti-fish, $šn$-fish, dss-fish. The fish are more plentiful than the sands of the shore; one cannot reach the end of them.

Amun himself established it. The plantations are his in truth. You sit in their shade; you eat their fruit. Garlands are made for you of their (13a,1) branches; you are drunken with their wines. Boats are built for you of their pines, a chariot of their $t3g3$-trees. You flourish and prosper every day. The sustenance of Amun is with you, O Raia, chief overseer of the cattle of Amun!

11. An encomium of the teacher

You are nimble-handed with the censer, before the Lord of Gods at his every appearance.[10]

(13b,1) You are father of the god in command of the mysteries, with censer in your right, byssus in your left; the censer in your fist blesses your lord.

You are a noble priest in the House of Ptah, versed in all the mysteries in the House of the Prince.

You are the burial priest of Kamutef, chief seer of Re in Thebes, offerer of his oblations.

You are swift-footed at the Sokar-feast, drawing Egypt's people to your lord with the flail.

(13b,5) You are graceful with the libation vase, pouring, censing, and calling the praises.

You are nimble-handed when you circulate the offerings, foremost in calling the daily praises.

You are he who holds the Eye of Mut, mistress of heaven, on the first day of her procession in Ashru.

You are the water-pourer of Khons in Thebes, on the day of circulating offerings in the House of the Prince.

You are wise in planning, skilled in speech; farseeing at all times; what you do succeeds.

You are a judge of hearts; you resemble the Ibis; wise in all ways like the Eye and the Ear.[11]

(14,1) You are the good champion of your people; your great meals overflow like Hapy.

You are rich in food, you know how to proffer it, to all whom you love, like a surging sea.

You are a magistrate who is calm, a son of praised ones; loved by all, and praised by the king.

You are a man of high standing since birth; your house overflows with foods.

(14,5) You are rich in fields, your barns are full; grain clung to you on the day you were born.

You are rich in teams, your sails are bright; your barges on the deep are like jasper.

You are rich in crews skilled in rowing; their shouts please as they carry and load.

You are one weighty of counsel who weighs his answer; since birth you have loathed coarse language.

You are handsome in body, gracious in manner, beloved of all people as much as Hapy.

You are a man of choice words, who is skilled in saying them; all you say is right, you abhor falsehood.

(15,1) You are one who sits grandly in your house; your servants answer speedily; beer is poured copiously; all who see you rejoice in good cheer.

You serve your lord, you nourish your people; whatever you say soothes the heart.

You are one who offers the beer-jug and fills the bowl; one beloved of the herdsman[12] when the offering is made.

(15,5) You are one who directs the jubilees ⟨for⟩ his lord, one who lays the Nine Bows under his feet, one who provides for his army.

NOTES

1. *Bw3t*, the marsh thicket, signifies the joys of hunting and fishing.

2. The simile is mixed. It begins as a criticism of the pupil's heart (i.e., mind) which is "dense," and proceeds to describe the finished stone obelisk which fulfills its function, in contrast with the idle pupil who does not.

3. Compare the Middle Kingdom composition known as the *Satire of the Trades*. The Ramesside texts on this theme are in the same satirical vein. All occupations except that of the scribe are derided and ridiculed through exaggerated and farcical descriptions of their hardships.

4. I emend the unknown *bḥ* to *dbḥ*, "vat," which occurs in the *Satire of the Trades*: "The cobbler suffers much among his vats of oil" (P. Sallier II.8,1-2).

5. The word is obscure but the context suggests a man who guards and cleans the temple at night and makes it ready for the morning service.

6. A joking alteration of the teacher's title.

7. Despite the wrong determinative, *s3.f n i3wt.f* undoubtedly means "He whose back is turned to his job." This conclusion was also reached by H. Satzinger, *JEA*, 59 (1973), 227-228.

8. *Š3w* seems to be more than one type of plant. It is in parallelism with "vegetables" in the *Satire of the Trades* (P. Sallier II.6,7), and in the sun-temple of Ni-user-re it is a water plant eaten by fish; see Edel, *Inschriften*, I, 217.

9. Nickname of Nebmare-nakht.

10. The encomium is metrically structured. Each period begins with *mntk*, "you are," and consists of two, three, or four sentences or clauses.

11. Sight and hearing personified as divinities.

12. Literally, "he who drives the calves," that is, the king performing a harvest ceremony. It was studied by A. M. Blackman and H. W. Fairman in *JEA*, 35 (1949), 98-112, and *JEA*, 36 (1950), 63-81.

THE IMMORTALITY OF WRITERS

P. Chester Beatty IV = P. British Museum 10684

Verso 2,5-3,11

The verso of the papyrus contains a group of school texts to which Gardiner gave the name "A Student's Miscellany." On page 2, line 5, there begins the text here translated, an interesting disquisition on the immortality of books and authors. Writings, says the scribe, bestow on their authors an afterlife more real and durable than that provided by the stone-hewn tomb; for men's bodies turn to dust and their tombs crumble.

Here the skepticism concerning man's immortality, which first found expression in the Middle Kingdom *Harper's Song from the Tomb of King Intef*, reaches a remarkable climax. Where the Harper's Song had deplored the disappearance of tombs and the absence of solid knowledge about life after death, the Ramesside author found an answer: Bodies decay but books last, and they alone perpetuate the names of their authors. To make his point, the scribe enumerates the famous authors of the past. Yet the claim that only writers are immortal is astonishing on two counts. First the fact that the vast majority of Egyptian literary works were produced anonymously. Second, the writer's disregard for the belief in a *transformed* existence after death for which the buried corpse was merely the point of departure. Thus, unless the author was indulging in hyperbole, he is voicing a rationalist skepticism which surpasses that of the Harper' Song in boldness and radicalism.

The text is composed in the orational style. The presence of a metrical scheme was recognized by Schott in his translation. Since a metrical organization does not require perfect symmetry, the sentence division is not always entirely clear. It is, moreover, obscured by scribal errors. There are no verse-points; but the text is divided into sections by means of rubrication.

Publication: Gardiner, *Hieratic Papyri*, I, pp. 38-39, and II, pls. 18-19.

Translation: Schott, *Liebeslieder*, pp. 155-157.   J. A. Wilson in *ANET*, pp. 431-432.

(2,5) If you but do this, you are versed in writings.
As to those learned scribes,
Of the time that came after the gods,[1]
They who foretold the future,
Their names have become everlasting,
While they departed, having finished their lives,
And all their kin are forgotten.

They did not make for themselves tombs of copper,
With stelae of metal from heaven.[2]
They knew not how to leave heirs,
Children [of theirs] to pronounce their names;
They made heirs for themselves of books,
Of Instructions they had composed.

They gave themselves [the scroll as lector]-priest,
The writing-board as loving-son.[3]
Instructions are their tombs,
The reed pen is their child,
The stone-surface their wife.
People great and small
Are given them as children,
For the scribe, he is their leader.

Their portals and mansions have crumbled,
Their *ka*-servants are [gone];
Their tombstones are covered with soil,
Their graves are forgotten.
Their name is pronounced over their books,
Which they made while they had being;
Good is the memory of their makers,
It is for ever and all time!

Be a scribe, take it to heart,
That your name become (3,1) as theirs.
Better is a book than a graven stela,
Than a solid ⌐tomb-enclosure.¬
They[4] act as chapels and tombs
In the heart of him who speaks their name;
Surely useful in the graveyard
Is a name in people's mouth!

Man decays, his corpse is dust,
All his kin have perished;
But a book makes him remembered
Through the mouth of its reciter.
Better is a book than a well-built house,
Than tomb-chapels in the west;
Better than a solid mansion,
Than a stela in the temple!

Is there one here like Hardedef?
Is there another like Imhotep?
None of our kin is like Neferti,
Or Khety, the foremost among them.
I give you the name of Ptah-emdjehuty,
Of Khakheperre-sonb.
Is there another like Ptahhotep,
Or the equal of Kaires?[5]
Those sages who foretold the future,
What came from their mouth occurred;
It is found as ⟨their⟩ pronouncement,
It is written in their books.
The children of others are given to them
To be heirs as their own children.
They hid their magic (3,10) from the masses,
It is read in their Instructions.
Death made their names forgotten
But books made them remembered!

NOTES

1. I.e., the early days of mankind when the gods had ceased to live on earth.

2. Iron.

3. The person who maintained the funerary cult.

4. The books.

5. An interesting list of sages of the past, most of them known to us through the survival of works attributed to them.

PART SIX

Love Poems

Four manuscripts containing love poems are known. They are: Papyrus Chester Beatty I; Papyrus Harris 500; a Turin Papyrus fragment; and a fragmentary Cairo Museum Vase.

The handsome and well-preserved *Papyrus Chester Beatty I* contains, along with other texts, three collections of love poems. They are: (I.a) An integrated cycle of seven stanzas, each with a numbered stanza heading, and the whole introduced by a title. The cycle occupies Section C 1-5 on the *verso* of the papyrus. (I.b) A sequence of three poems, lacking a numbering device but held together by their interrelated content. It occupies Section G 1-2 of the *verso*. (I.c) A loose collection of seven poems, not integrated as a cycle but held together by an introductory title. It occupies a page and a half on pages 16 and 17 of the *recto*. The translations given below contain the complete cycles I.a and I.b, and poems 3, 4, 6, and 7 of collection I.c.

Papyrus Harris 500 (= P. British Museum 10060) also has three collections of love poems. Unfortunately, the papyrus is in a very poor state of preservation, and the poems have many lacunae, scribal errors, and other obscurities. The first collection (II.a) consists of eight poems not connected with one another. There probably was an introductory heading but it is lost. Of the eight poems, numbers 5, 6, and 7 are rendered below. The second collection (II.b) also has eight poems. These too are essentially independent of one another, but there is some continuity of themes and the introductory heading is preserved. Of this group, numbers 2, 3, 6, 7, and 8 are translated here. The third collection (II.c) is an integrated cycle of three poems, each beginning with the name of a flower. The first two poems are complete, the third is a fragment. Numbers 1 and 2 are given below.

The short and fragmentary collection of the Turin Papyrus has been omitted here. Our final selection (III) consists of two poems from the *Cairo Vase*.

In their introductory titles some of the collections are called "sayings," others are called "songs." Calling them "love poems" rather than "love songs" is not meant to deny the probability that many of them were sung, but is designed to emphasize their literary origin. The freshness, immediacy, and universality of these poems should not mislead the reader into believing them to be the spontaneous outpourings of unlettered young lovers. Their style, prosody, and choise of words, all bear the stamp of deliberate, literate artistry.

The form basic to all the poems is the direct first-person speech of either a young man or a young woman. It is a monologue addressed to the speaker's own heart. In the seven stanzas of the first Chester Beatty cycle there is a regular alternation of male and female speakers. The other collections do not have this regularity. The lovers refer to each other as "brother" and "sister," these words being the normal terms of endearment in ancient Egyptian usage.

Though sophisticated in the context of their own times, the poems have the conceptual simplicity and the terseness of language that are the hallmarks of ancient Egyptian literature. That simplicity and terseness must be retained in the translations. Some recent renderings of Egyptian love poems exhibit a typically modern lush and mannered eroticism which is quite alien to the ancient Egyptian. These renderings are so unfaithful to the letter and spirit of the originals as to be undeserving of the name "translations."

Publication: I. The poems of P. Chester Beatty I: Gardiner, *Chester Beatty I*, pp. 27-38 and pls. 16-17, 22-26, and 29-30.

II. The poems of P. Harris 500: Müller, *Liebespoesie*, pp. 14-28 and pls. 2-15.   E. A. W. Budge, *Facsimiles of Egyptian Hieratic Papyri in the British Museum, Second Series* (London, 1923), pls. 41-46.

III. The Cairo Vase: Posener, *Ostr. hiér.*, Vol. II, fasc. 3 (1972), pp. 43-44 and pls. 75-79a.

Translation: P. Gilbert, *La poésie égyptienne*, (2d ed.; Brussels, 1949), pp. 42-79.   Schott, *Liebeslieder*, pp. 39-69.   Simpson, *Literature*, pp. 296-325.

Study: A. Hermann, *Altägyptische Liebesdichtung* (Wiesbaden, 1959).

FROM PAPYRUS CHESTER BEATTY I

I.a A Cycle of Seven Stanzas[1]

Beginning of the sayings of the great happiness

The *One*, the sister without peer,
The handsomest of all!
She looks like the rising morning star
At the start of a happy year.
Shining bright, fair of skin,
Lovely the look of her eyes,
Sweet the speech of her lips,
She has not a word too much.
Upright neck, shining breast,
Hair true lapis lazuli;
Arms surpassing gold,
Fingers like lotus buds.
Heavy thighs, narrow waist,
Her legs parade her beauty;
With graceful step she treads the ground,
Captures my heart by her movements.
She causes all men's necks
To turn about to see her;
Joy has he whom she embraces,
He is like the first of men!
When she steps outside she seems
Like that other *One*![2]

Second Stanza

My *brother* torments my heart with his voice,
He makes sickness take hold of me;

He is neighbor to my mother's house,
And I cannot go to him!
Mother is right in charging him thus:
"Give up seeing her!"
It pains my heart to think of him,
I am possessed by love of him.
Truly, he is a foolish one,
But I resemble him;
He knows not my wish to embrace him,
Or he would write to my mother.
Brother, I am promised to you
By the Gold[3] of women!
Come to me that I see your beauty,
Father, Mother will rejoice!
My people will hail you all together,
They will hail you, O my *brother*!

Third Stanza

My heart *devised* to see her beauty
While sitting down in her house;
On the way I met Mehy on his chariot,
With him were his young men.
I knew not how to avoid him:
Should I stride on to pass him?
But the river was the road,
I knew no place for my feet.
My heart, you are very foolish,
Why accost Mehy?
If I pass before him,
I tell him my movements;
Here, I'm yours, I say to him,
Then he will shout my name,
And assign me to the first . . .
Among his *followers*.[4]

Fourth Stanza

My heart *flutters* hastily,
When I think of my love of you;
It lets me not act sensibly,[5]
It leaps ⟨from⟩ its place.
It lets me not put on a dress,
Nor wrap my scarf[6] around me;
I put no paint upon my eyes,
I'm even not anointed.

"Don't wait, go there,"[7] says it to me,
As often as I think of him;
My heart, don't act so stupidly,
Why do you play the fool?
Sit still, the brother comes to you,
And many eyes as well![8]
Let not the people say of me:
"A woman fallen through love!"
Be steady when you think of him,
My heart, do not *flutter*!

Fifth Stanza

I *praise* the Golden,[9] I worship her majesty,
I extol the Lady of Heaven;
I give adoration to Hathor,
Laudations to my Mistress!
I called to her, she heard my plea,
She sent my mistress to me;
She came by herself to see me,
O great wonder that happened to me!
I was joyful, exulting, elated,
When they said: "See, she is here!"
As she came, the young men bowed,
Out of great love for her.
I make devotions to my goddess,
That she grant me my sister as gift;
Three days now[10] that I pray[11] to her name,
Five days since she went from me!

Sixth Stanza

I *passed*[12] before his house,
I found his door ajar;
My brother stood by his mother,
And all his brothers with him.
Love of him captures the heart
Of all who tread the path;
Splendid youth who has no peer,
Brother outstanding in virtues!
He looked at me as I passed by,
And I, by myself, rejoiced;
How my heart exulted in gladness,
My brother, at your sight!
If only the mother knew my heart,
She would have understood by now;

O Golden, put it in her heart,
Then will I hurry to my brother!
I will kiss him before his companions,
I would not weep before them;
I would rejoice at their understanding
That you acknowledge me!
I will make a feast for my goddess,
My heart leaps to go;
To let me see my brother tonight,
O happiness in *passing*!

Seventh Stanza

Seven days since I saw my sister,
And sickness invaded me;
I am heavy in all my limbs,
My body has forsaken me.
When the physicians come to me,
My heart rejects their remedies;
The magicians are quite helpless,
My sickness is not discerned.
To tell me "She is here" would revive me!
Her name would make me rise;
Her messenger's coming and going,
That would revive my heart!
My sister is better than all prescriptions,
She does more for me than all medicines;
Her coming to me is my amulet,
The sight of her makes me well!
When she opens her eyes my body is young,
Her speaking makes me strong;
Embracing her expels my malady—
Seven days since she went from me!

NOTES

1. Text: Gardiner, *op. cit.*, pls. 22-26: *Verso*, C 1-5. The cycle consists
of seven stanzas, each headed by the word "house," which means
"stanza," or, "chapter," followed by a numeral. In addition, the first line
of each stanza repeats the appropriate numeral, or uses a homophone of
the numeral; and the same word recurs as the final word of the stanza.
Thus the first stanza begins and ends with the word "one," while the
second begins and ends with the word "brother," which is a homophone
of the numeral "two," and so on. The stanzas are spoken by a young man
and a young woman in alternating sequence.

The texts are written with verse-points; sometimes these are misplaced. The sentences form distichs and quatrains.

2. The "One" is the sun, viewed as the sole eye of heaven.

3. Hathor, patroness of love, was called "the gold" or "the golden one."

4. This whole stanza is unfortunately rather obscure. It has been concluded that Mehy, spelled like the word *mhy*, "flax," is the name of a prince (see P. C. Smither, *JEA*, 34 (1948), 116, and A. Hermann, *op. cit.*, pp. 105-108), but his role is enigmatic. Nor is it clear what the consequences of encountering him are, for the phrase *t3 kpyw tpy* is obscure. I agree with Hermann that the speaker of the stanza is the young man, not the young woman. The final *m-ḥt* hardly matches the beginning *ḥmt*.

5. Literally, "go about like a person."

6. *Bhn* has been rendered "fan." But the word for fan is *bḥt* and is written with the fan determinative, while the word written here as *bhn* has the cloth determinative.

7. *Pḥ ḥnw* can hardly mean "go home," for the girl's monologue indicates that she is in her home. I take it to mean "go to *his* home." The verse-point after *ḥnw* is misplaced.

8. I.e., Many people will be watching you.

9. Ever since I found "O golden" in the poem "Calypso's Island" by Archibald MacLeish ("She is not beautiful as you, O golden") I think it permissible to write "golden" rather than "golden one."

10. Literally, "Three days till yesterday."

11. The verse-point is misplaced.

12. The scribe wrote, "He passed," which is clearly wrong. The masculine and feminine suffixes are frequently garbled by the scribes of these texts.

FROM PAPYRUS CHESTER BEATTY I

I.b Three Poems[1]

I

O that you came to your sister swiftly!
Like a swift envoy of the king;
The heart of his lord frets for his message,
His heart is anxious to hear it.
All stables are held ready for him,
He has horses at the stations;
The chariot is harnessed in its place,
He may not pause on the road.
When he arrives at his sister's house,
His heart will jubilate!

II

O that you came to ⟨your sister swiftly⟩!
Like a horse of the king;

Picked from a thousand steeds of all kinds,
The choicest of the stables.
It is singled out in its feed,
Its master knows its paces;
When it hears the sound of the whip,
There's no holding it back.
There's no chief of charioteers
Who could overtake it.
Sister's heart is aware:
He is not far from her!

III

O that you came to your sister swiftly,
Like a bounding gazelle in the wild;
Its feet reel, its limbs are weary,
Terror has entered its body.
A hunter pursues it with his hounds,
They do not see ⟨it in⟩ its dust;
It sees a resting place as a ⌐trap⌐[2]
It takes the river as road.
May you attain her hiding-place,
Before your hand is kissed four times;
As you pursue your sister's love,
The Golden gives her to you, my friend!

NOTES

1. Text: Gardiner, *op. cit.*, pls. 29-30: *Verso*, G 1-2.
2. An illegible word.

FROM PAPYRUS CHESTER BEATTY I

I.c A Collection[1]

Beginning of the sweet sayings found in a text collection, made by[2]
the scribe of the necropolis, Nakht-Sobk.

3

How well she knows to cast the noose,
And yet not pay the cattle tax!
She casts the noose on me with her hair,
She captures me with her eye;
She curbs me with her necklace,
She brands me with her seal ring.

4

Why do you argue with your heart?
Go after her, embrace her!
As Amun lives, I come to you,
My cloak over my arm.

6

What my sister did to me!
Why keep silent about it?
Left me to stand at her house door,
While she herself went inside!
She didn't say, "Come in, young man,"
She was deaf tonight.

7

I passed by her house in the dark,
I knocked and no one opened;
A good night to our doorkeeper,
Bolt, I will open!
Door, you are my fate,
You are my own good spirit;
Our ox will be slaughtered inside,
Door, do not show your strength!
We'll offer a long-horn to the bolt,
A short-horn to the lock,
A wild goose to the door-posts,
Its fat to the key.
And the choice cuts of our ox
Are for the carpenter's boy;
So he'll make for us a bolt of reeds,
And a door of woven grass.
Now any time the brother comes,
He'll find her house is open;
He'll find a bed laid with fine sheets,
A lovely girl is with them.
The girl will tell me: "My house here,
Its owner is the mayor's son!"

NOTES

1. Text: Gardiner, *op. cit.*, pls. 16-17: *Recto*, 16-17. The text is written with verse-points and paragraph signs. The poems in this collection are gay, light, and humorous.

2. The formula *ir.n* usually means "copied by" a scribe who is not the author. But U. Luft in a new study (*ZÄS*, 99 (1973), 108-116) concludes that in Ramesside times *ir.n* could also convey the claim of authorship, whether or not the claim was true.

FROM PAPYRUS HARRIS 500

II.a The First Collection[1]

5

I fare north in the ferry
By the oarsman's stroke,
On my shoulder my bundle of reeds;
I am going to Memphis
To tell Ptah, Lord of Truth:
Give me my sister tonight!
The river is as if of wine,
Its rushes are Ptah,
Sakhmet is its foliage,
Iadet[2] its buds,
Nefertem its lotus blossoms.
[The Golden] is in joy
When earth brightens in her beauty;
Memphis is a bowl of fruit
Placed before the fair-of-face![3]

6

I shall lie down at home
And pretend to be ill;
Then enter the neighbors to see me,
Then comes my sister with them.
She will make the physicians unneeded,
She understands my illness!

7

The mansion of my sister,
With door in the center of her house,
Its door-leaves are open,
The bolt is sprung,
My sister is angry!
If only I were made doorkeeper!
Then I would make her rage at me,

Then I would hear her angry voice,
And be a child in fear of her!

1. Text: Müller, *op. cit.*, pls. 4-5: *Recto*, 2. No verse-points are used;
but the poems are separated by paragraph signs.
2. An unknown divinity.
3. Epithet of Ptah.

FROM PAPYRUS HARRIS 500

II.b The Second Collection[1]

Beginning of the delightful, beautiful songs of your beloved sister
as she comes from the fields.

2

The voice of the wild goose shrills,
It is caught by its bait;
My love of you pervades me,
I cannot loosen it.
I shall retrieve my nets,
But what do I tell my mother,
To whom I go daily,
Laden with bird catch?
I have spread no snares today,
I am caught in my love of you!

3

The wild goose soars and swoops,
It alights on the net;
Many birds swarm about,
I have work to do.
I am held fast by my love,
Alone, my heart meets your heart,
From your beauty I'll not part!

6

The voice of the dove is calling,
It says: "It's day! Where are you?"

O bird, stop scolding me!
I found my brother on his bed,
My heart was overjoyed;
Each said: "I shall not leave you,
My hand is in your hand;
You and I shall wander
In all the places fair."
He makes me the foremost of women,
He does not aggrieve my heart.

7

My gaze is fixed on the garden gate,
My brother will come to me;
Eyes on the road, ears straining,
I wait for him who neglects me.[2]
I made my brother's love my sole concern,
About him my heart is not silent;
It sends me a fleet-footed messenger
Who comes and goes to tell me:
"He deceives you, in other words,[3]
He found another woman,
She is dazzling to his eyes."
Why vex another's heart to death?[4]

8

My heart thought of my love of you,
When half of my hair was braided;
I came at a run to find you,
And neglected my hairdo.
Now if you let me braid my hair,
I shall be ready in a moment.

NOTES

1. Text: Müller, *op. cit.*, pls. 8-13: *Recto*, 4-6.
2. Not a personal name, but the verb *mhi*, "neglect," preceded by the article. Except for Prince Mehy (spelled *mhy*) no personal names occur in the love poems.
3. For *m ky dd*, as recognized by Müller, *op. cit.*, p. 25 n. 8, and discussed by Gardiner, *JEA*, 24 (1938), 243-244.
4. The whole second half of the poem is difficult and has been rendered in various ways.

FROM PAPYRUS HARRIS 500

II.c The Third Collection[1]

Beginning of the songs of delight

1

Portulaca:[2] apportioned to you is my heart,
I do for you what it desires,
When I am in your arms.
My longing for you is my eye-paint,
When I see you my eyes shine;
I press close to you to look at you,
Beloved of men, who rules my heart!
O happiness of this hour,
Let the hour go on forever!
Since I have lain with you,
You raised up my heart;
Be it sad or gay,
Do not leave me!

2

Saam-plants here summon us,
I am your sister, your best one;
I belong to you like this plot of ground
That I planted with flowers
And sweet-smelling herbs.
Sweet is its stream,
Dug by your hand,
Refreshing in the northwind.
A lovely place to wander in,
Your hand in my hand.
My body thrives, my heart exults
At our walking together;
Hearing your voice is pomegranate wine,
I live by hearing it.
Each look with which you look at me
Sustains me more than food and drink.

NOTES

1. Text: Müller, *op. cit.*, pls. 14-15: *Recto*, 7.
2. Each poem begins with the name of a flower, followed by a verb of similar sound. These wordplays cannot be imitated adequately. The *mḥmḥ*-flower has been guessed to be the portulaca.

FROM THE CAIRO VASE 1266 + 25218

III. A Collection[1]

My sister's love is on yonder side,
The river is between our bodies;
The waters are mighty at [flood]-time,
A crocodile waits in the shallows.
I enter the water and brave the waves,
My heart is strong on the deep;
The crocodile seems like a mouse to me,
The flood as land to my feet.
It is her love that gives me strength,
It makes a water-spell for me;
I gaze at my heart's desire,
As she stands facing me!

My sister has come, my heart exults,
My arms spread out to embrace her;
My heart bounds in its place,
Like the red fish in its pond.
O night, be mine forever,
Now that my queen has come!

NOTES

1. Before it was broken, this tall vase had been inscribed with a large collection of love poems. Three fragments of the vase have been known since 1897. Twenty-eight more fragments were found in the excavation of Deir el-Medina in 1949-1951. The thirty-one pieces have now been published as an integrated text by G. Posener in his *Ostr. hiér.*, II/3, pp. 43-44 and pls. 74-79a. The vase is still far from complete, hence most of the poems have lengthy lacunae. The poems are separated by paragraph signs; there are no verse-points.

Two complete poems are translated here. Both had been known in part from the original three fragments. But in translating them the lacunae, now filled by the new fragments, had not been correctly gauged and restored. Hence the earlier translations are obsolete. The two poems begin on plate 76, line 11.

PART SEVEN

Tales

Apart from *The Destruction of Mankind*, which is probably a tale of the Middle Kingdom, the five best preserved tales of the New Kingdom are assembled here. Except for the *Report of Wenamun*, which may be a true account, the New Kingdom tales are works of the imagination. This is not to say that they are folktales. They are, on the contrary, complex and deliberate artistic creations. The language they employ is the vernacular of the New Kingdom, handled by the different authors with greater or lesser verbal wealth and sophistication. Most New Kingdom tales, including the ones not translated here, make use of the authors' knowledge of foreign places and peoples, and exhibit the cosmopolitan outlook characteristic of Egypt's imperial age.

Mythological material is employed in varying degrees. The tale of *Horus and Seth* is set entirely among the gods. It is a coarsely humorous retelling of the ancient myth of the struggle between Horus and Seth for the kingship of Egypt, which had fallen vacant through the death of Osiris. The tale of *Truth and Falsehood* also takes place among the gods, but the protagonists are personified concepts, and their personalities and actions are those of human beings. Thus the tale is an allegory rather than a myth. In the story of the *Two Brothers* the mythological material forms a substratum and a background. Bata and Anubis are brothers who act out human lives, albeit that Bata is endowed with superhuman powers. Parts of the tale have some connection with a myth of the gods Anubis and Bata, who were worshiped in the Seventeenth Nome of Upper Egypt, a late version of which is found in the Papyrus Jumilhac. In the story of the *Doomed Prince* all the characters are completely human, but the animals possess fairytale powers. Thus all the tales employ a blending of the human and the divine spheres.

The *Report of Wenamun* does not fully belong in this company, for it is generally believed that the story is based on the account of an actual mission. Not that the *Report* is the official account; but rather that it is the imaginative and humorous literary reworking of an actual report. This is of course not a certainty. The story may be wholly fictitious, even though it sketches a true historical background. In its central theme it is a New Kingdom counterpart of the Middle Kingdom *Story of Sinuhe*. Where *Sinuhe* was a tale of personal success abroad, set on the background of Egypt's might and prestige, the *Report of Wenamun* is a tale of misfortunes and failures in the context of Egypt's loss of empire and loss of prestige. Its most remarkable quality is the ironic detachment with which the author describes the insults to which the Egyptian envoy is subjected. Wenamun's triumphs, such as they are, are due to the astute rhetoric of this lone envoy, who does not even have a ship of his own, and whose only protection abroad is the still effective renown of the god Amun.

THE DESTRUCTION OF MANKIND

This mythological tale forms the first part of a longer text known as "The Book of the Cow of Heaven," which is inscribed in five royal tombs of the New Kingdom (the tombs of Tutankhamun, Seti I, Ramses II, Ramses III, and Ramses VI). The first part relates how the sun-god Re set out to destroy the human race because mankind was plotting rebellion against him. But after an initial slaughter, carried out by the "Eye of Re," the sun-god relented and devised a ruse to stop the goddess from further killing. The interest of the tale lies, of course, in the theme of human wickedness arousing the divine wrath and resulting in a partial destruction of mankind, a theme that received its classic treatment in the Mesopotamian and Biblical stories of the Flood.

The second part of the text (not translated here) tells how the sun-god, weary of government, withdrew into the sky and charged the other great gods with the rule of heaven and earth.

Though recorded in the New Kingdom, the text is written in Middle Egyptian, and it probably originated in the Middle Kingdom. The tale thus stands apart from the other stories in this section, all of which are written in Late Egyptian, the vernacular of the New Kingdom.

Publication: Ch. Maystre, "Le livre de la vache du ciel," *BIFAO*, 40 (1941), 53-115: the whole text; 58-73: The Destruction of Mankind.

Translation: Erman, *Literature*, pp. 47-49.   Wilson in *ANET*, pp. 10-11.   A. Piankoff, *The Shrines of Tut-Ankh-Amon* (New York, 1955; Harper Torchbook, 1962), pp. 27-29.   Brunner-Traut, *Märchen*, pp. 69-72.

(1) It happened [⌜in the time of the majesty of ⌝] Re, the self-created, after he had become king of men and gods together: Mankind plotted against him, while his majesty had grown old, his bones being silver, his flesh gold, his hair true lapis lazuli. When his majesty perceived the plotting of mankind against him, his majesty said to his followers: "Summon to me my Eye,[1] and Shu, Tefnut, Geb, Nut, and the fathers and mothers who were with me when I was in Nun,[2] and also the god Nun; and he shall bring his courtiers (5) with him. But bring them stealthily, lest mankind see, lest they lose heart.[3] Come with them (the gods) to the Palace, that they may give their counsel. In the end I may return to Nun, to the place where I came into being."

The gods were brought, the gods were lined up on his two sides, bowing to the ground before his majesty, that he might make his speech before the eldest father, the maker of mankind, the king of people.[4] They said to his majesty: "Speak to us, that we may hear it." Then Re said to Nun: "O eldest god in whom I came into being, and ancestor gods, look, mankind, which issued from my Eye,[5] is plotting against me. Tell me what you would do about it, for I am searching. I would not slay them until I have heard what you might (10) say about it."

Then spoke the majesty of Nun: "My son Re, god greater than his maker, more august that his creators, stay on your throne! Great is fear of you when your Eye is on those who scheme against you." Said the majesty of Re: "Look, they are fleeing to the desert, their hearts fearful that I might speak to them." They said to his majesty: "Let your Eye go and smite them for you, those schemers of evil!" No Eye is more able to smite them for you. May it go down as Hathor!"

The goddess returned after slaying mankind in the desert, and the majesty of this god said: "Welcome in peace, Hathor, Eye who did what I came for!" Said the goddess: "As you live for me, I have overpowered mankind, and it was balm to my heart." Said the majesty of Re: "I shall have power over them as king (15) by diminishing them." Thus the Powerful One (Sakhmet) came into being.[6]

The beer-mash of the night for her who would wade in their blood as far as Hnes.[7] Re said: "Summon to me swift, nimble messengers that they may run like a body's shadow!" The messengers were brought immediately, and the majesty of this god said: "Go to Yebu and bring me red ochre[8] in great quantity!" The red ochre was brought to him, and the majesty of this god ordered the Side-Lock Wearer in On[9] to grind the ochre, while maidservants crushed barley for beer. Then the red ochre was put into the beer-mash, and it became like human blood; and seven thousand jars of beer were made. Then the majesty of the King of Upper and Lower Egypt, Re came together with the gods to see the beer.

Now when the day dawned (20) on which the goddess would slay mankind in their time of traveling south,[10] the majesty of Re said: "It is good;[11] I shall save mankind by it!" And Re said: "Carry it to the place where she plans to slay mankind!" The majesty of King Re rose early before dawn, to have this sleeping draught poured out. Then the fields were flooded three palms high with the liquid by the might of the majesty of this god. When the goddess came in the morning she found them flooded, and her gaze was pleased by it.[12] She drank and it pleased her heart. She returned drunk without having perceived mankind. The majesty of Re said to the goddess: "Welcome in peace, O gracious one!" Thus beautiful women came into being in the town of Imu.[13]

NOTES

1. The eye of the sun-god is viewed as a being distinct from him.
2. The primordial water in which creation began.
3. Literally, "lest their heart flee."
4. The god Nun.
5. An allusion to the idea that mankind (*rmṯ*) issued from a tear (*rmyt*) of the sun-god.
6. A word play on *sḫm*, "power," and *sḫmt*, the lion-goddess Sakhmet.
7. This sentence serves as introduction to what follows.
8. Or hematite.
9. The high priest of Re in Heliopolis.
10. Emend to "her time of traveling south"?
11. I.e., "the beer is good."
12. Or, "her face was beautiful in it"?
13. A word play on *im3*, "gracious."

THE DOOMED PRINCE

P. Harris 500, Verso

Though usually called *The Doomed Prince*, the tale is more accurately called "The prince who was threatened by three fates"; for most scholars have come to the conclusion that the now missing ending of the tale was a happy one. A happy ending would be in keeping with the fairy-tale character of the story. Moreover, the ancient Egyptian concept of fate was a fluid one. There was no rigid determinism, no firm belief in an inescapable fate. Rather a sense that righteousness would triumph and innocence would overcome adversity.

The tale occupies pages 4,1-8,14 on the *verso* of the papyrus.

Publication: E. A. W. Budge, *Facsimiles of Egyptian Hieratic Papyri in the British Museum, Second Series* (London, 1923), pls. 48-52.   Möller, *Lesestücke*, II, 21-24.   Gardiner, *LES*, pp. 1-9.

Translation: T. E. Peet, *JEA*, 11 (1925), 227-229.   Lefèbvre, *Romans*, pp. 114-124.   Schott, *Liebeslieder*, pp. 188-192.   Brunner-Traut, *Märchen*, pp. 24-28.   E. F. Wente in Simpson, *Literature*, pp. 85-91.

Comments: W. Spiegelberg, *ZÄS*, 64 (1929), 86-87.   M. Pieper, *ZÄS*, 70 (1934), 95-97.   A. Hermann in *Mélanges Maspero*, I, 313-325.   G. Posener, *JEA*, 39 (1953), 107.

(4,1) It is said, there once was a king to whom no son had been born. [After a time his majesty] begged a son for himself from the gods of his domain, and they decreed that one should be born to him. That night he slept with his wife and she [became] pregnant. When she had completed the months of childbearing, a son was born.

Then came the Hathors to determine a fate for him. They said: "He will die through the crocodile, or the snake, or the dog." When the people who were with the child heard (it), they reported it to his majesty. Then his majesty's heart became very very sad. His majesty had [a house] of stone built [for him] upon the desert, supplied with people and with every good thing of the palace, and the child was not to go outdoors.

Now when the boy had grown, he went up to his roof, and he saw a greyhound following a man[1] who was walking on the road. He said to his servant, who was beside him: "What is it that is walking behind the man who is coming along the road?" He told him: "It is a greyhound." The boy said to him: "Have one like it brought to me." Then the servant went and reported (4,10) it to his majesty. His majesty said: "Bring him a little puppy, [so that] his heart [will not] grieve." So they brought him a greyhound.

Now when many days had passed and the boy was fully grown in all his body, he sent to his father saying: "To what purpose is my sitting here? I am committed to Fate. Let me go, that I may act according to my heart, until the god does what is in his heart." Then a chariot was harnessed for him, equipped [with] (5,1) all sorts of weapons, and [a servant was given him] as an attendant. He was ferried over to the eastern shore and was told: "Go wherever you wish," and his greyhound was with him. He went northward across the desert, following his heart and living on the best of all the desert game.

He reached the Prince of Nahrin.[2] Now the Prince of Nahrin had no children except one daughter. For her a house had been built whose window was seventy cubits away from the ground. He had sent for all the sons of all the princes of Khor[3] and told them: "He who reaches the window of my daughter, his wife she shall be." Now when many days had passed and they were at their daily pursuit, the youth passed by them. Then they took the youth to their house. They washed him; they gave fodder to his team. They did everything for the youth. They anointed him; they bandaged his feet; they (5,10) gave food to his attendant. And they said to him by way of conversation: "Whence have you come, you good youth?" He said to them: "I am the son of an officer of the land of Egypt. My mother died; my father took another wife, a stepmother. She came to hate me, and I went away, fleeing from her." Then they embraced him and kissed him on [all his body].

[Now when many days had passed], he said to the sons: "What is this you are doing [here?" They said]: "For three [months] now we are here passing (6,1) the time [in leaping. For he] who reaches [the] window of the daughter of the Prince of Nahrin [will] get her as [wife]." [He] said to them: "If only my feet did [not] hurt, I would go leaping with you." They went leaping in their daily manner, while the youth stood at a distance watching, and the gaze of the daughter of the Prince of Nahrin was upon him.

Now when many days had passed, the youth came to leap with the sons of the princes. He leaped, he reached the window of the daughter of the Prince of Nahrin. She kissed him, she embraced him on all his body. One went to inform her father and told him: "One man has reached the window of your daughter." Then the Prince questioned him saying: "Which prince's son?" They said to him: "The son of an officer who came fleeing from Egypt, away from his stepmother." Thereupon (6,10) the Prince of Nahrin became exceedingly angry. He said: "Am I to give my daughter to this fugitive from Egypt? Make him go away!"

They went and told him: "Go back where you came from!" But the daughter held him, and she swore by the god saying: "As Pre-Harakhti lives, if he is taken from me, I shall not eat, I shall not drink, I shall die right away!" The messenger went and reported to her father every ⟨word⟩ that she had said. And her ⟨father⟩ sent men to

slay him on the spot. But the daughter said to ⟨them⟩ : "As Pre lives, if
they slay him, when the sun sets I shall be dead. I will not live an hour
longer than he!"

They [went] to tell it to her father. Then her (7,1) [father had] the
[youth brought] before him [together with] his daughter. And when
[the youth stood before him] his dignity impressed[4] the Prince. He
embraced him, he kissed him on all his body; he said to him: "Tell me
about yourself, for now you are my son." He said to him: "I am the
son of an officer of the land of Egypt. My mother died; my father
took another wife. She came to hate me; I left fleeing from her."
Then he gave him his daughter as wife. He gave him a house and
fields as well as cattle and all sorts of good things.

Now when many days had passed, the youth said to his wife: "I am
given over to three fates: the crocodile, the snake, the dog." Then she
said to him: "Have the dog that follows you killed." He said to her:
"What foolishness! I will not let my dog be killed, whom I raised when
it was a puppy." So she began to watch her husband very much and did
not let him go out alone.

Now on the day on which the youth had left Egypt in his
wandering, the crocodile, (7,10) his fate [ʿhad followed himʾ] –––. It
came to be opposite him in the village in which the youth was, [ʿand it
dwelled inʾ] the lake. But there was a demon in it. The demon did not
let the crocodile come out; nor did the crocodile let the demon come
out to stroll about. As soon as the sun rose [they] stood and fought
each other every day for three months now.

And when more days had passed, the youth sat down to a feastday
in his house. Then when night had come, the youth lay down on his
bed, and sleep overwhelmed his body. Then (8,1) his wife filled a
[bowl] with [ʿwineʾ] and another bowl with beer. Thereupon a [snake]
came out [of its] hole to bite the youth. But his wife was sitting beside
him, not sleeping. [ʿShe placed the bowls beforeʾ] the snake. It drank,
it became drunk, it lay down on its back. Then [the woman had] it
hacked to pieces with her axe. They woke her husband ––––––. She
said to him: "Look, your god has given one of your fates into your
hand. He will protect [you ʿfrom the others alsoʾ]." [Then he] made
an offering to Pre, praising him and extolling his might every day.

Now when many days had passed, the youth went out for a pleasure
stroll on his estate. [ʿHis wifeʾ] did not go out [with him], but his dog
was following him. Then his dog began to speak[5] [saying: "I am your
fate]." Thereupon he ran before it. He reached the lake. He de-
scended into [the water in flight from the] dog. Then the crocodile
[seized] him and carried him off to where the demon was. [But he was
gone. The] crocodile said to the youth: "I am your fate that has come
after you. But [for three months] now I have been fighting with the

demon. Now look, I shall release you. If my [enemy returns] to fight [you shall] help me to kill the demon. For if you see the —————— the crocodile." Now when it dawned and the next day had come, [the demon] returned ——————.

NOTES

1. Literally, "a big man," i.e., an adult.
2. The kingdom of Mitanni on the upper Euphrates.
3. Syria.
4. Literally, "entered the prince."
5. E. F. Wente in Simpson, *op. cit.*, p. 90 rendered *t̠i tp-r* as "take a bite" and referred to the meaning "bite" for *tp-r*, which occurs in the medical texts. The usual meaning of *tp-r*, however, is "speech," and this meaning seems preferable to me. See also the term *t̠i-r* in *Amenemope*, 4,7 and 15,13.

THE TWO BROTHERS

P. D'Orbiney = P. Brit. Mus. 10183

This is a complex and vivid tale, rich in motifs that have parallels in later literatures. The two protagonists have some connection with a myth of the two gods, Anubis and Bata, that was told as a tradition of the Seventeenth Nome of Upper Egypt. The myth is preserved in a late form in the Papyrus Jumilhac (see below). More important than the mythological connection is the depiction of *human* characters, relationships, and feelings in a narration of sustained force. The episode of Bata and his brother's wife has a remarkable similarity with the tale of Joseph and Potiphar's wife, a similarity that has often been commented on. References to the recurrence in other literatures of the tale's folkloristic motifs will be found in the works cited, especially in Lefèbvre's and Brunner-Traut's comments to their translations.

Papyrus D'Orbiney is written in a beautiful hand by the scribe Ennana who lived at the end of the Nineteenth Dynasty.

Publication: *Select Papyri in the Hieratic Character from the Collections of the British Museum*, Part II (London, 1860), pls. 9-19.   Möller, *Lesestücke*, II, 1-20.   Gardiner, *LES*, pp. 9-29.

Translation: Lefèbvre, *Romans*, pp. 137-158.   Schott, *Liebeslieder*, pp. 193-204.   Brunner-Traut, *Märchen*, pp. 28-40.   E. F. Wente in Simpson, *Literature*, pp. 92-107.

Comments: J. Yoyotte, *RdE*, 9 (1952), 157-159.   J. Vandier, *Le Papyrus Jumilhac* (Paris [1962]), pp. 45-46, 105-106, and 114-115.   F. Jesi, *Aegyptus*, 42 (1962), 276-296.   E. Blumenthal, *ZÄS*, 99 (1973), 1-17.   For additional references see Lefèbvre, *op. cit.*, pp. 141-142, and Blumenthal, *op. cit.*, *passim*.

(1,1) It is said, there were two brothers, of the same mother and the same father. Anubis was the name of the elder, and Bata the name of the younger. As for Anubis, he had a house and a wife; and his young brother was with him as if he were a son. He was the one who made clothes for him, and he went behind his cattle to the fields. He was the one who did the plowing, and he harvested for him. He was the one who did for him all kinds of labor in the fields. Indeed, his young brother was an excellent man. There was none like him in the whole land, for a god's strength was in him.

Now when many days had passed, his young brother [was tending] his cattle according to his daily custom. And he [returned] to his house in the evening, laden with all kinds of field plants, and with milk, with wood, and with every [good thing] of the field. He placed them before his [elder brother], as he was sitting with his wife. Then he drank and ate and [went to sleep in] his stable among his cattle.

Now when it had dawned and another day had come, [he took foods] that were cooked and placed them before his elder brother. Then he took bread for himself for the fields, and he drove his cattle to let them eat in the fields. He walked behind his cattle, and they would say to him: "The grass is good in such-and-such a place." And he heard all they said and took them to the place of (2,1) good grass that they desired. Thus the cattle he tended became exceedingly fine, and they increased their offspring very much.

Now at plowing time his [elder] brother said to him: "Have a team [of oxen] made ready for us for plowing, for the soil has emerged and is right for plowing. Also, come to the field with seed, for we shall start plowing tomorrow." So he said to him. Then the young brother made all the preparations that his elder brother had told him [to make].

Now when it had dawned and another day had come, they went to the field with their [seed] and began to plow. And [their hearts] were very pleased with this work they had undertaken. And many days later, when they were in the field, they had need of seed. Then he sent his young brother, saying: "Hurry, fetch us seed from the village." His young brother found the wife of his elder brother seated braiding her hair. He said to her: "Get up, give me seed, (3,1) so that I may hurry to the field, for my elder brother is waiting for me. Don't delay." She said to him: "Go, open the storeroom and fetch what you want. Don't make me leave my hairdo unfinished."

Then the youth entered his stable and fetched a large vessel, for he wished to take a great quantity of seed. He loaded himself with barley and emmer and came out with it. Thereupon she said to him: "How much is what you have on your shoulder?" He said to her: "Three sacks of emmer and two sacks of barley, five in all, are on my shoulder." So he said to her. Then she [spoke to] him saying: "There is [great] strength in you. I see your vigor daily." And she desired to know him as a man. She got up, took hold of him, and said to him:

"Come, let us spend an hour lying together. It will be good for you. And I will make fine clothes for you."

Then the youth became like a leopard in [ʿhisʾ] anger over the wicked speech she had made to him; and she became very frightened. He rebuked her, saying: "Look, you are like a mother to me; and your husband is like a father to me. He who is older than I has raised me. What (4,1) is this great wrong you said to me? Do not say it to me again! But I will not tell it to anyone. I will not let it come from my mouth to any man." He picked up his load; he went off to the field. He reached his elder brother, and they began to work at their task. When evening had come, his elder brother returned to his house. And his young brother tended his cattle, loaded himself with all things of the field, and drove his cattle before him to let them sleep in their stable in the village.

Now the wife of his elder brother was afraid on account of the speech she had made. So she took fat and grease and made herself appear as if she had been beaten, in order to tell her husband, "It was your young brother who beat me." Her husband returned in the evening according to his daily custom. He reached his house and found his wife lying down and seeming ill. She did not pour water over his hands in the usual manner; nor had she lit a fire for him. His house was in darkness, and she lay vomiting.

Her husband said to her: "Who has had words with you?" She said to him: "No one has had words with me except your (5,1) young brother. When he came to take seed to you, he found me sitting alone. He said to me: 'Come, let us spend an hour lying together; loosen[1] your braids.' So he said to me. But I would not listen to him. 'Am I not your mother? Is your elder brother not like a father to you?' So I said to him. He became frightened and he beat ⟨me⟩, so as to prevent me from telling you. Now if you let him live, I shall die! Look, when he returns, do [not let him live]![2] For I am ill from this evil design which he was about to carry out in the morning."[3]

Then his elder brother became like a leopard. He sharpened his spear and took it in his hand. Then his elder ⟨brother⟩ stood behind the door ⟨of⟩ his stable, in order to kill his young brother when he came in the evening to let his cattle enter the stable. Now when the sun had set he loaded himself with all the plants of the field according to his daily custom. He returned, and as the lead cow was about to enter the stable she said to her herdsman: "Here is your elder brother waiting for you with his spear in order to kill you. Run away from him." He heard what his lead cow said, and (6,1) when another went in she said the same. He looked under the door of his stable and saw the feet of his elder brother as he stood behind the door with his spear in his hand. He set his load on the ground and took off at a run so as to flee. And his elder brother went after him with his spear.

Then his young brother prayed to Pre-Harakhti, saying: "My good lord! It is you who judge between the wicked and the just!" And Pre heard all his plea; and Pre made a great body of water appear between him and his elder brother, and it was full of crocodiles. Thus one came to be on the one side, and the other on the other side. And his elder brother struck his own hand twice, because he had failed to kill him. Then his young brother called to him on this side, saying: "Wait here until dawn! When the Aten has risen, I (7,1) shall contend with you before him; and he will hand over the wicked to the just! For I shall not be with you any more. I shall not be in the place in which you are. I shall go to the Valley of the Pine."

Now when it dawned and another day had come, and Pre-Harakhti had risen, one gazed at the other. Then the youth rebuked his elder brother, saying: "What is your coming after me to kill me wrongfully, without having listened to my words? For I am yet your young brother, and you are like a father to me, and your wife is like a mother to me. Is it not so that when I was sent to fetch seed for us your wife said to me: 'Come, let us spend an hour lying together'? But look, it has been turned about for you into another thing." Then he let him know all that had happened between him and his wife. And he swore by Pre-Harakhti, saying: "As to your coming to kill me wrongfully, you carried your spear on the testimony of a filthy whore!" Then he took a reed knife, cut off his phallus, and threw it into the water; and the catfish swallowed it. And he (8,1) grew weak and became feeble. And his elder brother became very sick at heart and stood weeping for him loudly. He could not cross over to where his young brother was on account of the crocodiles.

Then his young brother called to him, saying: "If you recall something evil, will you not also recall something good, or something that I have done for you? Go back to your home and tend your cattle, for I shall not stay in the place where you are. I shall go to the Valley of the Pine. But what you shall do for me is to come and look after me, when you learn that something has happened to me. I shall take out my heart and place it on top of the blossom of the pine. If the pine is cut down and falls to the ground, you shall come to search for it. If you spend seven years searching for it, let your heart not be disgusted. And when you find it and place it in a bowl of cool water, I shall live to take revenge on him who wronged me. You will know that something has happened to me when one puts a jug of beer in your hand and it ferments. Do not delay at all when this happens to you."

Then he went away to the Valley of the Pine; and his elder brother went to his home, his hand on his head and smeared with dirt.[4] When he reached his house, he killed his wife, cast her to the dogs, and sat mourning for his young brother.

Now many days after this, his young brother was in the Valley of the Pine. There was no one with him, and he spent the days hunting desert game. In the evening he returned to sleep under the pine on top of whose blossom his heart was. And after (9,1) many days he built a mansion for himself with his own hand ⟨in⟩ the Valley of the Pine, filled with all good things, for he wanted to set up a household.

Coming out of his mansion, he encountered the Ennead as they walked about administering the entire land. Then the Ennead addressed him in unison, saying: "O Bata, Bull of the Ennead, are you alone here, having left your town on account of the wife of Anubis, your elder brother? He has killed his wife and you are avenged of all the wrong done to you." And as they felt very sorry for him, Pre-Harakhti said to Khnum: "Fashion a wife for Bata, that he not live alone!" Then Khnum made a companion for him who was more beautiful in body than any woman in the whole land, for ⟨the fluid of⟩ every god was in her. Then the seven Hathors came ⟨to⟩ see her, and they said with one voice: "She will die by the knife."

He desired her very much. She sat in his house while he spent the day (10,1) hunting desert game, bringing it and putting it before her. He said to her: "Do not go outdoors, lest the sea snatch you. I cannot rescue you from it, because I am a woman like you. And my heart lies on top of the blossom of the pine. But if another finds it, I shall fight with him." Then he revealed to her all his thoughts.

Now many days after this, when Bata had gone hunting according to his daily custom, the young girl went out to stroll under the pine which was next to her house. Then she saw the sea surging behind her, and she started to run before it and entered her house. Thereupon the sea called to the pine, saying: "Catch her for me!" And the pine took away a lock of her hair. Then the sea brought it to Egypt and laid it in the place of the washermen of Pharaoh. Thereafter the scent of the lock of hair got into the clothes of Pharaoh. And the king quarreled with the royal washermen, saying: "A scent of ointment is in the clothes of Pharaoh!" He quarreled with them every day, and (11,1) they did not know what to do.

The chief of the royal washermen went to the shore, his heart very sore on account of the daily quarrel with him. Then he realized[5] that he was standing on the shore opposite the lock of hair which was in the water. He had someone go down, and it was brought to him. Its scent was found to be very sweet, and he took it to Pharaoh.

Then the learned scribes of Pharaoh were summoned, and they said to Pharaoh: "As for this lock of hair, it belongs to a daughter of Pre-Harakhti in whom there is the fluid of every god. It is a greeting to you from another country. Let envoys go to every foreign land to search for her. As for the envoy who goes to the Valley of the Pine, let many men go with him to fetch her." His majesty said: "What you have said is very good." And they were sent.

Now many days after this, the men who had gone abroad returned to report to his majesty. But those who had gone to the Valley of the Pine did not return, for Bata had killed them, leaving only one of them to report to his majesty. Then his majesty sent many soldiers and charioteers to bring her back, and (12,1) with them was a woman into whose hand one had given all kinds of beautiful ladies' jewelry. The woman returned to Egypt with her, and there was jubilation for her in the entire land. His majesty loved her very very much, and he gave her the rank of Great Lady. He spoke with her in order to make her tell about her husband, and she said to his majesty: "Have the pine felled and cut up." The king sent soldiers with their tools to fell the pine. They reached the pine, they felled the blossom on which was Bata's heart, and he fell dead at that moment.

When it had dawned and the next day had come, and the pine had been felled, Anubis, the elder brother of Bata, entered his house. He sat down to wash his hands. He was given a jug of beer, and it fermented. He was given another of wine, and it turned bad. Then he took his (13,1) staff and his sandals, as well as his clothes and his weapons, and he started to journey to the Valley of the Pine. He entered the mansion of his young brother and found his young brother lying dead on his bed. He wept when he saw his young brother lying dead. He went to search for the heart of his young brother beneath the pine under which his young brother had slept in the evening.[6] He spent three years searching for it without finding it.

When he began the fourth year, his heart longed to return to Egypt, and he said: "I shall depart tomorrow." So he said in his heart. When it had dawned and another day had come, he went to walk under the pine and spent the day searching for it. When he turned back in the evening, he looked once again in search of it and he found a fruit. He came back with it, and it was the heart of his young brother! He fetched a bowl of cool water, placed it in it, and sat down according to his daily ⟨custom⟩.

When night had come, (14,1) his heart swallowed the water, and Bata twitched in all his body. He began to look at his elder brother while his heart was in the bowl. Then Anubis, his elder brother, took

the bowl of cool water in which was the heart of his young brother and
⟨let⟩ him drink it. Then his heart stood in its place, and he became as
he had been. Thereupon they embraced each other, and they talked
to one another.

Then Bata said to his elder brother: "Look, I shall change myself
into a great bull of beautiful color, of a kind unknown to man, and
you shall sit on my back. By the time the sun has risen, we shall be
where my wife is, that I may avenge myself. You shall take me to
where the king is, for he will do for you everything good. You shall be
rewarded with silver and gold for taking me to Pharaoh. For I shall be
a great marvel, and they will jubilate over me in the whole land. Then
you shall depart to your village."

When it had dawned (15,1) and the next day had come, Bata
assumed the form which he had told his elder brother. Then Anubis,
his elder brother, sat on his back. At dawn he reached the place where
the king was. His majesty was informed about him; he saw him and
rejoiced over him very much. He made a great offering for him,
saying: "It is a great marvel." And there was jubilation over him in the
entire land. Then the king rewarded his elder brother with silver and
gold, and he dwelled in his village. The king gave him many people
and many things, for Pharaoh loved him very much, more than anyone else in the whole land.

Now when many days had passed, he[7] entered the kitchen, stood
where the Lady was, and began to speak to her, saying: "Look, I am
yet alive!" She said to him: "Who are you?" He said to her: "I am Bata.
I know that when you had the pine felled for Pharaoh, it was on
account of me, so that I should not live. Look, (16,1) I am yet alive! I
am a bull." The Lady became very frightened because of the speech
her husband had made to her. Then he left the kitchen.

His majesty sat down to a day of feasting with her. She poured
drink for his majesty, and he was very happy with her. Then she said
to his majesty: "Swear to me by God, saying: 'Whatever she will say, I
will listen to it!" He listened to all that she said: "Let me eat of the liver
of this bull; for he is good for nothing." So she said to him. He became
very vexed over what she had said, and the heart of Pharaoh was very
sore.

When it had dawned and another day had come, the king pro-
claimed a great offering, namely, the sacrifice of the bull. He sent one
of the chief royal slaughterers to sacrifice the bull. And when he had
been sacrificed and was carried on the shoulders of the men, he shook
his neck and let fall two drops of blood beside the two doorposts of his
majesty, one on the one side of the great portal of Pharaoh, and the

other on the other side. They grew into two (17,1) big Persea trees, each of them outstanding. Then one went to tell his majesty: "Two big Persea trees have grown this night—a great marvel for his majesty—beside the great portal of his majesty." There was jubilation over them in the whole land, and the king made an offering to them.

Many days after this, his majesty appeared at the audience window of lapis lazuli with a wreath of all kinds of flowers on his neck. Then he ⟨mounted⟩ a golden chariot and came out of the palace to view the Persea trees. Then the Lady came out on a team behind Pharaoh. His majesty sat down under one Persea tree ⟨and the Lady under the other. Then Bata⟩ spoke to his wife: "Ha, you false one! I am Bata! I am alive ⌐in spite of you⌐. I know that when you had ⟨the pine⟩ felled for Pharaoh, it was on account of me. And when I became a bull, you had me killed."

Many days after this, the Lady stood pouring drink for his majesty, and he was happy with her. Then she said to his majesty: "Swear to me by God, saying: 'Whatever she will say, I will listen to it!' So you shall say." He listened (18,1) to all that she said. She said: "Have the two Persea trees felled and made into fine furniture." The king listened to all that she said. After a short while his majesty sent skilled craftsmen. They felled the Persea trees of Pharaoh, and the Queen, the Lady, stood watching it. Then a splinter flew and entered the mouth of the Lady. She swallowed it, and in a moment she became pregnant. The king ⟨ordered⟩ made of them[8] whatever she desired.

Many days after this, she gave birth to a son. One went to tell his majesty: "A son has been born to you." He was fetched, and a nurse and maids were assigned to him. And there was jubilation over him in the whole land. The king sat down to a feastday and held him on his lap. From that hour his majesty loved him very much, and he designated him as (19,1) Viceroy of Kush. And many days after this, his majesty made him crown prince of the whole land.

Now many days after this, when he had spent [many years] as crown prince of the whole land, his majesty flew up to heaven.[9] Then the king[10] said: "Let my great royal officials be brought to me, that I may let them know all that has happened to me." Then his wife was brought to him. He judged her in their presence, and they gave their assent. His elder brother was brought to him, and he made him crown prince of the whole land. He ⟨spent⟩ thirty years as king of Egypt. He departed from life; and his elder brother stood in his place on the day of death.

Colophon.—It has come to a good end under the scribe of the treasury, Kagab, and the scribes of the treasury, Hori and Meremope. Written by the scribe Ennana, the owner of this book. Whoever maligns this book, Thoth will contend with him.

NOTES

1. *Wnḥ* here does not mean "to put on"; on the contrary, it means "to loosen" one's braids, as a woman does when she lies down. This meaning of *wnḥ* is known from the medical texts; see H. von Deines and W. Westendorf, *Wörterbuch der medizinischen Texte* (Berlin, 1961-1962), II, 194, where the authors write: "Der Terminus *wnḥ* bezeichnet eine Lösung zweier Teile von einander, ohne dass eine vollständige Trennung erfolgt."

2. Or restore: "You shall kill him."

3. Literally, "yesterday." The day ended at sunset.

4. Gestures of mourning.

5. *Smn*, "to establish," evolved to include the meanings "to record," and "to determine." Hence the chief washerman did not "stand still," but rather he "determined" or "realized" that he was standing opposite the lock of hair.

6. The phrasing fails to take into account that the pine has been felled.

7. The bull.

8. The Persea trees.

9. I.e., the king died.

10. Bata.

TRUTH AND FALSEHOOD

P. Chester Beatty II = P. Brit. Mus. 10682

The papyrus dates from the Nineteenth Dynasty. The tale occupies the eleven pages of the *recto*, and four pages of the *verso*. The beginning is lost, and the first four pages have numerous lacunae.

Publication: Gardiner, *LES*, pp. 30-36.   Gardiner, *Hieratic Papyri*, I, 2-6 and 135, and II, pls. 1-4.

Translation: Lefèbvre, *Romans*, pp. 159-168.   Schott, *Liebeslieder*, pp. 205-208.   Brunner-Traut, *Märchen*, pp. 40-44.   E. F. Wente in Simpson, *Literature*, pp. 127-132.

Comments: M. Pieper, *ZÄS*, 70 (1934), 92-97.   J. G. Griffiths, *JEA*, 53 (1967), 89-91.   A. Théodoridès, *RdE*, 21 (1969), 85-105.

The lost beginning may be summarized as follows: Truth and Falsehood are brothers. Falsehood, the younger brother, has denounced Truth to the Ennead. He claims that he had lent to Truth a wondrous dagger of extraordinary size, and Truth had failed to return it to him. He proceeds to describe the dagger:

[All the copper of Mount Yal had gone into the making of its blade. The timber of the grove of Coptus was its haft]. The god's tomb was its sheath. The cattle of Kal formed its belt.[1] Then Falsehood (2,2) said to the Ennead: "Let Truth [be brought], let him be blinded in both eyes, and let him be given to me as door-keeper of my house." And [the] Ennead did all that he had asked.

Now many days after this, Falsehood raised his eyes to see, and he observed the virtue of Truth, his elder brother. Then Falsehood said to two servants of Truth: "Take your master and [cast] him to a

savage lion with many lionesses ------. [So they] took him. Now as
they went up with him, Truth [said to his servants]: "Do not take [me]
------. Find me a little bread ------. Go and tell Falsehood: 'When
[we] had left [him] ------ [a lion] came out of ------.'"

Now many days after this, the Lady[2] went out [of her] house,
[accompanied by her servants. They] saw him (Truth) [lying beneath
a thicket,[3] and he was a handsome man; there was none] like [him in
the] whole land. They went [to where] the Lady was and [said]:
"Come [with] us and see (4,1) [the blind man] lying beneath the
thicket. He should be brought back and made door-keeper of our
house." The Lady said: "Hasten to him, I want to see him." They
went and brought him back. [And when the Lady] saw him she
desired him very much, for she saw that he was [handsome] in all his
[body]. He slept with her that night and knew her with the knowledge
of a man. And she conceived a son that night.

Now many days after this, she gave birth to a boy whose like did not
exist in the [whole] land. [He was] tall ------; he was like the child of
a god. He was sent to (5,1) school and learned to write very well. He
practiced all the arts of war, and he surpassed his older companions
who were at school with him. Then his companions said to him:
"Whose son are you? You don't have a father!" And they reviled him
and mocked him: "Hey, you don't have a father!"

Then the youth said to his mother: "What is the name of my
father?" I want to tell it to my companions, for they quarrel with me.
'Where is your father?' So they say; and they mock me." His mother
said to him: "You see the blind man who sits by the door; he is your
father." (6,1) So she said to him. Then he said to her: "You deserve
that your family be gathered and a crocodile be summoned."[4] The
youth brought his father inside; made him sit on an armchair; placed
a footrest under his feet; and put food before him. He gave him to
eat, he gave him to drink. Then the youth said to his father: "Who
blinded you? I will avenge you!" He said to him: "My young brother
blinded me." And he told him all that had happened to him.

He went off to avenge (7,1) his father. He took ten loaves of bread,
a staff, a pair of sandals, a waterskin, and a sword. He fetched an ox
of very beautiful color. And he went to where the herdsman of Falsehood was. He said to him: "Take for yourself these ten loaves, the
staff, the waterskin, the sword and the sandals, and guard my ox for
me until I return from town."

Now many days after this, when his ox had spent many months with
Falsehood's herdsman, Falsehood (8,1) came to the fields to view his
cattle. Then he saw the ox of the youth which was exceedingly
beautiful in color. He said to his herdsman: "Give me this ox, I want

to eat it. The herdsman said to him: "It is not mine; I cannot give it to you." Then Falsehood said to him: "Look, all my cattle are in your charge; give one of them to its owner."

Then the youth heard that Falsehood had taken his ox. He came to where the herdsman of Falsehood was and said to him: "Where is my ox? I do not see it among your cattle." The herdsman said to him: "All my cattle are yours; take (9,1) one you like. The youth said to him: "Is there another ox as big as my ox? If it stood on Amun's Island,⁵ the tip of its tail would lie on the papyrus marshes, while one of its horns would be on the western mountain and the other on the eastern mountain. The Great River⁶ is its resting place, and sixty calves are born to it daily." The herdsman said to him: "Does there exist an ox as big as you say?" Then the youth seized him and took him to where Falsehood was. And he took (10,1) Falsehood to court before the Ennead.

Then ⟨they⟩ said to the youth: "[What you have said] is false. We have never seen an ox as big as you say." The youth [said to the Ennead]: "Is there a dagger as big as you said? One that has Mount Yal in it for copper, in whose haft is [the grove] of Coptus, whose sheath consists of the tomb of the god, and its belt of the herds of Kal?" And he said to the Ennead: "Judge between Truth and Falsehood! I am his son; I have come to avenge him!"

Then Falsehood took an oath by the lord, saying: "As Amun lives, as the Ruler lives, if Truth is found alive, I shall be blinded in both eyes and shall be made door-keeper of the house of Truth!" Then (11,1) the youth [led the Ennead to where his father was] and he was found to be alive. Then they [inflicted punishment upon Falsehood. He was smitten] with five open wounds, blinded in [both his eyes, and made door-keeper of] the house of Truth. ------ [thus they settled the dispute] between Truth and Falsehood ------.

Colophon: [It has been finished successfully under the scribe of] the temple, the pure of hands, Amen---, [the scribe of] the palace ------.

NOTES

1. I.e., all the copper of the mountain was required for its blade; the timber of a whole grove had gone into its haft; its sheath was the size of a rock-tomb shaft, and its leather belt was made from the hides of all the cattle of the Nubian province of Kal.

2. The word for the lady occurs four times, each time in a lacuna. Lefèbvre rendered it as "Lady X," while Schott and Brunner-Traut took her to be a personified concept comparable to "Truth" and "Falsehood." Schott rendered "Goodness," and Brunner-Traut, "Desire," the latter being more plausible, since the behavior of the lady is not good.

3. *Bw3t*, the reed thicket, as in P. Lansing, 2,1. See p. 175, n. 1.
4. I.e., The callous behavior of the woman deserves to be punished by death.
5. Modern El-Balamun in the northern Delta.
6. The name for the Nile in its main course.

HORUS AND SETH

P. Chester Beatty I, Recto

Written in a beautiful hand, the papyrus dates from the reign of Ramses V and comes from Thebes. The tale occupies the first fifteen pages of the *recto* and the first eight lines of page 16.

Publication: Gardiner, *Chester Beatty I*, pp. 8-26 and pls. 1-16. Gardiner, *LES*, pp. 37-60.

Translation: J. Capart, *CdE*, 8, (1933), 243-255.   Lefèbvre, *Romans*, pp. 178-203.   Brunner-Traut, *Märchen*, pp. 93-107.   E. F. Wente in Simpson, *Literature*, pp. 108-126.

Translation and study: J. Spiegel, *Die Erzählung vom Streite des Horus und Seth in Pap. Beatty I als Literaturwerk*. Leipziger ägyptologische Studien, 9 (Glückstadt, 1937).

On the myth of Horus and Seth see: H. Kees, *Horus und Seth als Götterpaar*. 2 vols. Mitteilungen der vorderasiatisch-ägyptischen Gesellschaft, Berlin, vols. 28, 1 and 29, 1 (Leipzig, 1923-1924).   J. G. Griffiths, *The Conflict of Horus and Seth from Egyptian and Classical Sources* (Liverpool, 1960).   H. te Velde, *Seth, God of Confusion* (Leiden, 1967).

(1,1) [This is] the judging of Horus and Seth, they of mysterious forms, mightiest of existing princes and lords. A [divine] youth was seated before the All-Lord, claiming the office of his father Osiris, he of beautiful appearances, [the son of] Ptah, who brightens [the netherworld] with his lustre, while Thoth presented the Eye to the great prince of On.[1]

Then spoke Shu, the son of Re, before [Atum], the great prince of On: "Right rules might. Do it by saying: 'Give the office to Horus.'" Then Thoth said to the Ennead: "That is right a million times!" Then Isis uttered a loud shout and was overjoyed. She [stood] before the All-Lord and said: "Northwind, go west, give the news to Wennofer!"[2] Then said Shu, the son of Re: "Presenting the Eye (to Horus) seems right to the Ennead." Said the All-Lord: "What is this, your making decisions on your own?" Then [⌜Onuris⌝] said: "He (Thoth) shall take the royal name-ring to Horus, and the White Crown shall be placed on his head!" Then the All-Lord was silent for a long moment, for he was angry with the Ennead.

Then Seth, the son of Nut, spoke: "Let him be sent outside with me, and I shall let you see my hand prevailing over his hand in the presence of the Ennead, since one knows no other means [of] dispossessing him." Then Thoth said to him: "Do we not know what is wrong? Shall one give the office of Osiris to Seth while his son Horus is there?" Then Pre-Harakhti became exceedingly angry, for it was Pre's wish (2,1) to give the office to Seth, great of strength, the son of Nut. And Onuris uttered a loud cry before the Ennead, saying: "What shall we do?" Then said Atum, the great prince of On: "Summon Banebdjede,³ the great living god, that he may judge between the two youths."

They brought Banebdjede, the great god who dwells in Setit, before Atum, along with Ptah-Tatenen. He said to them: "Judge between the two youths, so that they will stop wrangling here every day!" Then Banebdjede, the great living god, replied to what he had said: "Let us not decide in ignorance. Have a letter sent to Neith the Great, the divine mother. What she will say, we will do."

Then the Ennead said to Banebdjede, the great living god: "They have been judged once already in the hall "Way-of-Truth."" And the Ennead said to Thoth in the presence of the All-Lord: "Write a letter to Neith the Great, the divine mother, in the name of the All-Lord, the Bull of On." And Thoth said: "I will, I will." He sat down to write the letter, which said:

"The King of Upper and Lower Egypt: Re-Atum, beloved of Thoth; The Lord of the Two Lands, the Heliopolitan; the Aten who illumines the Two Lands with his lustre; the Hapy mighty in his rising: Re-Harakhti; to⁴ Neith the Great, the divine mother, who shone on the first face, who is alive, hale, and young. The living *Ba* of the All-Lord, the Bull of On who is the good King of Egypt, (says) as follows: I your servant spend the night on behalf of Osiris taking counsel for the Two Lands every day, while Sobk endures forever. What shall we do about these two people, who for eighty years now have been before the tribunal, and (3,1) no one knows how to judge between the two? Write us what we should do!"

Then Neith the Great, the divine mother, sent a letter to the Ennead, saying: "Give the office of Osiris to his son Horus, and don't do those big misdeeds that are out of place. Or I shall get angry and the sky will crash to the ground! And let it be said to the All-Lord, the Bull of On: Double Seth's possessions. Give him Anat and Astarte, your two daughters. And place Horus on the seat of his father!"

The letter of Neith the Great, the divine mother, reached the Ennead as they sat in the hall "Horned-Horus," and the letter was placed in the hand of Thoth. Then Thoth read it aloud before the

All-Lord and the whole Ennead. And they said with one voice: "This goddess is right!" Thereupon the All-Lord became angry at Horus and said to him: "You are feeble in body, and this office is too big for you, you youngster whose breath smells bad." Then Onuris became angry a million times and so was the Ennead, the Council of Thirty.[5] The god Baba[6] got up and said to Pre-Harakhti: "Your shrine is empty!"[7] Then Pre-Harakhti felt offended by the answer given him, and he lay down on his back, his heart very sore. Then the Ennead came out, shouting loudly at Baba and saying to him: "Go away; you have committed a very great crime!" And they went to their tents.

The great god spent a day (4,1) lying on his back in his pavilion, his heart very sore and he was alone. After a long while, Hathor, Lady of the southern sycamore, came and stood before her father, the All-Lord. She uncovered her nakedness before him; thereupon the great god laughed at her. He got up and sat with the great Ennead; and he said to Horus and Seth: "Speak for yourselves!"

Then Seth, great of strength, the son of Nut, said: "I, I am Seth, greatest of strength among the Ennead. For I slay the enemy of Pre every day, standing in the prow of the Bark-of-Millions, and no other god can do it. I should receive the office of Osiris!" Then they said: "Seth, the son of Nut, is right." Then Onuris and Thoth cried aloud, saying: "Shall one give the office to the uncle while the bodily son is there?" Then Banebdjede, the great living god, said: "Shall one give the office to the youngster while Seth, his elder brother, is there?"[8]

Then the Ennead cried out aloud to the All-Lord and said to him: "What are these words you spoke which are not worthy of being heard?"[9] Then said Horus, the son of Isis: "It is not good to defraud me before the Ennead and to take the office of my father Osiris away from me!" And Isis was angry with the Ennead, and she took an oath by the god before the Ennead, saying: "As my mother lives, the goddess Neith, and as Ptah-Tatenen lives, the tall-plumed horn-curber of gods, these matters shall be laid before Atum, the great prince of On, and also Khepri in his bark!" Then the Ennead said to her: "Don't be angry. Right will be given to him who is right. All that you said shall be done."

Then Seth, the son of (5,1) Nut, was angry with the Ennead because of the words they had said to Isis the Great, the divine mother. And Seth said to them: "I shall take my scepter of 4,500 pounds and kill one of you each day!" And Seth took an oath by the All-Lord, saying: "I shall not contend in court as long as Isis is in it!" Then Pre-Harakhti said to them: "Cross over to the Island-in-the-Midst and judge them there. And tell Nemty, the ferryman: 'Do not ferry across any woman who looks like Isis.'" So the Ennead crossed over to the Island-in-the-Midst, and they sat down to eat bread.

Isis came and approached Nemty, the ferryman, as he was sitting near his boat. She had changed herself into an old woman who walked with a stoop, and a small signet ring of gold was on her hand. She said to him: "I have come to you in order that you ferry me across to the Island-in-the-Midst. For I have come with this bowl of flour for the young boy who is tending some cattle on the Island-in-the-Midst these five days, and he is hungry." He said to her: "I have been told: 'Don't ferry any woman across.'" She said to him: "It was on account of Isis that this was said to you." He said to her: "What will you give me for ferrying you across to the Island-in-the-Midst?" Isis said to him: "I will give you this cake." He said to her: "What is it to me, your cake? Shall I ferry you across to the Island-in-the-Midst when I was told, 'Ferry no woman across,' in exchange for your cake?" (6,1) Then she said to him: "I will give you the signet ring of gold that is on ⟨my⟩ hand." He said to her: "Give me the signet ring of gold." She gave it to him, and he ferried her across to the Island-in-the Midst.

Now as she walked under the trees, she looked and saw the Ennead as they sat eating bread before the All-Lord in his pavilion. And Seth looked and saw her coming from afar. Thereupon she pronounced a spell of hers and changed herself into a young girl of beautiful body, the like of which did not exist in the whole land. Then he desired her very much.

Seth got up from sitting and eating bread with the great Ennead and went to meet her, while no one but himself had seen her. He stood behind a sycamore, called to her, and said to her: "I am here with you, handsome girl!" She said to him: "Let me tell, my great lord: As for me, I was the wife of a herdsman and I bore him a son. My husband died, and the boy began to tend the cattle[10] of his father. But then a stranger came. He sat down in my stable and spoke thus to my child: 'I shall beat you, I shall take your father's cattle, and I shall throw you out!' So he spoke to him. Now I wish to make you his defender." Then Seth said to her: "Shall one give the cattle to the stranger while the man's son is here?" Thereupon Isis changed herself into a kite, flew up, and sat on top of an acacia. She called to Seth and said to him: "Weep for yourself! Your own mouth has said it. Your own cleverness (7,1) has judged you! What do you want?"

Then he began to weep; and he want to where Pre-Harakhti was and wept. Pre-Harakhti said to him: "What do you want?" Seth said to him: "That evil woman came to me again. She has cheated me again. She had changed herself into a beautiful girl before me, and she said to me: 'I was the wife of a herdsman who is dead. I had born him a son; he tended the cattle of his father. Then a stranger intruded in my stable to be with my son, and I gave him food. And many days after this the intruder said to my son: "I shall beat you; I shall take your father's cattle; it shall be mine." Thus he spoke to my son.' So she said to me." Then Pre-Harakhti said to him: "What did you say to her?" And Seth told him: "I said to her: 'Shall one give the cattle to the stranger while the man's son is there?' So I said to her. 'One must beat the intruder with a stick, and throw him out, and set the son in the place of his father.' So I said to her."

Then Pre-Harakhti said to him: "Now look, you yourself have judged yourself. What do you want?" Seth said to him: "Let Nemty, the ferryman, be brought, and let a great punishment be done to him, saying: 'Why did you ferry her across?' So one shall say to him." Then Nemty, the ferryman, was brought before the Ennead, and they removed his toes. And (8,1) Nemty forswore gold to this day before the great Ennead, saying: "Gold shall be an abomination to me in my town!"

The Ennead crossed over to the western shore and sat on the mountain. Now when evening had come, Pre-Harakhti and Atum, Lord of the Two Lands, the Heliopolitan, wrote to the Ennead, saying: "Why are you sitting here again? Are you going to make the two youths spend their lifetime in the court? When my letter reaches you, you shall place the White Crown on the head of Horus, son of Isis, and appoint him to the position of his father Osiris."

Thereupon Seth became exceedingly angry, and the Ennead said to him: "Why are you angry? Should one not act according to the word of Atum, Lord of the Two Lands, the Heliopolitan, and Pre-Harakhti?" Then the White Crown was placed on the head of Horus, son of Isis. And Seth cried out aloud to the Ennead in anger and said: "Shall the office be given to my young brother while I, his elder brother, am here?" And he took an oath, saying: "The White Crown shall be removed from the head of Horus, son of Isis, and he shall be thrown into the water! I shall yet contend with him for the office of ruler!" Then Pre-Harakhti acted accordingly.

Seth said to Horus: "Come, let us change ourselves into two hippopotamuses and plunge into the depth in the midst of the sea. And he who emerges in the course of three whole months, he shall not receive the office." So they plunged together. Then Isis sat down weeping and said: "Seth will kill Horus, my son!" She took a quantity of yarn and made a rope. She took a *deben* of copper and cast it into a harpoon. She tied the rope to it and threw it into the water at the spot where Horus and Seth had plunged. (9,1) Then the weapon bit into the body of her son Horus. And Horus cried out aloud, saying: "Come to me, mother Isis, my mother! Tell your weapon to let go of me! I am Horus, son of Isis!" Then Isis cried out aloud and said to her weapon: "Let go of him! He is Horus my son." And the weapon let go of him.

Then she threw it again into the water, and it bit into the body of Seth. And Seth cried out aloud, saying: "What have I done to you, my sister Isis? Call to your weapon to let go of me! I am your maternal brother, O Isis!" Then she felt very sorry for him. And Seth called to her, saying: "Do you love the stranger more than your maternal brother Seth?" Then Isis called to her weapon, saying: "Let go of him! It is the maternal brother of Isis whom you are biting." And the weapon let go of him.

Thereupon Horus, son of Isis, was angry with his mother Isis. He came out, his face fierce like that of a leopard and his knife of 16 *deben* in his hand. He cut off the head of his mother Isis, took it in his arms, and went up the mountain. Then Isis changed herself into a statue of flint without a head. And Pre-Harakhti said to Thoth: "Who is she who is coming and has no head?" Thoth said to Pre-Harakhti: "My good lord, she is Isis the Great, the divine mother. Her son Horus has cut off her head." Then (10,1) Pre-Harakhti cried out aloud and said to the Ennead: "Let us go and punish him severely!" So the Ennead went up into the mountains to search for Horus, son of Isis.

As for Horus, he was lying under a *shenusha*-tree in the oasis country. Then Seth found him, seized him, and threw him on his back on the mountain. He removed his two eyes from their places and buried them on the mountain. Toward morning his two eyeballs became two bulbs, and they grew into lotuses. And Seth came and told Pre-Harakhti falsely: "I did not find Horus," although he had found him. Then Hathor, Mistress of the southern sycamore, went and found Horus as he lay weeping on the desert. Thereupon she caught a gazelle, milked it, and said to Horus: "Open your eyes, that I may put this milk in." He opened his eyes and she put the milk in. She put it in the right eye; she put it in the left eye; she said to him: "Open your eyes!" He opened his eyes. She looked at them; she found them healed. Then she went to tell Pre-Harakhti: "I found Horus deprived of his eyes by Seth, but I restored him. Now here he comes."

Then the Ennead said: "Horus and Seth shall be summoned and judged!" So they were brought before the Ennead. The All-Lord spoke before the great Ennead to Horus and Seth: "Go and heed what I tell you: Eat, (11,1) drink, and leave us in peace! Stop quarreling here every day!"

Then Seth said to Horus: "Come, let us have a feast day at my house." And Horus said to him: "I will, I will." Now when evening had come, a bed was prepared for them, and they lay down together. At night, Seth let his member become stiff and he inserted it between the thighs of Horus. And Horus placed his hands beween his thighs and caught the semen of Seth. Then Horus went to tell his mother Isis: "Come, Isis my mother, come and see what Seth did to me." He opened his hand and let her see the semen of Seth. She cried out aloud, took her knife, cut off his hand and threw it in the water. Then she made a new hand for him. And she took a dab of sweet ointment and put it on the member of Horus. She made it become stiff, placed it over a pot, and he let his semen drop into it.

In the morning Isis went with the semen of Horus to the garden of Seth and said to the gardener of Seth: "What plants does Seth eat here with you?" The gardener said to her: "The only plant Seth eats here with me is lettuce." Then Isis placed the semen of Horus on them. Seth came according to his daily custom and ate the lettuces which he usually ate. Thereupon he became pregnant with the semen of Horus.

Then Seth went and said to (12,1) Horus: "Come, let us go, that I may contend with you in the court." And Horus said to him: "I will, I will." So they went to the court together. They stood before the great Ennead, and they were told: "Speak!" Then Seth said: "Let the office of ruler be given to me, for as regards Horus who stands here, I have done a man's deed to him." Then the Ennead cried out aloud, and they spat out before Horus. And Horus laughed at them; and Horus took an oath by the god, saying: "What Seth has said is false. Let the semen of Seth be called, and let us see from where it will answer. Then let mine be called, and let us see from where it will answer."

Thoth, lord of writing, true scribe of the Ennead, laid his hand on the arm of Horus and said: "Come out, semen of Seth!" And it answered him from the water in the midst of the ⌜marsh.⌝ Then Thoth laid his hand on the arm of Seth and said: "Come out, semen of Horus!" And it said to him: "Where shall I come out?" Thoth said to it: "Come out of his ear." It said to him: "Should I come out of his ear, I who am a divine seed?" Then Thoth said to it: "Come out from the top of his head." Then it came out as a golden sun-disk on the head of Seth. Seth became very angry, and he stretched out his hand to seize the golden sun-disk. Thereupon Thoth took it away (13,1) from him and placed it as a crown upon his (own) head. And the Ennead said: "Horus is right, Seth is wrong." Then Seth became very angry and cried out aloud because they had said: "Horus is right, Seth is wrong."

Seth took a great oath by the god, saying: "He shall not be given the office until he has been dismissed with me, and we shall build ships of stone and race each other. He who wins over his rival, he shall be given the office of ruler." Then Horus built himself a ship of pine, plastered it over with gypsum, and launched it on the water in the evening, while no one in the whole land saw it. And Seth looked at the ship of Horus and thought it was of stone. He went to the mountain, cut off a mountain peak, and built himself a ship of stone of 138 cubits. Then they went into their ships in the presence of the Ennead. Thereupon the ship of Seth sank in the water. Seth changed himself into a hippopotamus and wrecked the ship of Horus. Then Horus seized his weapon and hit the body of Seth. Then the Ennead said to him: "Do not hit him."

So he took his sailing gear, placed it in his boat, and journeyed downstream to Sais to tell Neith the Great, the divine mother: "Let me be judged with Seth! For it is now eighty years that we are in the court, (14,1) but they don't know how to judge between us. He has not been vindicated against me; and a thousand times now I have been in the right against him day after day. But he pays no attention to what the Ennead says. I have contended with him in the hall "Way-of-Truth." I was found right against him. I have contended with him in the hall "Horned-Horus." I was found right against him. I have contended with him in the hall "Field-of-Rushes." I was found right against him. I have contended with him in the hall "Field-Pool." I was found right against him. The Ennead has said to Shu, son of Re: 'Horus, son of Isis, is right in all that he has said.'"

Thoth spoke to the All-Lord: "Have a letter sent to Osiris, that he may judge between the two youths." And Shu, son of Re, said: "Right a million times is what Thoth has said to the Ennead." Then the All-Lord said to Thoth: "Sit down and write a letter to Osiris, that we may hear what he has to say." So Thoth sat down to compose a letter to Osiris as follows: "The Bull:[11] Hunting Lion; Two Ladies: Protector of gods, Curber of the Two Lands; Gold Horus: Inventor of mankind in the beginning; King of Upper and Lower Egypt: Bull who dwells in On; Son of Ptah: Benefactor of the Two Shores, who arose as father of his Ennead, who lives on gold and all precious glazes: Life, prosperity, health! Write us what we should do about Horus and Seth, so that we do not take action in ignorance!"

⟨Many days⟩ after this, the letter reached the King, the son of Re, Great in Bounty, Lord of Sustenance. He cried out aloud when the letter was read before him. He replied in great haste to where the All-Lord was with the Ennead, saying: "Why is my son Horus being defrauded when it was I who made you strong? It was I who made barley and emmer to nourish the gods, and the cattle after the gods, while no god or goddess was able to do it!"

The (15,1) letter of Osiris arrived at the place where Pre-Harakhti was, as he sat with the Ennead in the White Field at Xois. It was read to him and the Ennead, and Pre-Harakhti said: "Answer this letter of

Osiris for me quickly, and tell him concerning his letter: 'If you had not existed, if you had not been born, barley and emmer would yet exist!'"

The letter of the All-Lord reached Osiris and was read before him. Then he wrote to Pre-Harakhti again, saying: "Very good is all you have done and what the Ennead has found to do! Maat has been made to sink into the netherworld! Now you pay attention to this matter! The land in which I am is full of savage-looking messengers who fear no god or goddess. If I send them out, they will bring me the heart of every evildoer, and they will be here with me![12] What good is my being here, resting in the west, while all of you are outside? Who among you is mightier than I? But they have invented wrongdoing! When Ptah the Great, South-of-his-Wall, Lord of Memphis, created the sky, did he not say to the stars in it: 'You shall go to rest in the west every night, in the place where King Osiris is? And after the gods all mankind shall also go to rest where you are!' So he said to me."

⟨Many days⟩ after this, the letter of Osiris arrived at the place where the All-Lord was with the Ennead. Thoth received the letter and read it to Pre-Harakhti and the Ennead. Then they said: "He is right, he is right in all he says, the Great in Bounty, the Lord of Sustenance!" Then Seth said: "Let us be taken to the Island-in-the-Midst, that I may contend with him!" And he went to the Island-in-the-Midst. But Horus was declared in the right against him.

Then Atum, Lord of the Two Lands, the Heliopolitan, sent to Isis, saying: "Bring Seth bound in fetters." So Isis brought Seth bound in fetters as a prisoner. Atum said to him: "Why have you resisted being judged and have taken for yourself the office of Horus?" Seth said to him: "Not so, my good lord. Let Horus, son of Isis, be summoned, and let him be given the office of (16,1) his father Osiris!"

They brought Horus, son of Isis. They placed the White Crown on his head. They placed him on the seat of his father Osiris and said to him: "You are the good King of Egypt! You are the good lord of all lands for ever and ever!" Then Isis uttered a loud shout to her son Horus, saying: "You are the good King! My heart rejoices that you will brighten the earth with your lustre!" Then said Ptah the Great, South-of-his-Wall, Lord of Memphis: "What shall we do for Seth, now that Horus has been placed on the seat of his father?" Then Pre-Harakhti said: "Let Seth, son of Nut, be given to me to dwell with me and be my son. And he shall thunder in the sky and be feared."

They came to say to Pre-Harakhti: "Horus, son of Isis, has risen as Ruler." Then Pre rejoiced greatly and said to the Ennead: "Jubilate throughout the land, jubilate throughout the land for Horus, son of Isis!" And Isis said:

"Horus has risen as Ruler, life, prosperity, health!
The Ennead is in feast, heaven in joy!
They take garlands seeing Horus, son of Isis
Risen as great Ruler of Egypt.
The hearts of the Ennead exult,
The entire land rejoices
As they see Horus, son of Isis
Given the office of his father,
Osiris, lord of Busiris."

Colophon: It has come to a good ending in Thebes, the place of truth.

NOTES

1. The All-Lord is the sun-god Re (or Pre) in all his manifestations which include Re-Harakhti, Atum, and Khepri. In this tale, however, Pre-Harakhti and Atum are in some instances viewed as one person and in some others as two distinct personalities. The Sacred Eye that Thoth presents to the sun-god is a complex symbol which here signifies the kingship of Egypt.
2. Name of Osiris.
3. Or, "Ba, lord of Mendes"; he is the ram-god of the Delta town of Mendes, the metropolis of the Sixteenth Nome of Lower Egypt. By calling him a dweller in Setit (the island Sehel in the first cataract) he is associated with the southern ram-god Khnum.
4. Emending *iw* to *n.*
5. The Ennead is sitting as the supreme tribunal of Egypt, called the Council of Thirty.
6. Or, Bebon; a deity associated with Seth; see P. Derchain, *RdE*, 9 (1952), 23-47.
7. This apparently means: "Go home."
8. In the dominant form of the myth, Osiris and Seth were brothers. But in an even older tradition, Horus and Seth were brothers. The two traditions are intermingled here.
9. The passage appears to be garbled, for the sun-god has not spoken.
10. The tale that Isis tells Seth plays on the words for "cattle" and "office" which sound alike.
11. Osiris is addressed as king of Egypt with a royal titulary of five names.
12. The netherworld over which Osiris rules includes a place of punishment.

THE REPORT OF WENAMUN

P. Moscow 120

In its present state the papyrus consists of two pages with a total of 142 lines. The first page has numerous lacunae, and the end of the story is missing. The papyrus was written at the end of the Twentieth Dynasty, that is to say, directly after the events which the report relates. Whether or not the report reflects an actual mission, it depicts a true historical situation and a precise moment. It is the third decade of the reign of Ramses XI, 1090-1080 B.C., during which the king yielded power to the two men who shared the effective rule of Egypt: Herihor in the south and Smendes in the north. The empire had been lost, and thus so simple an enterprise as the purchase of Lebanese timber could be depicted as a perilous adventure.

What makes the story so remarkable is the skill with which it is told. The Late-Egyptian vernacular is handled with great subtlety. The verbal duels between Wenamum and the prince of Byblos, with their changes of mood and shades of meaning that include irony, represent Egyptian thought and style at their most advanced. What *Sinuhe* is for the Middle Kingdom, *Wenamun* is for the New Kingdom: a literary culmination. The differences between them are not only that the one reflects political power and the other political decline, but more importantly that almost a millennium of human history has gone by, a time during which the peoples of the ancient world lost much of their archaic simplicity. Wenamun stands on the threshold of the first millennium B.C., a millennium in which the modern world began, a world shaped by men and women who were the likes of ourselves.

Publication: V. S. Golenishchev, *RT*, 21 (1899), 74-102.   Gardiner, *LEM*, pp. 61-76.   M. A. Korostovtsev, *Puteshestvie Un-amuna v Bibl.* (Moscow, 1960).

Translation: Erman, *ZÄS*, 38 (1900), 1-14.   Erman, *Literature*, pp. 174-185.   Lefèbvre, *Romans*, pp. 204-220.   J. A. Wilson in *ANET*, pp. 25-29.   Gardiner, *Egypt*, pp. 306-313.   E. Edel in Galling, *Textbuch*, pp. 41-48.   E. F. Wente in Simpson, *Literature*, pp. 142-155.

Comments: C. F. Nims, *JEA*, 54 (1968), 161-164. Additional references will be found in the works cited.

(1,1) Year 5,[1] fourth month of summer, day 16, the day of departure of Wenamun, the Elder of the Portal of the Temple of Amun, Lord of Thrones-of-the-Two-Lands, to fetch timber for the great noble bark of Amen-Re, King of Gods, which is upon the river and [is called] Amen-user-he.[2]

On the day of my arrival at Tanis, the place where Smendes and Tentamun are,[3] I gave them the dispatches of Amen-Re, King of Gods. They had them read out before them and they said: "I will do, I will do as Amen-Re, King of Gods, our lord has said."

I stayed until the fourth month of summer in Tanis. Then Smendes and Tentamun sent me off with the ship's captain Mengebet,[4] and I went down upon the great sea of Syria in the first month of summer,[5] day 1. I arrived at Dor,[6] a Tjeker town; and Beder, its prince, had fifty loaves, one jug of wine, (1,10) and one ox-haunch brought to me. Then a man of my ship fled after stealing one vessel of gold worth 5 *deben*, four jars of silver worth 20 *deben*, and a bag with 11 *deben* of silver; [total of what he stole]: gold 5 *deben*, silver 31 *deben*.

That morning, when I had risen, I went to where the prince was and said to him: "I have been robbed in your harbor. Now you are the prince of this land, you are the one who controls it. Search for my money! Indeed the money belongs to Amen-Re, King of Gods, the lord of the lands. It belongs to Smendes; it belongs to Herihor, my lord, and (to) the other magnates of Egypt. It belongs to you; it belongs to Weret; it belongs to Mekmer; it belongs to Tjekerbaal, the prince of Byblos!"[7] He said to me: "Are you serious? ⌐Are you joking?⌐ Indeed I do not understand the demand you make to me. If it had been a thief belonging to my land who had gone down to your ship and stolen your money, I would replace it for you from my storehouse, until (1,20) your thief, whatever his name, had been found. But the thief who robbed you, he is yours, he belongs to your ship. Spend a few days here with me; I will search for him."

I stayed nine days moored in his harbor. Then I went to him and said to him: "Look, you have not found my money. [Let me depart] with the ship captains, with those who go to sea."

[*The next eight lines are broken. Apparently the prince advises Wenamun to wait some more, but Wenamun departs. He passes Tyre and approaches Byblos. Then he seizes thirty deben of silver from a ship he has encountered which belongs to the Tjeker. He tells the owners that he will keep the money until his money has been found. Through this action he incurs the enmity of the Tjeker*].

They departed and I celebrated [in] a tent on the shore of the sea in the harbor of Byblos. And [I made a hiding place for] Amun-of-the-Road[8] and placed his possessions in it. Then the prince of Byblos sent to me saying: "[Leave my] harbor!" I sent to him, saying: "Where shall [I go]? ------. If [you have a ship to carry me], let me be taken back to Egypt." I spent twenty-nine days in his harbor, and he spent time sending to me daily to say: "Leave my harbor!"

Now while he was offering to his gods, the god took hold of a young man [of] his young men and put him in a trance. He said to him:[9] "Bring [the] god up! Bring the envoy who is carrying him! (1,40) It is Amun who sent him. It is he who made him come!" Now it was while the entranced one was entranced that night that I had found a ship headed for Egypt. I had loaded all my belongings into it and was watching for the darkness, saying: "When it descends I will load the god so that no other eye shall see him."

Then the harbor master came to me, saying: "Wait until morning, says the prince!" I said to him: "Was it not you who daily took time to come to me, saying: 'Leave my harbor'? Do you now say: 'Wait this night,' in order to let the ship that I found depart, and then you will come to say: 'Go away'?" He went and told it to the prince. Then the prince sent to the captain of the ship, saying: "Wait until morning, says the prince."

When morning came, he sent and brought me up, while the god rested in the tent where he was on the shore of the sea. I found him seated in his upper chamber with his back against a window, and the waves of the great sea of Syria broke behind (1,50) his head. I said to him: "Blessings of Amun!" He said to me: "How long is it to this day since you came from the place where Amun is?" I said to him: "Five whole months till now." He said to me: "If you are right, where is the dispatch of Amun that was in your hand? Where is the letter of the High Priest of Amun that was in your hand?" I said to him: "I gave them to Smendes and Tentamun." Then he became very angry and said to me: "Now then, dispatches, letters you have none. Where is the ship of pinewood[10] that Smendes gave you? Where is its Syrian crew? Did he not entrust you to this foreign ship's captain in order to have him kill you and have them throw you into the sea? From whom would one then seek the god? And you, from whom would one seek you?" So he said to me.

I said to him: "Is it not an Egyptian ship? Those who sail under Smendes are Egyptian crews. He has no Syrian crews."[11] He said to me: "Are there not twenty ships here in my harbor that do business with Smendes? As for Sidon, (2,1) that other ⟨place⟩ you passed, are there not another fifty ships there that do business with Werekter and haul to his house?"

I was silent in this great moment. Then he spoke to me, saying: "On what business have you come?" I said to him: "I have come in quest of timber for the great noble bark of Amen-Re, King of Gods. What your father did, what the father of your father did, you too will do it." So I said to him. He said to me: "True, they did it. If you pay me for doing it, I will do it. My relations carried out this business after Pharaoh had sent six ships laden with the goods of Egypt, and they had been unloaded into their storehouses. You, what have you brought for me?"

He had the daybook of his forefathers brought and had it read before me. They found entered in his book a thousand *deben* of silver and all sorts of things. (2,10) He said to me: "If the ruler of Egypt were the lord of what is mine and I were his servant, he would not have sent silver and gold to say: 'Carry out the business of Amun.' It was not a royal gift that they gave to my father! I too, I am not your servant, nor am I the servant of him who sent you! If I shout aloud to the Lebanon, the sky opens and the logs lie here on the shore of the

sea! Give me the sails you brought to move your ships, loaded with
logs for ⟨Egypt⟩! Give me the ropes you brought [to lash the pines]
that I am to fell in order to make them for you ---. ------ that I am
to make for you for the sails of your ships; or the yards may be too
heavy and may break, and you may die ⟨in⟩ the midst of the sea. For
Amun makes thunder in the sky ever since he placed Seth beside
him![12] Indeed, Amun has (2,20) founded all the lands. He founded
them after having first founded the land of Egypt from which you
have come. Thus craftsmanship came from it in order to reach the
place where I am! Thus learning came from it in order to reach the
place where I am![13] What are these foolish travels they made you do?"

I said to him: "Wrong! These are not foolish travels that I am
doing. There is no ship on the river that does not belong to Amun.
His is the sea and his the Lebanon of which you say, 'It is mine.' It is a
growing ground for Amen-user-he, the lord of every ship. Truly, it
was Amen-Re, King of Gods, who said to Herihor, my master: 'Send
me!' And he made me come with this great god. But look, you have let
this great god spend these twenty-nine days moored in your harbor.
Did you not know that he was here? Is he not he who he was? You are
prepared to haggle over the Lebanon with Amun, its lord? As to your
saying, the former kings sent silver and gold: If they had owned life
and health, they would not have sent these things. (2,30) It was in
place of life and health that they sent these things to your fathers! But
Amen-Re, King of Gods, he is the lord of life and health, and he was
the lord of your fathers! They passed their lifetimes offering to
Amun. You too, you are the servant of Amun!

If you will say 'I will do' to Amun, and will carry out his business,
you will live, you will prosper, you will be healthy; you will be
beneficent to your whole land and your people. Do not desire what
belongs to Amen-Re, King of Gods! Indeed, a lion loves his possessions! Have your scribe brought to me that I may send him to
Smendes and Tentamun, the pillars Amun has set up for the north of
his land; and they will send all that is needed. I will send him to them,
saying: 'Have it brought until I return to the south; then I shall
refund you all your expenses.'"[14] So I said to him.

He placed my letter in the hand of his messenger; and he loaded
the keel, the prow-piece, and the stern-piece, together with four other
hewn logs, seven in all, and sent them to Egypt. His messenger who
had gone to Egypt returned to me in Syria in the first month of
winter, Smendes and Tentamun having sent: (2,40) four jars and one
kakmen-vessel of gold; five jars of silver; ten garments of royal linen;
ten *ḥrd*-garments[15] of fine linen; five-hundred smooth linen mats;
five-hundred ox-hides; five-hundred ropes; twenty sacks of lentils;
and thirty baskets of fish. And she had sent to me:[16] five garments of

fine linen; five ḫrd-garments of fine linen; one sack of lentils; and five baskets of fish.

The prince rejoiced. He assigned three hundred men and three hundred oxen, and he set supervisors over them to have them fell the timbers. They were felled and they lay there during the winter. In the third month of summer they dragged them to the shore of the sea. The prince came out and stood by them, and he sent to me, saying: "Come!" Now when I had been brought into his presence, the shadow of his sunshade fell on me. Then Penamun, a butler of his,[17] intervened, saying: "The shadow of Pharaoh, your lord, has fallen upon you." And he was angry with him and said: "Leave him alone."

As I stood before him, he addressed me, saying: "Look, the business my fathers did in the past, I have done it, although you did not do for me what your fathers did for mine. Look, the last of your timber has arrived and is ready. Do as I wish, and come to load it. For has it not been given to you? (2,50) Do not come to look at the terror of the sea. For if you look at the terror of the sea, you will see my own! Indeed, I have not done to you what was done to the envoys of Khaemwese,[18] after they had spent seventeen years in this land. They died on the spot." And he said to his butler: "Take him to see the tomb where they lie."

I said to him: "Do not make me see it. As for Khaemwese, the envoys he sent you were men and he himself was a man. You have not here one of his envoys, though you say: 'Go and see your companions.' Should you not rejoice and have a stela [made] for yourself, and say on it: 'Amen-Re, King of Gods, sent me Amun-of-the-Road, his envoy, together with Wenamun, his human envoy, in quest of timber for the great noble bark of Amen-Re, King of Gods. I felled it; I loaded it; I supplied my ships and my crews. I let them reach Egypt so as to beg for me from Amun fifty years of life over and above my allotted fate.' And if it comes to pass that in another day an envoy comes from the land of Egypt who knows writing and he reads out your name on the stela, you will receive water of the west like the gods who are (2,60) there."

He said to me: "A great speech of admonition is what you have said to me."[19] I said to him: "As to the many ⟨things⟩ you have said to me: if I reach the place where the High Priest of Amun is and he sees your accomplishment, it is your accomplishment that will draw profit to you."

I went off to the shore of the sea, to where the logs were lying. And I saw eleven ships that had come in from the sea and belonged to the Tjeker (who were) saying: "Arrest him! Let no ship of his leave for the land of Egypt!" Then I sat down and wept. And the secretary of the prince came out to me and said to me: "What is it?" I said to him: "Do you not see the migrant birds going down to Egypt a second time? Look at them traveling to the cool water![20] Until when shall I be left here? For do you not see those who have come to arrest me?"

He went and told it to the prince. And the prince began to weep on account of the words said to him, for they were painful. He sent his secretary out to me, bringing me two jugs of wine and a sheep. And he sent me Tentne, an Egyptian songstress who was with him, saying: "Sing for him! Do not let his heart be anxious." And he sent to me, (2,70) saying: "Eat, drink; do not let your heart be anxious. You shall hear what I will say tomorrow."

When morning came, he had his assembly summoned. He stood in their midst and said to the Tjeker: "What have you come for?" They said to him: "We have come after the blasted[21] ships that you are sending to Egypt with our enemy." He said to them: "I cannot arrest the envoy of Amun in my country. Let me send him off, and you go after him to arrest him."

He had me board and sent me off from the harbor of the sea. And the wind drove me to the land of Alasiya.[22] Then the town's people came out against me to kill me. But I forced my way through them to where Hatiba, the princess of the town was. I met her coming from one of her houses to enter another. I saluted her and said to the people who stood around her: "Is there not one among you who understands Egyptian?" And one among them said: "I understand it." I said to him: "Tell my lady that I have heard it said as far away as Thebes, the place where Amun is: 'If wrong is done in every town, in the land of Alasiya right is done.' Now is wrong done here too every day?"

She said: "What is it (2,80) you have said?" I said to her: "If the sea rages and the wind drives me to the land where you are, will you let me be received so as to kill me, though I am the envoy of Amun? Look, as for me, they would search for me till the end of time. As for this crew of the prince of Byblos, whom they seek to kill, will not their lord find ten crews of yours and kill them also?" She had the people summoned and they were reprimanded. She said to me: "Spend the night —————[23]

NOTES

1. The year date is reckoned by the "Renaissance Era" introduced by Herihor in the nineteenth regnal year of Ramses XI. The month dates given for the beginning of Wenamun's journey are garbled and require emendation. This first date might be emended to "second month of summer."

2. The name of the great processional bark of Amun of Thebes.

3. Smendes, the ruler of Tanis, subsequently became the first king of the Twenty-First Dynasty. The fact that, in the tale, his wife Tentamun

is always mentioned together with him suggests that she was an important person, perhaps a Ramesside princess, who shared the rule with her husband.

4. The captain is a Syrian, and so apparently is the crew; but the ship is in the service of Egypt.

5. Emend to: "first month of the inundation."

6. A port town on the coast of northern Palestine, controlled by the Tjeker, a people belonging to the "sea peoples" who, having failed to invade Egypt, had settled on the Palestinian coast.

7. I.e., the stolen money was intended for the persons with whom Wenamun expected to do business.

8. The statuette which represented Amun in his aspect of protector of travelers.

9. I.e., the man in a trance says to the prince.

10. Or, "for (the transport of) the pinewood."

11. Wenamun claims that Syrian crews who sail for Egypt are Egyptian crews.

12. Seth was equated with the Syrian Baal and both were storm gods.

13. The gist of the prince's speech is that, though Egypt was created by Amun before all other lands and is thus the motherland of all the arts, the civilization of Syria is now fully grown and no longer dependent on Egypt.

14. I.e., after Wenamun has returned to Thebes, his master Herihor will reimburse Smendes and Tentamun.

15. The nature of *ḥrd* is not known. In *BIFAO*, 57 (1958), 208-209, J. Černý suggested the meanings "awning," and "veil." To my knowledge Egyptian art never depicts the wearing of veils.

16. Tentamun had sent a personal gift to Wenamun.

17. An Egyptian in the service of the prince of Byblos.

18. We do not know to whom the prince is referring. A vizier Khaemwese served under Ramses IX.

19. This reply of the prince seems to be ironic.

20. I.e., Wenamun has now been abroad for more than a year and is thus witnessing for the second time the annual flight to Egypt of migratory birds.

21. It looks as if the verb *knkn*, "to beat," is here used idiomatically as a curse word. *Cf.* the name *knkn-t3* given to a lonely foreign place in P. Anastasi IV.12,6 (Gardiner, *LEM*, p. 48.)

22. Alasiya is thought to be Cyprus, but the identification is not certain.

23. The remainder of the report is lost.

Indexes

Indexes

I. DIVINITIES

Amen-Re, 26, 31, 35, 38, 43, 44, 45, 46, 52, 53, 105, 106, 111, 112, 168, 169, 172, 224, 225, 226, 227, 228

Amen-Re-Atum, 41

Amun, 3, 5, 16, 18, 21, 25, 26, 27, 28, 30, 31, 32, 33, 39, 40, 41, 42, 43, 44, 45, 46, 47, 48, 53, 54, 55, 57, 60, 62, 63, 64, 65, 66, 67, 68, 69, 71, 72, 76, 81, 85, 86, 87, 89, 105, 106, 107, 109, 111, 112, 115, 122, 171, 173, 188, 197, 213, 224, 226, 227, 228, 229, 230

Amun-of-the-Road, 225, 228

Anat, 215

Anubis, 16, 86, 92, 197, 203

Apopis, 89, 100, 103, 153

Astarte, 42, 215

Aten, 6, 25, 26, 27, 29, 44, 45, 48, 49, 50, 51, 83, 84, 85, 86, 87, 89, 90, 91, 92, 93, 94, 95, 96, 97, 98, 99, 100, 101, 153, 161, 172, 206, 215

Atum, 28, 40, 53, 62, 86, 89, 120, 214, 215, 216, 218, 222, 223

Baal, 64, 67, 69, 71, 230

Baba, Babi, Bebon, 128, 216, 223

Banebdjede, 215, 216

Bastet, 127

Bata, 197, 203

Ennead, Enneads (= Nine Gods), 16, 18, 26, 52, 54, 55, 57, 75, 82, 83, 84, 102, 103, 109, 110, 113, 120, 207, 211, 213, 214, 215, 216, 217, 218, 219, 220, 221, 222, 223

Geb, 40, 82, 83, 84, 85, 122, 130, 198

Hapy, 18, 19, 21, 44, 45, 85, 94, 98, 99, 100, 174, 215

Harakhti, 26, 31, 39, 86, 87, 89, 102, 124

Harmakhis, 39, 42

Hathor, Hathors, 16, 184, 186, 198, 199, 200, 207, 216, 219

Horus, 18, 29, 32, 38, 39, 41, 53, 54, 56, 74, 81, 84, 86, 87, 128, 132, 149, 197, 214, 215, 216, 218, 219, 220, 221, 222, 223

Horus (as designation of Pharaoh), 25, 26, 27, 30, 38, 39, 42, 43, 49, 52, 53, 74

Iadet, 189

Isis, 16, 28, 39, 54, 56, 83, 84, 85, 214, 216, 217, 218, 219, 220, 221, 222, 223

Kamutef, 26, 174

Khentamentiu (Foremost-of-the-Westerners), 16, 85

Khepri, 26, 86, 87, 88, 89, 216, 223

Khnum, 87, 121, 154, 207, 223

Khons, 174

Mertseger, 107, 108

Min, 16, 127, 131, 149

Min-Kamutef, 149

Mont, 32, 41, 42, 60, 62, 63, 64, 66, 67, 69, 70, 71

Mut, 46, 70, 72, 174

Nefertem, 127, 189

Neith, 39, 215, 216, 221

Nekhbet, 16, 20, 21

Nekhebkau, 127

Nemty, 216, 217, 218

Nephthys, 39, 131

Nepri, 84, 122

Nun, 16, 45, 47, 82, 127, 198, 199

Nut, 28, 41, 82, 83, 87, 88, 122, 198, 215, 216, 222

Ogdoad (= Eight Gods), 122

Onuris, 214, 215, 216

Osiris, 6, 16, 20, 39, 54, 56, 81, 84, 85, 86, 92, 100, 101, 103, 116, 121,

233

II. KINGS AND QUEENS

III. PERSONAL NAMES

IV. GEOGRAPHICAL AND ETHNICAL TERMS

V. EGYPTIAN WORDS

VI. SOME MAJOR CONCEPTS